Trout Streams of Southern New England

The Bantam River in Connecticut

Trout Streams of Southern New England

Tom Fuller

An Angler's Guide to the Watersheds
of Massachusetts, Connecticut, and
Rhode Island

BACK COUNTRY

A Backcountry Guide
Woodstock, Vermont

Library of Congress Cataloging-in-Publication Data

Fuller, Tom, 1948–
  Trout streams of southern New England : an angler's guide to the watersheds of Connecticut, Rhode Island, and Massachusetts / Tom Fuller. — 1st ed.
     p. cm.
  ISBN 0-88150-470-X (pbk. : alk. paper)
  1. Fly fishing—New England Guidebooks. 2. Trout fishing—New England Guidebooks. 3. New England Guidebooks.
SH456.F85   1999
I. Title.
799.1'757'0974—dc21   99–28587
                           CIP

Maps by Paul Woodward, © 1999 The Countryman Press
Book design by Joanna Bodenweber
Cover photograph by Tom Fuller
Author photo by Patricia Fuller
Interior photographs by Tom and Patricia Fuller

Backcountry Guides is a division of The Countryman Press, P.O. Box 748, Woodstock, Vermont 05091

Distributed by W. W. Norton & Company, Inc., 500 Fifth Avenue, New York, NY 10110

Printed in the United States of America

10 9 8 7 6 5 4 3

DEDICATION

For my father, Louis E. Fuller, whose steady, loving guidance throughout my life has been all that a son could ask for, and more. He was a gentleman in every sense of the word to his family, to his community, and to everyone who knew him. And he was a gentle man. He died as this book was being completed, leaving a void in all of our lives.

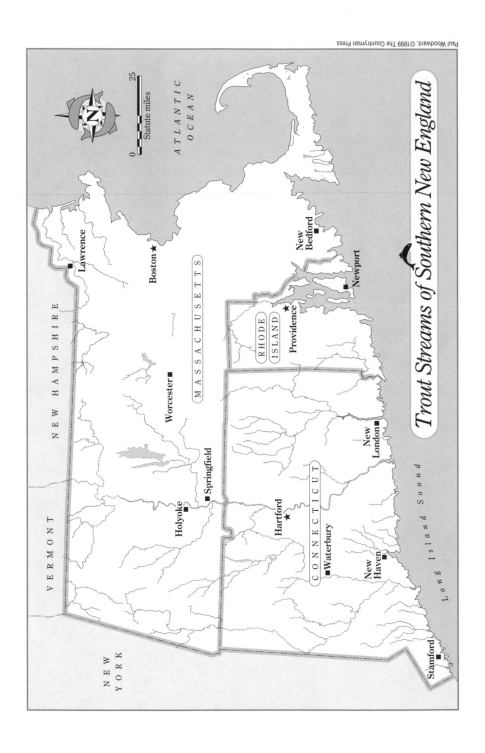

Trout Streams of Southern New England

ATLANTIC OCEAN

Statute miles

0   25

N

NEW HAMPSHIRE

VERMONT

NEW YORK

MASSACHUSETTS

RHODE ISLAND

CONNECTICUT

Long Island Sound

Lawrence

Boston ★

Worcester ■

Springfield ■

Holyoke ■

Hartford ★

Waterbury ■

New Haven ■

Stamford ■

New London ■

Providence ★

Newport ■

New Bedford ■

Contents

The book you hold in your hands is a labor of love—love for a region, its trout waters, and its history. New England, for all its faults, is still the place we call home, where our roots are as long as any place in the country, and where many of us developed our great passion for nature in general and for her waters in particular.

For me, New England is where I started my own love affair with fly-fishing nearly fifty years ago, and it is where I have chased trout dreams for nearly 100 days a year for the last twenty. Because I have lived here all of my life, when I have needed to get on a stream, I have done so close to home, on a little brook across the street, on the cold waters of Swift River where it emerges from expansive Quabbin Reservoir, on the variety of waters in the Westfield River complex, or on the Western-look meanderings of the Deerfield River in the Berkshires. And these streams are all within an hour of my house.

I have, of course, had dreams of other waters in other areas of the continent. The siren song of the West has drawn me there regularly to drop my flies in its pure, productive waters. Their big fish and blizzardlike hatches are not to be denied, and the very space and span of the West is something to behold. The addictive attractions of a 20-pound Atlantic salmon screaming line off your reel is also an experience that is matched by no other in fly-fishing. And with Atlantic Canada so close at hand, how could I even begin to intimate that New England anglers can find experiences to rival that one in their own territory? I can't.

But what I can do is state unequivocally that there is ample excellent fly-fishing for trout right here in southern New England. We fly-fishers may be a group of dreamers, always anxious to test waters a day or two or three away (who among us hasn't dreamed of fly-fishing New Zealand?), but we're also realists who need to put flies in front of trout regularly. And we can do it right here close to home, on a variety of fertile waters matched by no other place in the world that I know of.

Make no mistake, our trout waters have suffered all of the insults that a modern industrial society can throw at them. They have been soiled and dammed and abused like no other waters in the country. Yet we lovers of free-flowing, clean water can take pride in the job that we and our fellow citizens have done in remedying past wrongs.

The weight of our numbers—and there is no higher concentration of concerned anglers than in the Northeast—has forced improvements in our water-quality standards and has not only stopped the pollution of our streams, but also seen the reversal of the damage. And for the first time ever, our voices have been heard in the fight to give equal weight to the needs of all people for the use of rivers. We have seen dams removed on the Clyde River in Vermont and the Kennebec River in Maine. Five more on the Naugatuck in Connecticut will soon be gone. These temples of greed and disregard for the public good have long stood as symbols of a bygone era. Now that they are gone, a new era of respect has dawned, not only for the cleanliness of our waters but for their very real aesthetic value.

This does not mean that we can let our guard down. It means that we need to support the coalitions of river users—all river users—who together have given a single voice to all of us who would guard our precious resources. Anyone who would enjoy a river or pond or lake, be they a hiker, a rafter, a canoeist, or a fly-fisherman, becomes a steward. And together they become a force to be reckoned with. So join Trout Unlimited (TU), or the Appalachian Mountain Club, or your local watershed group, and be active. We've come a long way, and we need to keep going forward.

This book is intended to help anyone who would like to scratch their angling itch to do so more easily. It is not—indeed cannot be—all-inclusive, but I have tried to cover the most important waters in all three southern New England states. I hope that this book will help you find and enjoy the wealth of good water to be found here. In addition, I hope it leads you to appreciate the long struggle to restore these waters and to learn something about the important part that flowing and still water has played in defining this region and the country.

This book is organized geographically and geologically. In Massachusetts and Connecticut, the waters are presented from west to east. In Rhode Island, they are presented north to south. I then focus on particular watersheds within each state. At the beginning of each major river system you'll find a map pinpointing location; the pertinent United States Geological Survey (USGS) topographical map name; and capsule descriptions of water type, regulations, access, necessary patterns, and some of the highlights (and low points) of the particular drainage. These capsules allow you to flip to the targeted water and quickly get the essential information you need. The remainder of the text gives a more in-depth profile.

What you'll find here is that even within the tiny confines of southern New England, there are more trout streams, rivers, lakes, and ponds than any one angler can fully appreciate in a lifetime. The variety of waters in itself is quite astonishing, and their fertility and ability to sustain trout year-round will surprise you. This variety and fertility will also reinforce what many angling veterans of the area have always believed—namely, that southern New England does not contain only marginal or barren trout waters, that it is not the overcrowded, overfished region that many casual observers perceive it to be. It is, rather, a fly-fisherman's delight with opportunities and trout for all.

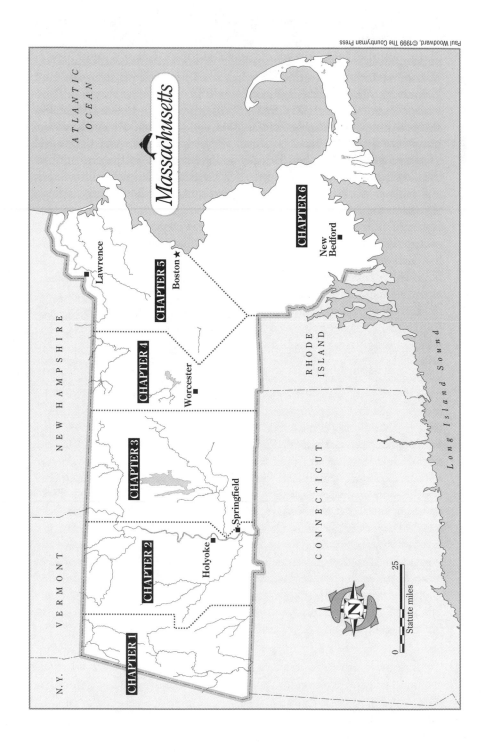

Massachusetts

I | MASSACHUSETTS

Massachusetts spans the southern New England trout-fishing spectrum, both geographically and ecologically. The state is the home of some of the very best examples of the region's trout streams, rivers, lakes, and ponds, but it also harbors too many examples of past abuses that are still waiting to be resolved. Where the trout waters are good, they're often spectacular, with plenty of strong holdover and stream-born trout, heavy hatches and forage bases, and plenty of room and access for fly-fishermen. And even where serious pollution problems remain, specifically persistent mercury and (PCB) contamination, trout often thrive, albeit on a de facto catch-and-release basis.

Nowhere in the state is this contrast more evident than in the waters of the west slope of the Berkshire Hills. The two main watersheds of Berkshire County, the Housatonic and the Hoosic, flow in opposite directions, south and north respectively, and contain alarming levels of PCBs. They also hold very big trout, in spite of an official shunning of their waters by the Division of Fisheries and Wildlife and the stocking trucks. Yet several of the streams that feed into these rivers, like the Green Rivers in Great Barrington and Williamstown and the Konkapot River, offer some of the most rewarding angling in the state in their pure waters and pristine settings.

The Connecticut River Valley shows the same contrast even more acutely. The Deerfield River and the Westfield River watershed flow into the Connecticut from the west, and they are truly magnificent. They're big; they're pure; they are surrounded by protected lands; and they hold trout, insects, and forage exceptionally well. Yet nearly opposite the mouth of the Deerfield, the Millers River has a consumption advisory because of mercury and PCB pollution. South of the Millers River in the Chicopee River watershed—where the population is denser and you'd expect to find even more focused pollution problems—the Ware, Quaboag, and Swift Rivers are first-class, pollution-free trout streams.

This pattern continues throughout the state. The Nashua River flows through the central highlands and contains mercury, but the Squannacook and the Nissitisset Rivers, two of the state's finest, feed into it. The Sudbury River, in the northeast, is polluted, but the pure Parker and Ipswich Rivers are nearby.

It must be said, however, that the situation with the polluted rivers is not static. In almost all cases, the industrial sources of heavy metals have been identified and new pollution stopped. Historic source sites of the heavy metals have also been identified, and there is, finally, some movement to clean them up. And the rivers themselves have begun to flush some of these pollutants out, although not with the rapid, miraculous cleansing that we saw with the more soluble pollutants when the Clean Water Act was first instituted.

So Bay State anglers can opt for pristine waters that are justly famous or can ply the not-so-pristine waters where the angling pressure is substantially reduced. Both types hold trout, and both types can be enormously rewarding.

In Massachusetts, anglers can also choose from a broad variety of types of water. Meadow meanders resembling fertile limestone streams are available throughout the state, as are mountain-type freestone streams. Diligent searchers can find hidden, wooded headwater streams that literally teem with native brookies. There are even broad, flowing cold waters with enough hidden backwaters to keep canoeing anglers happy for years. Landlocked salmon run up into rivers that feed both the Quabbin and Wachusett Reservoirs. And on Cape Cod, sea-run brown trout and brookies chase up into freshwater streams seeking food and spawning areas.

Still-water anglers can likewise choose from the full array of waters. Huge, fertile Quabbin Reservoir is an oasis of wilderness that holds landlocked salmon, lake trout, rainbows, and brown trout. On the other extreme, there are innumerable beaver ponds where brookies thrive, especially now that myopic urban voters have banned trapping in the state. And there are hundreds of examples of trout-holding still waters in between.

The highlight of all of these still waters, however, may well be the unique kettle holes of Cape Cod. These small—even tiny—bodies of water are deep, spring fed, and astoundingly fertile. Most have direct access to the sea, adding the bonus of river herring forage. And nowhere in the state do trout grow so large so quickly. These waters are a shore-wader's or belly-boat aficionado's dream.

The contrasts that exist in the state's waters are paralleled by contrasts in the state's administration of its waters. Visionary leaders of the Division of Fisheries and Wildlife long ago eliminated any closed season on trout throughout the state. While some traditionalists still bemoan the lack of an opening day, anglers more attuned to the needs of the trout realize that ultimately a year-round open season provides better angling. Stocking can be done when water levels, pH, and temperatures are optimal. The lack of a closed season allows stocked trout to acclimate to their new habitat. They discover where the food is, even what it is. They find the best holding areas away from the stocking sites. They become wilder and more challenging.

The division also flagged the most important rivers in the commonwealth and imposed a reduced daily trout limit of three fish on them. And they labeled several important stretches of streams as either fly-fishing-only waters or catch-and-release, artificial-lure-only waters. All of these moves have helped.

Yet somewhere along the line, the division became complacent. An important study intended to catalogue the trout waters of the state so that they might be better managed was initiated haphazardly and quickly abandoned. (Connecticut has effectively organized and completed just such a study.) This lack of information means, for instance, that fine brook trout waters still receive disruptive stockings of jumbo-sized rainbows and browns—fish that quickly migrate out of the tiny streams, but not until they've displaced the brookies.

Further refinements to the catch-and-release program have run afoul of politics and perceived revenue flows, rather than responding to the needs of the waters and the anglers who use them. Recent proposals, for instance, to adopt a more extensive catch-and-release section on the Swift River—or to establish at least short, protected areas on the Quinapoxet and Quaboag Rivers—have been quickly pushed aside.

So while much has been accomplished, much remains to be done. In the meantime, the waters of Massachusetts remain. They're very attractive to anglers now, it cannot be denied; but they still need our attention and help. As we enjoy their bounty, we must be ever watchful to maintain and improve them.

Below, some 70 of the most important waters of Massachusetts are discussed, many in detail. And all of the waters in the commonwealth that the Division of Fisheries and Wildlife stock with trout are either discussed or listed. No one in the state is more than a few minutes' drive from decent trout fishing, and all of us are no more than an hour's drive from spectacular angling. Enjoy.

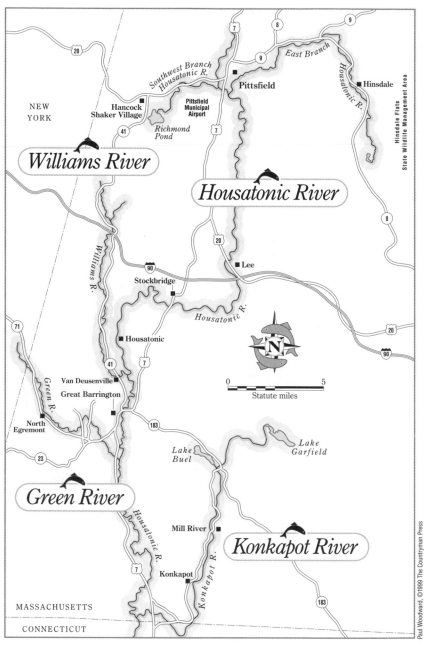

NEW YORK

20

Southwest Branch
Housatonic R.

Hancock
Shaker Village

Pittsfield
Municipal
Airport

Richmond
Pond

41

7

9

East Branch

Housatonic R.

■ Pittsfield

9

8

9

■ Hinsdale

8

Hinsdale Flats
State Wildlife Management Area

Williams River

Housatonic River

Williams R.

20

90

Stockbridge

■ Lee

Housatonic R.

■ Housatonic

71

7

N

41

Green R.

Van Deusenville
Great Barrington

■ North
Egremont

23

183

Green River

Lake
Buel

Lake
Garfield

20

90

0   5
Statute miles

■ Mill River

Konkapot River

Housatonic R.

7

Konkapot R.

■ Konkapot

183

MASSACHUSETTS

CONNECTICUT

Paul Woodward, ©1999 The Countryman Press

West Slope of the Berkshire Hills

HOUSATONIC RIVER

Maps *USGS:* Ashley Falls (Connecticut border to Sheffield), Great Barrington (Sheffield to Housatonic), Stockbridge (Housatonic to Lee), East Lee (Lee to Lenox), Pittsfield East (Lenox to Pittsfield).

Description The Housatonic River makes an impressive 36-mile-long meander through some of western Massachusetts' most beautiful mountains and farmlands. It is fertile, it is accessible, and it should be one of the state's crown jewels for trout fishermen. Yet there is no mention of the Housatonic in the state's fishing and hunting abstracts. It has not been labeled a major trout stream, as have many other lesser streams in the commonwealth. It is not stocked with trout and has not been for years. And there is no mention in any trout-fishing guide of its attractions.

The reason for this universal shunning of the Housatonic River is its extreme pollution by PCBs, a potent, proven carcinogen. As one U.S. Fish and Wildlife official told me, it is "so polluted with PCBs that it should fairly glow after dark."

Yet the Housatonic does have trout, a good supply of stream-born browns that have been documented by the state to average 1–3 pounds, and it even holds some lunker browns as large as 6 pounds. These trout are the by-products of stocking in many of the tributaries of the Housatonic that do flow pollution-free (see below). And the river is fertile, with strong hatches of mayflies and caddis and a good supply of forage fish such as sculpins and dace.

Should you fish the Housatonic? Yes, emphatically, but we all should take an active interest in the restoration of the Housatonic River to a clean-flowing, nonthreatening resource. It could easily become southern New England's premier trout river.

Access Major highways intertwine to follow the Housatonic for its entire flow through Massachusetts from the city of Pittsfield to the Connecticut border.

US Routes 7 and 20 lead south out of Pittsfield along the river. In Lenox, US 20 bears southeast toward Lee and stays along the river, and US 7 cuts cross-country to Stockbridge, where it again picks up the river (which has taken a sweeping westward turn in Lee). MA 102 follows this aberration of flow between Lee and Stockbridge and provides good access. In Stockbridge, US 7 merges with MA 102, but soon US 7 bends to the south, right in the middle of that famous town. Stay on Main Street, which becomes Glendale Middle Road and soon crosses the river and joins MA 183. Turn south, and fish this section, one of the most attractive of the entire river, all the way to Great Barrington. There you'll again join US 7, which then closely follows the river to Connecticut.

Regulations The Housatonic River in Massachusetts has no closed season and no tackle restrictions. However, the presence of heavy PCB pollution makes the river a de facto catch-and-release river. Do not eat fish, or anything else for that matter, from the Housatonic.

Don't miss The river south of Great Barrington is a meandering, trout-growing factory that flows through pastoral farmland and along mature woodlands. East Sheffield Street, a country lane along its east shore, is remote and lovely and gives plenty of easy access to the river. The river here can be waded in many places, and a convenient canoe access at Brush Hill Road makes it possible to float this entire run of river. If you have only a short day to ply the waters of the Housatonic, do it here.

Best asset The irony of the Housatonic's pollution is that the river is largely abandoned. You could fish its trout runs and riffles for a week and not see another angler. Yet this is fertile water. Indeed, just a short run downstream, in Connecticut, the catch-and-release area there (see chapter 8) is world famous. In years to come, you might just be able to say you fished the famous waters of Massachusetts' Housatonic before it became the East's best-known trout water.

Biggest drawback PCB pollution is easily the Housatonic's biggest problem, and because of it, other pollution sources have not been pressed as hard as they might be. There are places where it is just plain not pleasant to be on the river, yet with renewed attention to the cleanup of PCBs, the entire river should improve.

Necessary patterns *Underwater:* Pheasant Tail Nymph (#14–20), Hare's Ear Nymph (#12–16), Hendrickson Nymph (#12–16), Leadwing Coachman (#12–14), Caddis Larva (#14–18), Caddis Emerger (#12–18), Black-Nosed Dace (#4–10), Sculpin (#4–12), Matuka (#2–12), Clouser Deep Minnow

(#4–10). *Dry flies:* Quill Gordon (#12–16); Hendrickson (#12–16); Red Quill (#12–16); Rusty Spinner (#12–16); March Brown (#12–14); Gray Fox (#12–14); Mahogany Dun (#12–16); Mahogany Spinner (#10–16); Sulphur Dun (#14–16); Light Cahill (#14–16); Green Drake (#6–10); Brown Drake (#10–12); Golden Drake (#8–12); White Mayfly (#12–14); Tan, Yellow, Brown, Green or Black Caddis (#12–18); Blue-Winged Olive (#12–20); Cream Midge (#18–22); Trico (#18–24); Alder (#16–18); Cricket (#10–14); Hopper (#4–12); Black or Cinnamon Ant (#10–20).

Stocked feeder streams worth a look Konkapot River (see below), Green River (see below), Williams River, Southwest Branch of the Housatonic, East Branch of the Housatonic, Iron Works Brook, Hubbard Brook, Larrywaug Brook, West Branch Beartown Brook, Hop Brook, Goose Pond Brook, Washington Mountain Brook, Yokum Brook, Sackett Brook.

Other feeders (from downstream to upstream) Roaring Brook, Thomas and Palmer Brook, Mohawk Brook, Konkapot Brook, Kampoosa Brook, Willow Brook, Barnes Brook, Laurel Brook, Codding Brook, Willow Creek, Roaring Brook, Mill Brook, Sykes Brook, Wampenum Brook.

The Housatonic River is both a revelation for anyone seeking little-used but rich trout water, and a tragedy. The river could become the premier trout water in the state, but not until its severe PCB pollution problem has been addressed and cleaned up. The source of this pollution was long ago identified and halted, but PCBs, unlike many other pollutants, do not flush out of a river. Instead, they become embedded in the silt and gravel and infect all of the living organisms there, including insects, forage, and ultimately fish.

Yet recently there has been a movement to clean up the Housatonic River. Finally, state and federal environmental officials are beginning to get tough about eliminating PCBs, and have even threatened to list the entire river as a federal Superfund site. Negotiations with General Electric, whose Pittsfield plant was the source of the pollution, have been contentious and ongoing, and no firm cleanup plan has been agreed on to date. But at least there has been a general consensus that the river is polluted and needs to be attended to. It will certainly be years before the river is free from PCBs, but perhaps in our lifetime the Housatonic River will assume its rightful place as the crown jewel of Massachusetts trout angling.

The main stem of the Housatonic is formed in the heart of Pittsfield where the Southwest Branch joins the East Branch. Quickly the river flows east, then south into a surprisingly wild section of habitat, which has been largely protected by the Division of Fisheries and Wildlife. To fish this upper area, you'll need to cut across the southern tier of the city to East New

The Housatonic River just below Stockbridge has both moving water and some decent slow water angling.

Lenox Road, which parallels the river on its east bank all the way into Lee. The best route is via Crofut Street, a left (east) turn off US 7 and 20 just past Memorial Park. Bear right onto Pomeroy Street, take your first left onto Brunswick Street and your first right onto Williams Street, which runs east for 2 miles to East New Lenox Road. Turn right (south).

East New Lenox Road parallels the river through Pittsfield and into Lenox, where much of the river is included in the Housatonic River State Wildlife Management Area (WMA). New Lenox Road crosses the river to the west (a right turn) and leads to the John F. Decker Canoe Access, which is important for this slow, mostly unwadeable water.

South of New Lenox Road, East New Lenox Road becomes Roaring Brook Road. The name is a misnomer, for the river here is a series of deep, sweeping oxbows and backwaters, with better pike and bass fishing than trout fishing, but there are some hidden and large brown trout. October Mountain State Forest borders the eastern side of Roaring Brook Road, which becomes a dirt road that is quite rough, though usually passable, all the way south, through the town of Washington and into Lenoxdale. The road's name in Lee is officially Woodland Road, and Woods Pond, which is formed by a dam on the river, shortly comes into view. On the south edge of Woods Pond, Valley Street bears right (west), but the bridge across the Housatonic here is for foot traffic only. You can launch a canoe or car-top boat, however.

Continue along Woodland Road to Willow Hill Road, bear right, cross the river at the Mill River bridge, and turn right (north) onto Crystal Street. It borders the river here, below Woods Pond, where there is a more natural flow and some decent pocket water and pools. Be aware, however, that the Lenox station sewage disposal plant is nearby and can blanket the area with a foul stench. Check for wind direction.

Mill Street, on the south end of Crystal Street, leads to Columbia Street. Follow it south to Main Street, Lee, which is US 20. Turn left (south) here to where US 20 crosses under I-90, the Massachusetts Turnpike. At this intersection, MA 102 heads west along the river toward Stockbridge. Again, the river is little fished here, but there is access to it at several locations, and it has some decent plunge pools and riffles.

On the west side of Stockbridge, Main Street becomes Glendale Middle Road and, just after crossing the river, bumps into MA 183. Turn left (south) and fish anywhere along the highway. This meandering country lane is just far enough away from urban Pittsfield and Lee, and from the bustle of tourist-choked Stockbridge, to make you believe you're back in pristine country. You aren't, of course, as MA 183 soon rejoins US 7 just north of Great Barrington, itself a thriving community of antiques stores, schools, and commerce.

Travel along US 7, past the fairgrounds, to Brookside Road, a left (east) turn. An arched steel bridge crosses the river, and there is a canoe access and parking lot just west of the bridge. The river is large here, but you can carefully wade along its shores and fish the riffles and runs. In addition, there are deep pools at the turns and along the undercut bankings, some 15 feet and deeper, where lunker browns lurk. If you prefer, you can float a canoe downstream, but stop above the good pools and runs so you don't alert these wary and impressively large browns.

Just east of the Brookside Road bridge, East Sheffield Road turns right (south) and parallels the river into the town of Sheffield, where its name changes to Boardman Road. About 2 miles along, Kellogg Road turns right (west) and returns to US 7. You can take out your canoe here.

Follow US 7 south all the way to the Connecticut border, and use any of the rest stops and turnouts along it to get onto the river. If you have the time, you can meander through any of the 25 antiques shops in Sheffield or fish at the Covered Bridge Lane bridge (yes, it's covered and newly restored) or at the bridge on Maple Avenue.

The trout in the Housatonic in Massachusetts are browns, survivors of earlier stockings in the feeders. They're mostly stream born and wary, and they grow large. As a plus, they're not fished over very often, so presenting good artificials that match the current hatch, or drifting big nymphs or streamers into the depths of the plunge pools and undercut bankings, can produce exciting hard strikes from big trout.

Konkapot River

The Konkapot River originates from Lake Garfield in the town of Monterey as a small swamp-laden rill, then gathers the waters from Lake Buel in northern New Marlboro and from a few small feeders as it rushes south toward Connecticut. These upper reaches do provide some decent small-water opportunities for anglers, but much of the land around it is posted. Be sure that you know you are welcome or get landowner permission to cross onto the stream.

From the little community of Mill River, downstream through the town of Konkapot to the crossroads at Clayton, the river is much more attractive for fly-fishermen and much more accessible. A good road, the Clayton Mill River Road, follows the river closely, and you can park along it almost anywhere and step into a pretty stream that has good water quality and decent stocked and holdover trout. At Clayton, the river takes a 2-mile-long oxbow meander into Connecticut before sweeping back into Massachusetts and dumping into the Housatonic.

Find Clayton Mill River Road from the north via MA 57 (from the east or west). Turn south onto the Hartsville Mill River Road at the outlet from Lake Buel. This road leads to the town of Mill River. From US 7 and Sheffield, take the Clayton Road east just before the Connecticut state line, turn north (left) in Clayton and onto the Clayton Mill River Road. Note that there is another Clayton Road just over the Connecticut line, which some maps note as CT 124, but which has no such markings on the road. It too leads to the town of Clayton and Clayton Mill River Road.

If all of these directions sound like you're headed out into the country, you are, and that's the charm of the Konkapot River. Each of the towns mentioned above is little more than a crossroads with a few well-kept colonial houses on their corners, and the rolling hills and gentle farmland that border the river and the roads are lightly populated and inviting. The river is, too, because its trout are not pressured and easily rise to decent hatches of mayflies and caddis.

Green River (Great Barrington)

The Green River in Great Barrington (not to be confused with the Green River in Williamstown) is a small version of the best river you've ever fished. It has the highest quality of water in the county, supports prolific and varied hatches of mayflies and caddis, holds stream-born browns and brookies as well as stocked rainbows, and is easily accessible. If only it was 100 feet wide, not 15.

The quality of the Green's water and its gravel bottom are what make it such a fertile trout brook. On a late August day, after a long and oppressive

The Green River in Great Barrington is cold and home to a strong core of stream-bred trout.

heat wave, I took the temperature of the stream not far from where it empties into the Housatonic. It was 64 degrees cold in three different locations. (The nearby Williams River was 78 degrees.) And in each of these locations, the flowing water meandered and turned and cut deep into the banks to form ideal, protected trout havens of tangled roots and dark shadows. In addition, the river stayed shaded and sheltered, and deadfalls helped gouge out inviting pools.

That's the good news. The bad is that these same trout meccas, the undercut banks and roots and deadfall pools, are not easy to fish. And this fragile little river could be vulnerable to overfishing if it became too well-known. Still, a short 3-weight travel rod and an adventurous spirit can lead to a full day of superb angling on the Green.

Find the best angling by turning west in Great Barrington from US 7 onto MA 23 and 41. The road passes over the Green within a mile, and you can park at the bridge and fish up- or downstream. Soon, MA 71 bears right, and three right (north) turns (Hurlburt, Seekonk Cross, and Pumpkin Hollow

Roads) all lead to the river. To fish its small headwaters, stay on MA 71 into Egremont and Alford, as the river flows beside the road.

Williams River

The Williams River originates in West Stockbridge near Massachusetts Turnpike Exit 1 and flows due south into Great Barrington; with it joins the Housatonic in the village of Van Deusenville. MA 41, where a number of crossroads and bridges provide access, parallels the river for its entire run.

The Williams also parallels the Housatonic River, but is separated from it by a ridge of rocky hills, making it more a freestone stream and lacking the supplemental nutrients that enrich many other flows in the floodplain of the Housatonic. Still, the Williams flows through some very attractive country and does generate enough forage to feed its trout, most of which are stocked annually. There are a few holdover fish, but the river can suffer from high summer temperatures.

Southwest Branch of the Housatonic

The Southwest Branch of the Housatonic River is an urban, slow-moving water that originates in Richmond Pond, just southwest of Pittsfield and the Pittsfield Municipal Airport. Its leisurely pace and crowded surroundings belie a very good early-season trout stream with water that maintains the high quality that emerges from Richmond Pond. It has very decent hatches of mayflies and, particularly, caddis.

Although the river is capable of holding trout throughout the year, it does receive substantial angling pressure, making stream-born and holdover trout rare. Access is limited to bridges and areas close to the highway, but there are plenty of them.

US 20 follows the flow of the river west out of downtown Pittsfield, and Lebanon Avenue, a left (south) turn 2 miles from downtown, connects with Chapel Street. They both parallel the river upstream near Richmond Pond.

East Branch of the Housatonic

The East Branch of the Housatonic River originates as a swampy, brush-choked brook just south of the town of Hinsdale. This upriver section is very difficult to fish, but this leads to very little pressure and some very nice holdover brookies and browns. Access here is very good because the state owns the Hinsdale Flats Wildlife Management Area (WMA), but the wading and casting can be difficult because of the boggy, close-growing vegetation.

Just north (downstream) of the WMA, MA 8 finds the river and follows it through the town of Hinsdale before both the river and the road turn west toward Dalton, just east of Pittsfield. The most attractive angling water can be found along the highway, which has a number of pullouts for parking and decent riffles, rapids, and pools all along the way. In and below Dalton, that familiar Housatonic River problem, PCB pollution, again becomes present, and the state does no stocking.

The East Branch is of note because it is an excellent early-season stream that rarely overflows its banks. When all of the other streams in the region are high and roiled and unfishable, the East Branch is an excellent choice. Conversely, it does suffer from very low summer flows, and only in the upstream swampy area will trout hold over.

OTHER IMPORTANT REGIONAL RIVERS

Hoosic River

The Hoosic River consists of three major reaches: the South Branch, which originates in Lanesboro, gets interrupted by Cheshire Reservoir in Cheshire, then flows through Adams and into North Adams; the North Branch, which is a mountain stream in its headwaters in Clarksburg and joins the South Branch in North Adams; and the main stem, which flows out of North Adams, through Williamstown, into Vermont, and eventually into the Hudson River in New York.

The high quality of the fishing in the Hoosic River is little known beyond the local anglers. Those outside of the region know only that there is yet another pollution advisory, again for deadly PCBs, in the Hoosic. And they stay away in droves. Yet the South Branch is easily accessible, is very fertile, and holds trout well, and the North Branch has plenty of plunge pools, rapids, and riffle water. And neither of these streams is polluted—only the main stem from North Adams downstream contains the PCBs, making it a de facto catch-and-release river. In both the North and South Branches, the state stocks rainbows and brown trout, while the main stem holds stream-born browns, some to 3 pounds. And there are strong hatches of mayflies and caddis throughout the rivers.

The South Branch flows due north along MA 8 with its best angling downstream (north) of Cheshire Reservoir. In the town of Cheshire, turn east onto Church Street to where it crosses the river. An abandoned railroad bed follows the river up- and downstream, providing plenty of good access. The area from Cheshire to Cheshire Harbor, about 2 miles long, is more a slow, meandering type of water, but there are a few decent riffles and some nice trout pools. It becomes more of a classic trout stream between Cheshire Harbor and the flood control chutes in Adams, with MA 8 following close beside the west bank.

The short run of the North Branch in Massachusetts is paralleled by MA 8 from North Adams through Clarksburg and into Vermont. Travel north on

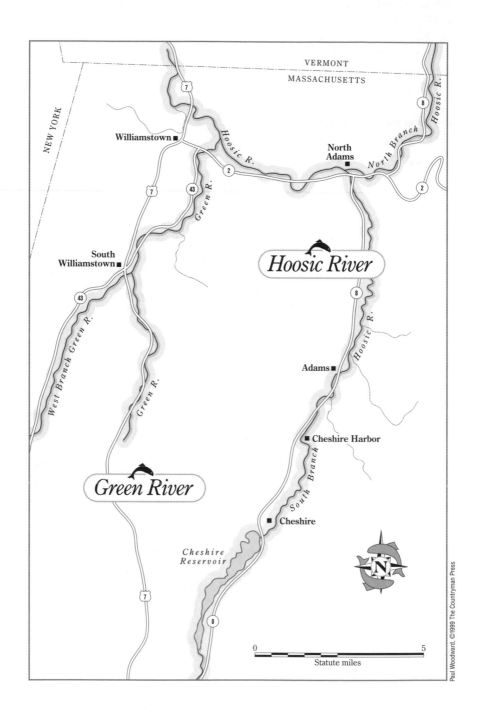

VERMONT

MASSACHUSETTS

NEW YORK

7

Hoosic R.

Williamstown ■

North
Adams ■

North Branch

Hoosic R.

8

2

7

43

Green R.

2

South
Williamstown ■

🐟
Hoosic River

43

8

West Branch Green R.

Hoosic R.

Green R.

Adams ■

🐟
Green River

■ Cheshire Harbor

South Branch

■ Cheshire

*Cheshire
Reservoir*

N

7

8

0   5
▮▯▮▯▮▯▮▮▮▮
Statute miles

Paul Woodward, ©1999 The Countryman Press

MA 8 toward the Clarksburg State Park to get away from the milky, murky water lower on the river.

The main stem of the Hoosic emerges from the cement flood-control pits in downtown North Adams and the downstream canals and travels through the highly developed area between North Adams and Williamstown. MA 2 is the main connecting highway and parallels the river along its south bank, but another road, Massachusetts Avenue, runs along the opposite shore. Look for the Ashton Avenue bridge, which is in the middle of the best reach for angling, and park at the canoe access on the south side of the bridge.

By the time the Hoosic reaches Williamstown, it has become a mature and inviting river, although still polluted with PCBs. The town itself (home of Williams College), the Williamstown Rural Lands Foundation, and the Hoosic Watershed Association have all been especially active in protecting the river corridor and surrounding land, so access to the river is relatively easy here.

US 7 runs north out of the town, and on the north side of the bridge over the river there is good access at the Bridges Pond Fish and Wildlife Access Area on the east. You can also turn left (west) just past the bridge onto the road that leads down to the water treatment plant and the Department of Public Works (DPW) complex and get onto good water. Look for a sign pointing to the DPW and treatment plant (there's no road name).

The Hoosic River could become a very fine trout stream, if there was a solution both to its PCB problem and to the general disrespect the river receives in Adams and North Adams. After all, it's hard to appreciate a river that is considered a dangerous threat because of flooding and that is sluiced into dirt and riprap canals and towering cement pits. In both communities, the river looks like it's just a big, wet catch basin. But the water quality is there, with good year-round temperatures and fertility, and it has a proven ability to hold and grow trout. And downstream it has the gradient, the pools, and the access that should lead to its being flagged for its huge potential. Cross your fingers for the Hoosic River's future.

Green River (Williamstown)

Feeding into the Hoosic River in Williamstown from the south is the Green River, and it is as different from the Hoosic as a sump pond is from a spring pool. The Green (not to be confused with the Green River in Great Barrington) is a lively, rural, freestone stream with plenty of formal and informal access that roams just far enough away from the hubbub of the Hoosic and MA 2 to make you feel that you've stepped into another century. And in a sense you have.

A short 3 miles south of Williamstown on MA 43 brings you to a stretch of river owned by the Massachusetts Division of Fisheries and Wildlife, and it's labeled for fishermen's access. Its southern border ends at a manicured lawn and stone gateway, labeled as Mount Hope Farm. The farm was developed as a getaway for a Rockefeller daughter and includes paved roads, an elegant mansion, spacious, sweeping stables that are visible from the road, and posters forbidding trespass or hunting. Apparently the money or interest in the project ran out and Williams College now owns the land, but signs along the river invite anglers (and picnickers) to enjoy the landscape. And the invitation extends for another 1½ miles upstream. Just beware of the electric fences that enclose some of the pastures. Stepping over them, if you've got short legs like mine, can provide a jolting experience.

The river itself and its West Branch tumble down out of the mountains from New Ashford and Hancock, respectively, and they're never far from the roads. MA 43 follows the main stem from Williamstown to South Williamstown to its intersection with US 7. There, US 7 continues upstream (south) along the main stem to its headwaters, and MA 43 stays along the banks of the West Branch.

Both the main stem and the West Branch of the Green River are heavily stocked by the state with rainbows and a few browns, and there are good populations of stream-bred brook trout in the headwaters. Hatches are not prolific, but there are some good caddis and a few mayflies.

Farmington River

The Farmington River runs through southeastern Berkshire County, originating in Shaw Pond in Becket and flowing through Otis, Sandisfield, and Tolland to Connecticut. Yes, it is the same Farmington River that forms Colebrook Reservoir and emerges as the great tailwater fishery in Connecticut (see chapter 9). In Massachusetts, however, the Farmington is a much different river than it is in Connecticut, with its own qualities and charms.

Although its headwaters in Becket and North Otis are small and often very boggy, starting in Otis the river becomes attractive to anglers because it is very accessible, yet still remote. Its location in the hill towns is far enough away from the Pittsfield–Great Barrington sprawl to the west and Westfield and Springfield to the east to make it a joy to fish. Yes, a few anglers find it, especially in spring, but for much of the year the Farmington is largely abandoned.

MA 8 follows the river for its entire productive run in the state, with uncounted turnouts for parking, but with plenty of water just a short hike away that rarely sees anglers. Start in Otis and fish anywhere along the road south to the Colebrook Reservoir, a distance of nearly 11 miles.

The river is not terribly large, and it has plenty of pools, riffles, and runs. Nearly all of it is easily waded, and it receives plenty of stocked trout, both rainbows and browns. In addition, there are very strong hatches of mayflies and caddis, and good numbers of stonefly nymphs. Good trout are

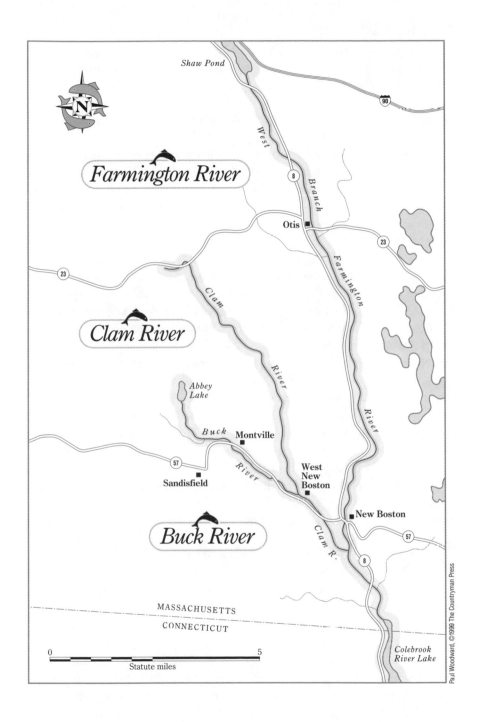

Shaw Pond

90

West

8

Branch

Otis

23

Farmington

Farmington River

23

Clam

Clam River

River

Abbey
Lake

River

Buck

Montville

57

River

West
New
Boston

Sandisfield

Buck River

Clam R.

New Boston

57

8

MASSACHUSETTS

CONNECTICUT

0   5

Statute miles

Colebrook
River Lake

taken on small streamers each year, too.

Clam and Buck Rivers

You've got to love two rivers called the Clam and the Buck, and in this case the streams back up their names with some excellent and often remote angling for stream-born brookies that are supplemented with stocked trout. These two mountain streams come together in West New Boston and feed into the Farmington River just a short distance upstream from Colebrook Reservoir in Sandisfield.

Of the two, the Clam is more remote, flowing as it does away from any nearby road access. You can get onto it via MA 57 in Montville by turning north onto the Montville Beech Plain Road, which is labeled Hammertown Road on some maps. The river emerges from a small flood-control dam and runs south through remote hills for 2 miles to its juncture with the Buck right on MA 57. Take hiking shoes rather than waders, because the river is a classic mountain stream with plenty of plunge pools and fast water.

The Buck originates just above Abbey Lake, another small flood-control impoundment in Sandisfield, and flows as a small mountain stream through Sandisfield State Forest until it crosses under Lower West Street to meet MA 57. Find this remote section of the Buck by hiking upstream from Lower West Street or by turning north onto West Street from MA 57 a mile west of Montville. East Hubbard Road turns east from West Street after about 2 miles, and near where it reverts to a dirt road, about a mile in, the Buck crosses under the road just upstream from Abbey Lake. Hike down to Abbey Lake and find the outlet on its southern end, then fish the Buck downstream to Lower West Road and MA 57. From here downstream to its confluence with the Clam, the Buck closely follows the path of MA 57 to New Boston, MA 8, and the Farmington River.

Both of these rivers offer good deep-woods angling for trout, with decent hatches of fast-water mayflies and some caddis. Because they see few anglers, however, a bright Royal Coachman dry fly might be all you'll need.

Other Stocked Trout Streams on the West Slope of the Berkshire Hills

Adams: Tophet Brook; *Alford:* Seekonk Brook; *Cheshire:* Dry Brook, Kitchen Brook, South Brook; *Clarksburg:* Hudson Brook; *Dalton:* Wahconah Falls Brook; *Great Barrington:* West Brook; Hancock: Kinderhook Creek; *Hinsdale:* Bennett Brook; *Lanesboro:* Town Brook, Secum Brook; *Lee:* Greenwater Brook; *New Marlboro:* Umpacheene Brook; *North Adams:* Notch Brook; *Pittsfield:* Daniel Brook, Lulu Cascade Brook, Smith Brook; *Richmond:* Cone Brook, Furnace Brook; *Washington:* Depot Brook; *Williamstown:* Broad Brook, Hemlock Brook.

Important Stocked Ponds and Lakes in the Region

Stocked spring and fall: *Lee:* Goose Pond, Laurel Lake; *Monterey:* Lake Buel; *Pittsfield:* Onota Lake, Lake Pontoosuc; *Stockbridge:* Stockbridge Bowl. **Stocked only in spring:** *Becket:* Greenwater Pond; *Great Barrington:* Mansfield Lake; *Hancock:* Berry Pond; *Hinsdale:* Plunkett Reservoir; *Monterey:* Lake Garfield; *New Marlboro:* York Pond; *North Adams:* Windsor Lake; *Richmond:* Richmond Pond.

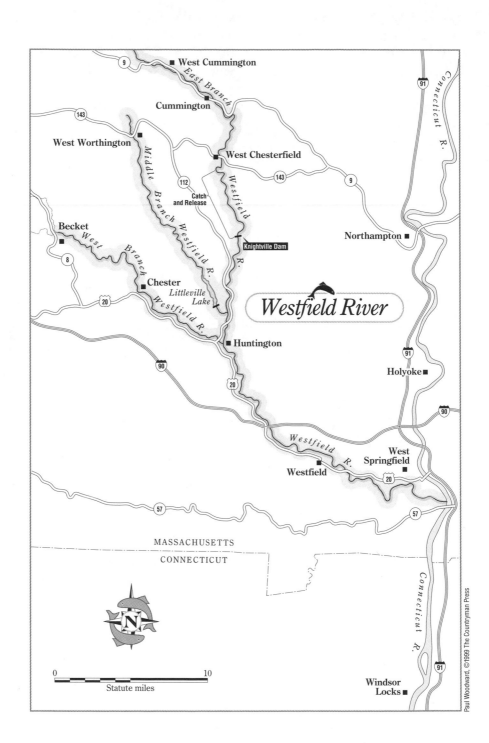

West Cummington

East Branch

9

Cummington

143

West Worthington

West Chesterfield

112

143

9

Catch
and Release

Northampton

Becket

West

Middle Branch Westfield R.

Knightville Dam

8

Chester

Littleville
Lake

Westfield River

Branch

20

Westfield R.

Huntington

90

20

91

Holyoke

90

Westfield R.

West
Springfield

57

Westfield

20

57

Connecticut R.

91

MASSACHUSETTS

CONNECTICUT

N

Connecticut R.

0   10
Statute miles

Windsor
Locks

91

Paul Woodward, ©1999 The Countryman Press

2 | Major Connecticut River Tributaries from the West

WESTFIELD RIVER

Maps *USGS:* Blandford (main stem), Chester (majority of the three branches), Goshen (headwaters of Middle and East Branches).

Description The three main branches of the Westfield River are wild and scenic and include more than 43 miles that are federally designated as such. These are the only Massachusetts waters thus protected. They're freestoners, subject to the whims of nature until they hit the Knightville Dam on the East Branch and the Littleville Dam on the Middle Branch. The West Branch flows free to its confluence with the main stem in Huntington. The branches are typical mountain streams—pocket water, pools, rapids, and riffles—and are stocked heavily by the state with rainbows, browns, and some brookies. There are reproducing populations of both browns and brookies in all of the branches, especially in the headwaters that stay cold year-round. The main stem, from Huntington to West Springfield, is big water, but fishable, and it produces big stocked and holdover trout.

Access Most of the river miles are easily accessible by car. The catch-and-release section on the East Branch is 7 miles long and is a walk-in on an easy dirt road. A few sections, like the "Pork Barrel" on the East Branch, are best accessed by canoe, and some of the more isolated pockets are an easy hike through the woods.

Regulations All branches and the main stem are designated major rivers with a daily creel limit of three trout. The catch-and-release section of the East Branch is artificial lures and flies only, zero daily limit. (There is no closed fishing season in Massachusetts.)

Don't miss The Chesterfield Gorge, off Route 143 in Chesterfield, is where the East Branch plunges through a deep granite fissure. Its tail also signals the start of the catch-and-release section, which runs through state and federally protected land that consists of totally undeveloped forests.

Best asset The fish ladder at the West Springfield Dam at the mouth of the river now allows anadromous fish—shad, herring, an occasional striped bass, and even Atlantic salmon—up into the main stem. Numbers are still meager, but increasing. And a local sports shop, B&G Sporting, annually stocks 300–600 lunker trout, to 8 pounds, in the main stem.

Biggest drawback Spring water releases from the flood-control dams on the East and Middle Branches can raise and roil the water downstream. And the Westfield River Canoe Races in early spring ensure a big gush of water. Head for the hills—above the dams or to the West Branch.

Necessary patterns *Underwater:* Cased Caddis (#6–10), Caddis Larva (#14–18), Pheasant Tail Nymph (#12–18), Baetis Nymph (#14–18), March Brown (#12–14), Hendrickson Nymph (#12–16), Hare's Ear Nymph (#12–16), Hornberg (#6–12), Black-Nosed Dace (#4–12), Olive Woolly Bugger (#2–8), Llama (#2–8), Olive Teeko Bug (#6–10). *Dry flies:* Mottled Caddis (#14–16), Blue-Winged Olive (#14–18), Quill Gordon (#12–16), Hendrickson (#12–16), March Brown (#12–14), Slate Caddis (#14–16), Adams (#12–20), Ausable Wulff (#10–12), Letort Hopper (#8–12), [Ant] (#14–20).

Stocked feeder streams worth a look *Main stem:* Stage Brook, Potash Brook, Little River and Munn Brook, Powder Mill Brook, Great Brook; *West Branch:* Sanderson Brook, Walker Brook, Factory Brook, Yokum Brook, Shaker Mill Brook; Middle Branch: Kinney Brook, Trout Brook; East Branch: Little River, North Branch of the Swift River, Mill Brook, Westfield Brook, Windsor Jambs Brook.

Other feeders (from downstream to upstream) Coles Brook, Depot Brook, Glendale Brook, Whiteside Brook, West Falls Branch, Tower Brook, Meadow Brook, Center Brook.

The Westfield River watershed offers the full range of angling opportunities—from tributary pocket hopping for small native brookies to main stem, big-water trout measured in pounds, and everything in between. It also perfectly illustrates the history of so many of the region's streams that were abused during the Industrial Revolution and then almost entirely redeemed.

Along the main stem and tributaries, there are no fewer than 29 dams and six water treatment sites. Granted, many of the dams are on smaller feeder streams, but four of the dams and all of the treatment sites are on the main stem below Huntington. And the two dams on the East and Middle Branches, the Knightville and Littleville respectively, can affect downstream angling because of springtime water releases. The treatment sites, however, are the solution to a long-standing problem and must adhere to strict water-quality standards. And the dams on the main stem were served notice that

The main stem of the Westfield River along US 20 is big water, but manageable.

fish ladders are imminent with the arrival of spawning Atlantic salmon below the West Springfield dam three years ago. A fish ladder there became operable last year.

Main Stem of the Westfield

The angler's first introduction to the Westfield comes as he or she enters the city of Westfield on US 202. Emerging from an underpass, the nemesis of many high-boxed semi trucks, an old iron bridge gives a good view of the river both up- and downstream. This is inviting water, and turning west (right) onto US 20 shortly brings into view some of the best water of the main stem.

There are virtually no access problems here, even before the river comes close to the highway, and the state has recently acquired frontage to provide fishermen an easy and obvious way into the river. A Division of Fisheries and Wildlife sign 3¾ miles after the turn onto US 20 identifies this area. And once you're on the river, you can go up- and downstream, legally, as long as it is not posted, as you can anywhere in Massachusetts.

The good angling on the main stem runs upstream for a full 18 miles through Westfield and the towns of Russell and Huntington right along US 20. There are plenty of decent-sized trout, especially rainbows and browns, throughout. And of course, B&G Sporting annually stocks as many as 600 browns and/or rainbows weighing from 3 to 8 pounds each.

One particular hot spot is under the I-90 Turnpike bridge near the state access; another is the tailwater below the Knightville Dam in Huntington. And veteran main stem anglers make it a point to go downstream from the local golf course, Tekoa, where there are some very deep pools and good summertime holding water.

The main stem hatches are varied and complex, as would be expected in a fertile, large chunk of water. Caddis thrive here, as do mayflies, stoneflies, and other forage, like dace, shiners, and crustaceans. For the traditionalist, the spring hatches arrive in mid-April, starting with quill Gordons and running through the Hendricksons, March browns, sulphurs, and cream variants, with blue-winged olives available most of the time. The caddis hatches can overwhelm the mayfly hatches, with slate and mottled caddis often swarming. Drifting big black and dark olive Stonefly Nymphs may well be the most consistent way to attract big fish, but local anglers swear by badger-winged Llama streamers, Olive Woolly Buggers verging on chartreuse, and a local concoction known as a Teeko Bug. Always remember that there are very big trout here, and if they are not focused on a particular hatch, they need big mouthfuls to be tempted to come to the fly.

West Branch of the Westfield

The West Branch joins the combined flows of the Middle and East Branches in the center of Huntington. Follow it by staying on US 20 west past Huntington toward Chester, and on the western fringe of Chester turn right onto Middlefield Road. You can fish this branch nearly anywhere along these roads by walking up the trail on the far side or along the railroad bed on the near side of US 20, or from Middlefield Road.

The West Branch flows unhindered from the high hill town of Becket for 20 miles to Huntington, with the 13.8 miles from Becket Center to the Huntington town line designated as Wild and Scenic. There are no dams on it, and it runs clear, cold, and clean for most of the year. This attribute attracts trout from the main stem and other branches when water levels there are high and roiled in the spring, and again in the summer when the other waters can warm to dangerous levels. And many an angler gasps at the size of the trout encountered. Although the West Branch cuts through steep valleys that provide plenty of shade to keep it cool, water levels do go down in summer, leaving the deep pockets the best places to find fish. Casting to them, however, requires careful approach, precise casting, and fine tippets.

Caddis predominate on the West Branch, but there are strong mayfly hatches and some stoneflies as well. The big fish in the cold, high, but clear water in the spring are deep feeders, so dredging a Hare's Ear Nymph, a Pheasant Tail Nymph, or a Cased Caddis or Larva works well. Always have some Blue-Winged Olives on hand, and watch for a spinner fall of these small bugs, using tiny dries down to sizes 20 and 22. Often even the biggest fish in the river will focus on them.

Middle Branch of the Westfield

The Middle Branch of the Westfield is often overlooked because of its close proximity to the West and East Branches and the main stem. It is a bit more difficult to get to, and the standing water of the Littleville Reservoir, covering better than 3 miles near its mouth, helps anglers to overlook it. However, these factors may also make it the most attractive of the three branches for fly-flingers seeking solitude and decent trout, because it does receive less angling pressure and because it has the excellent nursery waters of the reservoir. In addition, state stocking crews consider it the equal of the other branches, so it gets its own fair share of trout. To top it off, its 12.6-mile run through Worthington and Chester to the Littleville Reservoir is designated Wild and Scenic.

Find it by taking the immediate left after you cross the MA 112 bridge when you enter Huntington from US 20. This is Fiske Avenue. Take the first right from Fiske onto Basket Street, then shortly bear left onto Bromley Road. About a mile farther along, turn right onto the ineptly named East River Road, which follows the west shore all the way to the headwaters in West Worthington. If you are coming in from the north, in Worthington, take East River Road, a south turn, off MA 143.

The Middle Branch is a lovely mountain stream with plenty of pocket water, riffles, boulders, some plunge pools, and occasional deep holding water. While it requires some searching to find, its above-mentioned qualities, along with the same strong forage base found in the rest of the watershed, make it well worth the effort. Its own shaded, deep valley helps keep its waters cool in summer, and plenty of large, reservoir-born trout complement both stocked and stream-born fish.

While the Middle Branch does have strong caddis populations, they don't often reach the blizzard state that they can on the West and East Branches. They're still important, especially the mottled and chocolate caddis, but are more on a par with the mayflies than in the other streams. The mayflies follow the same progression as elsewhere in the system, although particular hatches can be a bit briefer and more intense. Along with the big black stonefly nymphs associated with highly oxygenated water like this, there are also a few yellow sallies.

East Branch of the Westfield

The East Branch of the Westfield garners the lion's share of fly-fishing attention in this watershed, and with good reason. Many maps label it simply as the Westfield. It is longer and larger by far than either the West or Middle Branches; its headwaters, high up in the Berkshire Hills in Savoy, rival the other two branches in scenic beauty and fishing productivity; and the state has designated the 7 miles from the Chesterfield Gorge to the Knightville flood control project as catch and release only, artificial lure only. (It's the longest catch-and-release area in Massachusetts.) Add to these attributes the fact that its headwaters in Savoy and Windsor are largely protected by state forests, and that the 16.5 miles of the East Branch from the Windsor-Cummington town line to the Knightville Dam are Wild and Scenic, and it becomes evident why the East Branch is locally renowned.

The upper, headwater sections of this branch are easily found off MA 9 in West Cummington. Simply follow the signs to Windsor State Forest from the highway. They lead to River Road, and the water flows right alongside. The river grows larger and rivals the size of the other branches as it flows downstream along MA 9 from west to east. There are plenty of pullouts along the highway, but this section does see its fair share of other users—canoeists, rafters, bathers, and others. Good pocket water and pool angling, however, are found nearly anywhere along the road.

In the little community of Swift River, the combined flows of the Westfield and the Swift take a sharp turn to the south and flow through mostly state forest and game management lands for 4.8 miles to the MA 143 bridge just above the Chesterfield Gorge. This is the Pork Barrel section of the river, and it is a very nice and short canoe trip through some fabled trout water. Indeed, the Pork Barrel is renowned as the home of many a legendary trout, probably because few anglers go to the trouble of either floating the river here or hiking in.

You can put your canoe onto the river nearly anywhere along MA 9 to take this trip, but be sure to pull out above the MA 143 bridge in West Chesterfield, the only man-made structure you'll encounter, because the gorge drops shortly below the bridge. Or you can make the half-mile hike down Jewell Brook, which flows in the Chesterfield State Forest. It's only a little trickle of water that starts right where Fuller Road intersects with Wilcutt and Loomis Roads, and it strikes the river about 3 miles upstream of the MA 143 bridge.

From the MA 143 bridge in West Chesterfied, turn south at the west end of the bridge and look for the signs that lead to the Chesterfield Gorge. A parking lot and facilities are near the gorge, and an impressive sight it is. From the parking lot downstream for 7 miles, the river is strictly catch-and-release, artificial-lure-only fishing. The state owns the forest on the upper end of the catch-and-release area, and the Corps of Engineers protects it lower down. An easy road, River Road, follows the west bank of the river. If you drive down this first mile, make sure that you park off the dirt, one-lane road.

A Corps of Engineers gate blocks vehicular access, but the road continues along, making the walk farther down into the catch-and-release area easy. And while the upper section does see plenty of fishing pressure, making the hike downstream will ensure that you are fishing alone and in some excellent water. This area is heavily stocked and harbors some very impressive holdover and stream-born brown and rainbow trout. And the fishing holds up well right into the Knightville Flood Control Project. Note that the reservoir is drained each spring of its winter runoff water, so that later in the season the river continues right to the dam.

Not to be missed is the section of the East Branch below the Knightville Dam. There are a good 3½ miles of river here that hold big trout coming up and out of the main stem, and again, the state fisheries crew stocks it heavily. It runs right along MA 112 north from Huntington.

You can also access the catch-and-release area from this end of the river by driving north on MA 112 to the same River Road, on the right, that follows the river in West Chesterfield. About a mile upstream there is another Corps of Engineers gate, and beyond it, a short hike takes you to all but abandoned water.

The East Branch has all of the standard aquatic insects in abundance, but caddis are especially plentiful. Black, mottled, and tan caddis adults can get into your mouth and eyes at times. And there is a good progression of mayfly hatches with sporadic blue-winged olives thrown in, as well as a strong population of stoneflies.

The water temperatures can get high in the catch-and-release area during summer because of the heat-holding qualities of the granite ledges and boulders, but the tailwater below the Knightville Dam remains productive throughout the year, as does the headwater section above Cummington. And there are enough deep holes, spring seeps, and cold-water feeders in the catch-and-release area to keep trout alive. As with any warm-water situation during the height of summer, fish this stretch at dawn, dusk, and after dark.

DEERFIELD RIVER

Maps *USGS:* Greenfield (Green River and lower Deerfield River); Ashfield (main stem Deerfield River in Charlemont); Rowe, MA-VT (Deerfield River, Charlemont to Vermont); Bernardston (Deerfield River oxbow, North River, upper Green River).

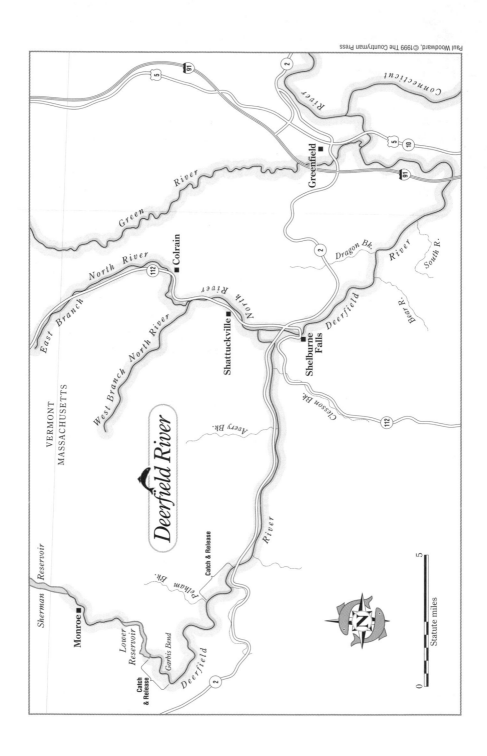

Deerfield River

Description The Deerfield River flows through the most rugged and picturesque country in Massachusetts; has a constant supply of high-quality, cold water; supports ample insect life and forage; is loaded with holdover and stream-born trout; gets ample annual stockings of hatchery trout; and is very accessible. Put all of these factors together and you have the state's premier blue-ribbon trout stream. In addition, it has two lengthy and fertile catch-and-release areas on some of the river's best water. And those qualities just describe the upstream section. Below, along the Mohawk Trail (MA 2), riffle and rapid sections are divided by long pools, some formed by dams and worth exploring with a canoe or belly boat. Even farther downstream, below Shelburne Falls, the river flows through a steep valley where few anglers tread and the fish, some to 6 pounds, rarely see a fly. Add to this two major high-quality tributaries, the North and the Green Rivers (see below), ,each of which could easily hold your attention for days, and it's easy to see why the Deerfield watershed attracts so much attention.

Access The Deerfield River is highly accessible from paved and dirt roads along its entire length, with the exception of the 6.6-mile downstream flow from New England Power Company's #2 power dam in Shelburne to the Stillwater bridge in Deerfield. Within this remote stretch of river, the 4.9 miles from the Bardwells Ferry bridge to the Stillwater bridge can be canoed over easy riffle water, and if you have the time, the canoe trip can take you right to the mouth of the river in the city of Greenfield. The 1.7 miles between the #2 dam and the Bardwells Ferry bridge can be hiked upstream from the bridge or downstream from the dam. Both the Green River and the North River are closely paralleled by dirt and paved roads, respectively.

Regulations The Deerfield, Green, and North Rivers and the West Branch of the North River are all designated as major rivers and have a daily creel limit of three trout. There are two catch-and-release sections on the Deerfield upstream of MA 2, where only artificial lures and flies may be used and a zero daily limit prevails. (Massachusetts has no closed fishing season.)

Don't miss Old Deerfield and its Main Street are lined with antique homes where visitors can experience colonial America and can learn particularly about the grit of this town, which suffered 58 attacks from the French and Indians from 1680 to the 1750s. And you can fish the section of the river behind the village where, on February 29, 1704, an overwhelming band of French and Indians crossed the frozen river and attacked the town, killing 48 and kidnapping 120 people.

Best asset When the eight dams along the Deerfield came up for relicensing recently, the New England Power Company, which owns them, and a coalition of users hammered out an agreement to present to FERC before the licensing process began. The agreement included increased minimum flows for fishermen below the dams, specific schedules for water releases for canoers and kayakers, and the deeding of large chunks of acreage along the river bank to land trusts and the state. It was only the second time in United States history that an agreement had been reached before the licensing process began, and it benefited all river users. Call 1-888-356-3663 for water release schedules.

Biggest drawback Although the river agreement has helped insure that all users can enjoy the Deerfield, the water releases, especially from the Fife Brook Dam at the head of the upper catch-and-release area, raise the river dramatically and quickly. Pay attention to water levels, and leave the water if it starts to rise, or you'll soon be swimming with the fishes.

Necessary patterns Underwater: Black-Nosed Dace (#2–8); Muddler Minnow (#2–8); Gray Ghost (#2–8); Black Ghost (#2–8); Olive, Gray, or Green Caddis Larva (#12–18); Deep Sparkle Pupa (#10–18); Hare's Ear Nymph and Wet (#8–14); Pheasant Tail Nymph (#12–18); Montana (#4–12); Ted's Stonefly (#6–12); Woolly Bugger (#2–8). Dry flies: Adams (#12–22), Light Cahill (#12–16), Hendrickson (#14–16), March Brown (#12–16), Black Caddis (#16–18), Mottled Caddis (#14–18), Wulff (#10–14).

Stocked feeder streams worth a look (from downstream to upstream) Dragon Brook, South River, Bear River, Clesson Brook, Avery Brook, Chickley River, Cold River, Pelham Brook, Dunbar Brook. **Other feeders:** Clark Brook.

The Deerfield River watershed takes you out of the overcommercialized and rampantly overdeveloped hubbub of the Northeast in the 20th century and plunks you squarely back in time—first in pastoral agricultural valleys reminiscent of the 19th century, and then, upstream, in the heart of the rugged Berkshire Hills that so effectively halted western expansion for better than 100 years in colonial times.

You can't help but feel the pace of life here palpably slow down, nor can you ignore the natural beauty of the narrow valleys and steep mountains. Whether you experience the tardy arrival of spring—which often comes a full month later than in the rest of the region—or marvel at the hillsides of blooming mountain laurel in early summer, or travel here during the bittersweet splendor of fall, you will not be unaffected. And the fishing is as good as it gets.

The energy potential of this strong river dropping out of the mountains did not go unrecognized, of course, and there are 10 dams along its length,

The lower catch and release area of the Deerfield River ends opposite the Mohawk Campground, where there is an excellent cliff pool.

including 3 on its headwaters in Vermont. Because of the steep valleys and fast drops of the river, however, the dams, especially in Massachusetts, are largely unobtrusive. They can affect river levels, particularly upstream, but the new agreement with the power company that owns them has somewhat leveled out the severe flows and improved the river habitat for the fish and the forage.

Lower Deerfield

The Deerfield can be effectively divided in two, with Shelburne Falls marking the dividing line. Downstream, the river is more inaccessible and includes nearly 7 miles that require a canoe or a fairly substantial hike to get to. Yet the fishing pressure here is light compared with the rest of the river; the broader flows, deeper pools, and larger tributaries are more conducive to bigger fish. And there are sections that can be accessed easily and give a taste of just how good the river can get.

Find the accessible section of the lower river by traveling north on US 5 from South Deerfield toward Greenfield. Turn west at Mill Village Road, the first left after I-91 Exit 24, and follow the road to a small stone building at an intersection. Going straight past the building takes you to the lower river, which will flow on the west (left). Turning left at the stone building takes you north, and the river shortly comes into view on the right. Fish at the I-91 overpass and up- and downstream from it, or travel a half mile farther and park at the Stillwater bridge, where there is a canoe access, the takeout if you canoe the river downstream from the Bardwells Ferry bridge.

To find the Bardwells Ferry bridge, take MA 116 west from I-91 Exit 24 and drive to the center of Conway, the first town you hit. Turn north, a right, onto Baptist Hill Road, which becomes Shelburne Falls Road, then bear right onto Bardwells Ferry Road about ⅔ mile farther along. The road leads down into the steep valley and to the old iron bridge that is the Bardwell's Ferry bridge. (Bill Cosby owns most of the land on the far side.)

An alternative to canoeing the 5-mile stretch between the Bardwells Ferry bridge and the Stillwater bridge is to drive past the Stillwater parking area and take your first right onto an abandoned railroad bed that follows the power line upstream. When you get to the height of land, you can park in several locations and hike down onto the river. It's a steep hike, but well worth the effort.

The lower river has the full complement of insects and hatches—plenty of varied caddis; strong, predictable mayflies; and abundant stoneflies—but to tempt the biggest trout (and some impressive smallmouth bass), get deep with big Montana or Black Stonefly Nymph, Hare's Ear Nymph, or Caddis Larva. And to fish for the biggest trout, dredge the depths with Muddler Minnows, streamers, or Woolly Buggers.

Upper Deerfield

To get to the upper Deerfield, leave I-91 at Exit 26, the MA 2/Mohawk Trail rotary, and travel west on MA 2 into the hills. You'll travel up the side of Greenfield Mountain with its spectacular views of the Connecticut River valley, and then back down toward Shelburne. MA 2 passes over the Deerfield twice (note the MA 112 turnoff here—it leads to the North River): once below the #4 dam, where the river flows freely, and once above the dam, where the backwaters are still and inviting. The dam itself is in view to the north (right).

Shortly, on the south side of the road, a state boat-launch ramp comes into view. Use it to canoe or belly-boat this section, and note that it is a good takeout spot if you canoe down the river from Charlemont. You can put in at any number of spots along MA 2, which parallels the river for the next 9½ miles right through Charlemont to the Indian Bridge at the Zoar

The upper catch-and-release section of the Deerfield River starts here at Fife Brook Dam.

Road turnoff. This stretch of the river is mostly wide and uninteresting, but there are a few spots where ledges, boulders, or short turns in the river provide good holding water. Most of them can be seen right from the road, and there are plenty of turnoffs and parking.

At the Indian Bridge on the west end of Charlemont, a road turns north on the east end of the bridge. It's the Zoar Road, and it leads to both of the catch-and-release areas. When you turn up this road, you climb for a quarter mile and then can look down at the Mohawk Campground on the left. You can also look upriver and see the lower boundary of the second, newer catch-and-release area. It runs upstream for 2.1 miles to approximately where Pelham Brook enters the river. You'll cross the Pelham Brook bridge just before a T-junction in the road.

There is plenty of good water throughout this lower section, with several long, deep pools interrupted by stretches of rapids and pocket water. Be sure to fish the Cold River pool, just upstream from a railroad bridge where the Cold River enters, under the bridge itself, and the Pelham Pool where Pelham Brook enters.

Take a left at the T-junction, drive under the railroad underpass with care (it's blind), and you'll shortly find a picnic area (there's some good pocket water behind it) and a new bridge that crosses the river just below the Zoar Gorge. You'll often find some of the nation's best kayakers practicing or competing in the gorge. If they're not, the deep plunge pools can produce some good trout.

Follow the river on this road all the way upstream to the Hoosic Tunnel

The North River feeds into the top of the oxbow of the Deerfield River near Shelburne Falls.

(on the left) and the railroad trestle bridge (on the right). There's a grade crossing over the tracks, and this marks the bottom of the upper catch-and-release area. For the next 1.6 miles upstream to the Fife Brook Dam runs the first and most popular catch-and-release area. To find the upper limit of the area, bear right on an access road just as the main road cuts up and away from the river. The good fishing starts right at the dam and runs downstream to a section of relatively barren flats that are shallow riffle water when minimum flows prevail, but become dangerous to cross when water is being released. These flats feed into the famous Carbis Bend pool, and the good water continues right downstream to the trestle bridge. Always beware of rising water here. It comes up fast.

Again in this area, the hatches run the full gamut, with plenty of black and mottled caddis and ample stoneflies. Recently, however, the mayfly hatches have been nothing short of spectacular with Hendricksons, March browns, and sulphurs coming off in droves. So be prepared. And when nothing is showing, float Stonefly and Mayfly Nymphs down through the deeper holes.

Green River

Find the Green River by taking Exit 26 off I-91 at the MA 2/ Mohawk Trail rotary, turning west onto MA 2, and taking your first right onto Colrain Road. At the intersection of Colrain Road and River Road, bear right onto River Road, and shortly bear left with River Road, which becomes dirt. If you stay on the paved road, you'll come to a covered bridge that crosses the river, but most of the interesting fishing is upstream.

The dirt road parallels the river and stays within sight of most of it all the way upstream, north, through West Leyden and Stewartsville and into Vermont, a distance of 8½ miles. Although it's steep in many places, hike down to the river almost anywhere along here and you'll find good pocket water and rapids and an occasional deep pool. The size of the trout and their willingness to take almost any fly—especially a bright attractor—will be surprising.

North River

To find the North River, you need to curlicue off MA 2 in Shelburne at MA 112. Follow the signs, and although you've just dropped into a residential neighborhood, the MA 112 signs will reappear. The road follows first the Deerfield and then the North into Vermont.

The North enters the Deerfield River at the top of the Deerfield's most pronounced oxbow. An arched steel bridge to the left cuts back across the North at its mouth and leads back to the Mohawk Trail. Be sure to fish the Deerfield and the mouth of the North here, because they hold some of the most productive and interesting water in both rivers.

Continue north on MA 112 as the North intertwines with the road for another 4½ miles upstream to Griswoldville, where a set of factory buildings identifies the entry of the West Branch of the North. Choose either to follow the West Branch via the paved Adamsville Road (a left turn in Griswoldville), or continue up MA 112 to Colrain and beyond it to the Vermont line. The West Branch runs to its headwaters in Heath, a distance of 8 miles, and the main stem also runs about 8 miles to Vermont. Either provides pretty country settings to chase after trout in riffles interspersed with rapids and a few pools. As in the Green, bright attractor flies draw attention, but occasional hatches need to be matched.

SMALLER CONNECTICUT RIVER FEEDERS FROM THE WEST

Mill River—Deerfield, Whately, and Hatfield

The Mill River flows out of Deerfield as a small meadow stream, but grows large enough to hold good populations of brown trout in both Whately and Hatfield. The river parallels both the Connecticut River and I-91 as it runs through some deep forest and occasional agricultural fields. Its meandering path, undercut banks, and silty bottom are perfect for the big, fickle browns.

Access is via the many crossroads that connect US 5 to the communities. From the south, on US 5, find the river at bridges on Elm Street and Mountain Road in Hatfield and on Claverack Road, Christian Lane, and Swamp Road in Whately.

As with any situation in which browns are the quarry, fish for them early and late in the day, and after dark using big dark dry flies or large Woolly Buggers and streamers.

Mill River—Williamsburg and Northampton

Not to be confused with the above-named Mill River, this Mill River flows along MA 9 in Williamsburg with excellent access right next to the highway. It's a freestoner here, but suffers from several dams and access problems nearer the Connecticut River in Northampton.

Its waters in Williamsburg flit and flow nicely in an array of pools, riffles, and easy rapids, but the stream does suffer from high summer temperatures. Nevertheless, it is stocked heavily in spring and early summer, has some strong mayfly hatches, and can provide some pleasant hours in a nice New England community.

Manhan River

The Manhan River is an interesting and surprising piece of water that meanders for almost 30 miles from its headwaters in the Berkshire Hills in Westhampton, through the foothills of Southampton, and into the flood plain of the Connecticut River in Easthampton. Each section has a distinct character.

In Westhampton, the river is a small mountain stream, often requiring quite a hike to get into its good water, but it's worth the effort because few anglers ply this section. It flows south from MA 66 to the White Reservoir and again below the White Reservoir for 1.2 miles to the Tighe-Carmody Reservoir in Southampton.

In Southampton, the Manhan is an inviting freestoner that receives an ample supply of hatchery rainbows and some browns, which supplement its good holdover fish. The river intertwines with MA 10 here, and several crossroads lead to its good water. Take the Russellville Road west from MA 10 to Manhan Road to find the stretch below the Tighe-Carmody Reservoir, or follow Brickyard Road, which parallels the river, just south of where it crosses under MA 10. Farther north, the river crosses under MA 10 again, just before the river and the road enter Easthampton.

In Easthampton, the river becomes a meandering flood-plain flow and must cross a dam before it reaches the Connecticut River. This is deep, fertile water that simply reeks of brown trout, and they are available in good numbers. Canoeing down this stretch is the best way to cover the water, but some wading can be done. The river runs right through the center of town, and you can access it from the MA 10 bridge or from Pleasant Street.

The hatches on the Manhan are as varied as the water. In the Southampton stretch you'll find the best insect life, with caddis predominating, but mayflies and some stoneflies are also present. In Easthampton, silt-loving mayflies are ample, as are dace, shiners, and sucker fry.

Other Stocked Streams That Flow from the Berkshire Hills toward the East and the Connecticut River

Berkshire County *Windsor:* Windsor Brook.

Franklin County *Bernardston:* Dry Brook, Falls River, Shattuck Brook; *Charlemont:* Maxwell Brook; *Conway:* Poland Brook; *Greenfield:* Allen Brook, Mill Brook; *Heath:* West Branch Brook; *Whately:* West Brook.

Hampshire County *Chesterfield:* West Branch Brook; *Easthampton:* Broad Brook, Hannums Brook, Basset Brook; *Goshen:* Stone Brook; *Northampton:* Parsons Brook; *Williamsburg:* Bradford Brook; *Worthington:* Bronson Brook, West Branch Brook.

Hampden County *Chester:* Walker Brook; *Granville:* Hubbard River; *Holyoke:* Broad Brook.

Important Stocked Lakes and Ponds

Berkshire County (stocked spring and fall) *Chester and Huntington:* Littleville Reservoir; *Florida:* North Pond; *Otis:* Otis Reservoir, Big Benton Pond; *Windsor:* Windsor Pond. **(Stocked only in spring)** *Otis:* Little Benton Pond.

Franklin County (stocked only in spring) *Ashfield:* Ashfield Pond; *Colrain:* McLeod Pond; *Monroe:* Sherman Reservoir.

Hampshire County (stocked spring and fall) *Easthampton:* Nashawannuck Pond; *Huntington:* Littleville Lake. **(Stocked only in spring)** *Goshen:* Upper Highland Lake; *Huntington:* Norwich Pond, Knightville Reservoir.

Hampden County (stocked spring and fall) *Southwick:* Congamond Lakes (North and Middle Ponds); *Westfield:* Hampton Pond.

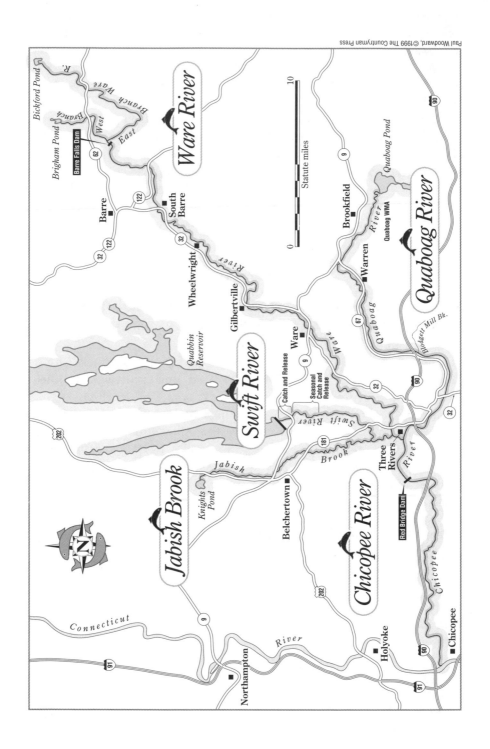

3 | Major Connecticut River Tributaries from the East

Chicopee River Watershed (Ware River, Swift River, Quaboag River)

The Chicopee River itself flows from the Three Rivers section of Palmer for 8 miles to the Connecticut River in the city of Chicopee. While it does have potential as a trout river, currently the Chicopee's waters are excessively warmed by overuse, backing up behind dams and pushed through too many manufacturing plants, to the point that trout cannot survive in the river for long. True, there is some trout angling in the impoundment behind the Red Bridge Dam near the Palmer–Chicopee boundary, but there is little stream fishing.

The watershed is of major importance, however, because the Ware River and the Quaboag River meet to form the Chicopee River in Three Rivers, and less than a mile upstream, the Swift River dumps into the Ware River. These three rivers offer good, often spectacular, fly-fishing for trout. They are all long and fertile, and they all have both convenient access areas and stretches of more remote water for those anxious to get away from the crowds. Taken individually, each of these rivers offers enough superb trout angling to warrant a special trip. Taken together, they are matched by no other area in southern New England for the quality and expansiveness of their trout waters.

Ware River

The Ware River is a long and interesting flow that is rather anonymous to most regional anglers. It forms where its two main feeders, the East and West Branches of the Ware, join just upstream from the Barre Falls flood-control dam in the northeastern corner of the town of Barre. The branches themselves offer average to decent small-stream angling but are somewhat difficult to get to. The main stem then flows for more than 25 miles through Barre, Hardwick, Ware, and Palmer to its confluence with the Quaboag River in the Three Rivers section of Palmer. Along the way, it has many reaches that provide a wide variety of angling, from gentle meadow-type back-waters and pools, to the riffle-run-pools typical of New England freestone streams, to full-blown mountain plunge pools. And it receives ample stock-ings of rainbow and brown trout from the state for nearly its entire run.

As with many other New England streams, the Ware River's potential for waterpower was amply tapped in the last century, and many of these dams are still present and still being used for manufacturing. Luckily, the waters that are returned to the river from the plants and from the towns are thor-oughly treated and clean, but the dams do contribute to a warm-water prob-lem, especially in the river's lower reaches in Ware and Palmer. Yet there are enough good trout sections on the Ware to make it a diamond in the rough, waiting to be discovered and enjoyed by anglers anxious to find new and largely untested waters.

Find the upper reaches of the Ware River by traveling upstream from the Gilbertville section of the town of Hardwick along MA 32 to Barre Plains. Just north of where MA 67 joins MA 32, take Nichols Road to MA 122, which then follows the river upstream to Coldbrook Road, which leads to the Barre Falls flood-control dam.

In Gilbertville itself, the river contains mountain-type water that can get high and wild during the spring runoff, but that has some good holding water up- and downstream during normal water levels. Find good access by turning west onto Covered Bridge Road and fishing upstream. A one-lane dirt road parallels the river. And yes, there is a large, well-maintained, attractive covered bridge that is not well known because it is difficult to photograph and leads only to a little-used country lane.

Once the river crosses into the town of Ware, the gradient becomes less severe and the effects of the several dams begin to show. While this section can offer some good trout fishing, it is best plied with a canoe. Below Ware, the water does warm up considerably. There is a put-and-take fishery below the center of town with access at the MA 32 bridge.

In Palmer, the river maintains this slow, canoeable character and is again dammed in Thorndike, but its last ¾-mile run to Three Rivers is vast-ly improved for trout angling by the infusion of the cold, clear waters of the Swift River. And few fly anglers make the effort to find this short run of the river, which holds excellent trout and produces abundant hatches. Access here is easy. Park at the Three Rivers Water Department pump house just south of the MA 181 bridge adjacent to Pathfinder Vocational School and hike down the river for ¼ mile to where the Swift enters on the opposite shore. Fish the big pool there and downstream.

SWIFT RIVER

Maps *USGS:* Palmer (Ware River to Belchertown), Winsor Dam (Belchertown to Quabbin Reservoir).

Description The Swift River in Belchertown is Massachusetts' only true tailwater fishery, fed by waters coming out of massive Quabbin Reservoir (see below) from 70 feet down. This means that the water is uniformly cold during the summer and marginally warmer during the winter, making year-round angling not only possible but also productive, even in the dog days of August and the middle of winter. In fact, I've caught trout rising to tiny dry flies on the Swift's famous Y-pool in mid-February and have fished over an astounding midge hatch with the air temperature hovering in the 90s.

The Swift River is not long, running a mere 7 miles from Quabbin Reservoir to the Ware River, and it is never a very large river. But it emerges nearly full grown from the reservoir, flows for 2½ miles before it backs up behind a pair of dams in the Bondsville section of Palmer, and then returns to its banks for a largely overlooked run to the Ware River. Because of this short run, the small dams in Bondsville do not affect the fertility and temperatures of the river, and the water stays ideally suited for holding and growing trout.

Access The year-round, fly-fishing-only, catch-and-release section of the Swift River is found by traveling to the boundary between the towns of Ware and Belchertown on MA 9. Park on the west side of the bridge and hike upstream to the Y-pool and Winsor Dam. The downstream section— including the 1½-mile-long seasonal artificial-lure-only, catch-and-release area—is adjacent to River Road on the east side of the river, 200 yards from the MA 9 bridge. Fish the lower river from Bondsville downstream via a number of crossroads off MA 181.

Regulations The mile-long run of river from Winsor Dam to the MA 9 bridge is fly-fishing only, catch and release only, year-round. The reach from the MA 9 bridge downstream to Cady Lane, about 1½ miles of river, is restricted to artificial lures, catch-and-release only from July 1 to December 31. From January 1 to June 30, this section is under general fishing regulations for major rivers, as is the rest of the river year-round, which limits the daily take to three fish.

Don't miss The stretch of river below the Bondsville dams is largely abandoned after the middle of May. It contains plenty of stream-born trout, as well as stocked and holdover trout. In addition, the hatches are more regular and predictable because of the infusion of groundwater nutrients to refertilize the largely barren water nearer the Winsor Dam.

Best asset The Swift River's excellent water quality and optimal year-round

The Swift River's famous Y-pool is formed near the base of Quabbin Reservoir at the junction of the spillway outflow and the water-generating release. The arched bridge here spans the spillway channel.

temperatures again illustrate the high quality of angling available from the tailwaters below bottom-release dams. Because this is a short river, the positive effect these waters have on the trout can be seen for its entire length, including the largely overlooked lower Bondsville water.

Biggest drawback Three problems plague the Swift. The first is that the fly-fishing-only water above MA 9 flows through the canal that was constructed when Winsor Dam was built in the 1930s. As such, you're really fishing in a big flat-bottomed ditch. The local TU chapter several years ago erected some deflector dams in an attempt to improve the holding water, and that helped. There are plans on the table to further restore the area to a more natural flow, but to date bureaucratic red tape has prevented any improvement.

The second problem involves the skewed compromise devised by the Massachusetts Division of Fisheries and Wildlife on the MA 9 to Cady Lane stretch of the river. This 1½ miles of river is governed by two sets of rules, and confusion reigns. Many local fly-fishermen feel that the section should be artificial lure, catch and release only year-round, especially because the upper fly-fishing-only area has virtually no natural streambed. This solution would allow spin or fly-fishermen to ply their trade. They would just be required to return the fish to the river unharmed.

The third problem is the renown of the Swift River itself. The fly-fishing-only section is famous and is often crowded, especially during the summer, when its waters stay cool while other rivers reach lethally high temperatures.

Necessary patterns *Underwater:* Pheasant Tail Nymph (#14–20), Hare's Ear Nymph (#12–16), Hendrickson Nymph (#12–16), Leadwing Coachman (#12–14), Caddis Larva (#14–18), Caddis Emerger (#12–18), Black-Nosed Dace (#4–10), Mickey Finn (#4–12). *Dry flies:* Quill Gordon (#12–16); Hendrickson (#12–16); Red Quill (#12–16); Rusty Spinner (#12–16); March Brown (#12–14); Sulphur Dun (#14–20); Light Cahill (#14–16); Tan, Yellow, Brown, Green or Black Caddis (#12–18); Blue-Winged Olive (#12–20); Cream Midge (#18–22); Trico (#18–24); Griffiths Gnat (#18–26); Black or Cinnamon Ant (#10–20).

Feeder streams worth a look Jabish Brook (see below).

The Swift River is a short gem of a stream that is the state's only tail water fishery. As such, it receives plenty of pressure from anglers, but also much attention from the stocking trucks. The fly-fishing-only area is famous and popular. Once the stream returns to its natural banks below MA 9, it is challenging, but fertile and interesting.

Access to the entire river is very good, but it is especially so above Bondsville, where an underground water main runs parallel to the east bank

Jabish Brook is the Swift River's only major feeder below the Quabbin Reservoir. It's not large, but it produces trout year-round.

on publicly owned property for the length of the free-flowing water. Travel down River Road in Ware and park nearly anywhere along the river. The opposite shore of the river is state owned for much of its run, with only a few privately held parcels preventing direct access to the river. The McLaughlin Fish Hatchery borders the river and uses some of its water to raise trout on the west shore along East Street near the MA 9 bridge. The Connecticut Valley District Offices of the Division of Fisheries and Wildlife are a bit farther south on East Street, and they maintain a cold-water fishing pool near their entrance that's a great place to introduce anyone—especially youngsters—to fly-fishing. They also maintain several trails down to the river.

At the south end of East Street, a left turn brings you almost immediately to the river and a boat-launch ramp (the bridge over the river here has been declared unsafe and is closed). The ramp is at the start of the water that backs up behind the first Bondsville dam, but anyone wanting to launch a canoe or small boat can find some very good still-water angling downstream.

Downstream from the first Bondsville dam there's a stretch of flowing water that can be accessed from a dirt road on the west bank. Find it on the west side of the MA 181 bridge. The dirt road runs upstream along the river. Few people take the trouble to find this short run, but it does hold good trout. (The vacant lot on the opposite bank is what's left of a mill complex that burned in 1968—the fire caused $25 million in damages—that's only now finally being rid of its hazardous material. No, it didn't pollute the river.)

The second of the two Bondsville dams is right in the center of town and is obvious. Park near the iron bridge that crosses the river just west of the center of town and fish from the dam downstream. The close proximity to the town is obvious from the litter on the shores, but the angling is great, starting in March with an excellent little black stonefly hatch and continuing right through the entire array of mayflies and caddis. Fish as far downstream as you like (the Ware River is only 2 miles away), or drive south on MA 181 to Fuller Road and turn into the industrial complex, which is right on the banks of the river. You'll have most of this run of river to yourself, because few anglers are willing to find it, especially with the excellent angling and access available upstream.

Jabish Brook

Jabish Brook is the only tributary to Swift River, but it's well worth exploring. It runs from just north of Belchertown, in Pelham, due south to the Swift, covering 12 miles. Much of its best angling is along US 202 from the Pelham line to the center of Belchertown. Then it parallels MA 181 with many crossroads providing access. It's a small stream, even in its lower reaches, because a portion of its water is redirected to a drinking-water reservoir, but it holds a good number of stream-born brook trout and receives ample stockings. Local angling legend Tim Lofland has caught native brookies to 16 inches in some of the more remote pools in Jabish Brook, but says that you must be willing to hike through the swamps and work hard to get them.

QUABOAG RIVER

Maps *USGS:* Palmer (Three Rivers to West Warren), Warren (West Warren to Quaboag Pond).

Description The Quaboag River is a fertile, midsized river that is very accessible, holds trout well all year, and is famous for its regular abundant rise of the full array of mayflies, caddis, and stoneflies. Its prime area is the 12-mile-long run from West Warren along MA 67 to the MA 32 bridge in Palmer. All along this section access is easy and the fishing often spectacular. It's a freestone-type stream with easy wading when the water levels are appropriate, and there is plenty of room to escape the crowds near the bridges and rest areas.

Access The Quaboag River is never far from auto access. If there aren't major highways near it, like US 20 in Palmer and MA 67 in Palmer and

Warren, then there are secondary roads and bridges all along it. The long reach along MA 67 is rural, but the lower river is never far from suburbia. Even so, a short hike away from the easy-access points leads to sections of the river that see very few anglers during the year.

Regulations The Quaboag River is a listed major river in Massachusetts, and as such, a three-trout-a-day limit is in force. There are no tackle restrictions on any part of the Quaboag.

Don't miss The Hendrickson hatch, in the middle of April, is as strong as anywhere in the state. Hordes of flies litter the surface, and it's the best time to cast over the trout that have held in the river over the winter. They're the ones anxious to slurp down these abundant meals.

Best asset The huge variety of hatching insects up and down the Quaboag River makes matching the hatch both invigorating and challenging. With so much forage available, the trout can afford to be picky, and you must match size, profile, and color precisely and present your flies realistically. But you'll rarely make a trip to the Quaboag when there isn't something drawing trout to the surface.

Biggest drawback The Quaboag River badly needs a catch-and-release section. With the entire river open to all methods of fishing, and with hatchery trucks stopping only at the bridges and easy-access points, the truck chasers are never far behind. And the majority of the stocked trout are snagged out of the water within a few days. You can still find trout if you're willing to hike up- or downstream, but a short section of the river reserved for catch and release would vastly improve the attraction of the Quaboag for all anglers.

Necessary patterns *Underwater:* Pheasant Tail Nymph (#14–20), Hare's Ear Nymph (#12–16), Hendrickson Nymph (#12–16), Leadwing Coachman (#12–14), March Brown Nymph (#10–14), Caddis Larva (#14–18), Caddis Emerger (#12–18), Zug Bug (#8–16), Black Stonefly (#4–10), Black-Nosed Dace (#4–10), Mickey Finn (#4–12), Woolly Bugger (#4–10). *Dry flies:* Adams (#10–20); Blue Quill (#14–18); Quill Gordon (#12–16); Hendrickson (#12–16); Red Quill (#12–16); Rusty Spinner (#12–16); March Brown (#12–14); Gray Fox (#12–14); Sulphur Dun (#14–16); Light Cahill (#14–16); Green Drake (#6–10); Brown Drake (#10–12); Golden Drake (#8–12); White Mayfly (#12–14); Humpy (#10–14); Tan, Yellow, Brown, Green, or Black Caddis (#12–18); Blue-Winged Olive (#12–20); Cream Midge (#18–22); Trico (#18–24); Alder (#16–18); Cricket (#10–14); Hopper (#4–12); Black or Cinnamon Ant (#10–20).

Stocked feeder streams worth a look (from downstream to upstream) Chicopee Brook, Blodgett Mill Brook, School Street Brook, Coys Brook.

Other feeders Foskett Mill Stream, Bottle Brook, Tufts Brook, Penny Brook, O'Neil Brook, Cheney Brook, Sullivan Brook, Naultaug Brook, Lambertown Brook, Burr Brook, Salmon Brook, Dunn Brook.

The Quaboag River is regionally and justly famed for its strong hatches throughout the season. Mayflies, caddis, stoneflies, and dobsonfly larva (hellgrammites) infest this stream and keep its trout fat and sassy throughout the year. Its regional fame stems from these hatches and the good trout that gorge on them, but it is also because nearly every inch of the Quaboag is open to anglers. Access to these miles of river is easy and always close to roads or highways. So, simply put, the hatches, the trout, and the access all should attract anglers, and do early in the season. But later in the year, the Quaboag can seem all but abandoned. Would that many of the more famous southern New England rivers had such a problem.

The most productive stretch of the Quaboag runs from West Warren downstream along MA 67 to US 20 and the MA 32 bridge, known locally as Fays Bridge. There are several roadside parks upstream—from where the Massachusetts Turnpike crosses over MA 67—that offer easy access, but hike up- or downstream from them because they are popular spots. Downstream from the Turnpike (south), Kings Bridge Road crosses the river and gives access to this area, which is a bit more remote than the upstream reaches.

From where MA 67 meets US 20, turn east; the river soon runs under the US 20 bridge. Park near the bridge and fish the good pools up- and downstream, or travel a bit farther east and turn back west onto Fenton Road, which parallels the river on its south bank, opposite the highway. Fenton is a more quiet country lane than US 20, and within a quarter mile a hiking trail bears off to the right. It's marked by a sign that states NOT MAINTAINED—PROCEED AT YOUR OWN RISK, but it's blocked to vehicular traffic. Hike down it right along the river for better than a mile, and you'll think you have the river to yourself. The trail comes back out onto Fenton Road, which leads to MA 32. Turn north and you'll be at Fays Bridge.

The lower Quaboag River—from the MA 32 bridge through the populated sections of Palmer and on to its confluence with the Ware River in Three Rivers—is almost never fished but has some interesting pools and runs that hold trout all year. Until recently, the last stocking spot was the MA 32 bridge, but with the improved water quality and recognized access, the river is now stocked all the way to Three Rivers. These trout, however, quickly adapt. They are never easy, but a well-presented dry or an enticing nymph or streamer can tempt them and some very large holdover fish, mostly browns, from the undercut banks and deep pools.

Three bridges offer decent access to the river here. The Bridge Street bridge is adjacent to downtown Palmer. Turn south onto it just opposite

Nick's Sport Shop (yes, they have flies) on Main Street. Just east of town, the Quaboag flows under another US 20 bridge, near the Mapletree Industrial Center. There's a rest area where you can park just east of the bridge. And the Palmer Street bridge connects Three Rivers to MA 181 just north of town, where the river takes a sweeping turn before it meets the Ware River.

It should be noted that upstream from Warren, the Quaboag River is a deep, slow-moving flow that comes out of Quaboag Pond in Brookfield. It's not trout water and it can't be waded, but it produces very big largemouth bass and an occasional lunker northern pike, as does the pond itself.

QUABBIN RESERVOIR AND ITS FEEDERS

Quabbin Reservoir

Quabbin Reservoir is Massachusetts' largest body of water, covering 25,000 acres and spanning more than 18 miles from north to south. In addition, it is a wilderness area, with its whole watershed entirely protected from development. Only fishing boats with outboard motors no larger than 20 horsepower are allowed on it, and if for no other reason, you should go to Quabbin Reservoir to wonder at its very existence. Here in southern New England, in the most crowded area of the most crowded region on the continent, sits an oasis of untouched Nature. Bald eagles and loons nest here. More than two dozen moose now call it home. And its waters, the purest in the northeast, fairly teem with fish.

Luckily for anglers, experiments in the past with rainbow and brown trout, northern pike, and walleyes have all ended, and the fisheries experts now concentrate on controlling resident lake trout numbers, while enhancing the landlocked salmon fishery. This is particularly attractive to fly-fishermen. In spring landlocks will gather near and feed on the spawning rainbow smelt, and in autumn the landlocks again concentrate near and in the feeders to answer their own spawning siren.

Fly casting for the landlocks in Quabbin is rare (most are caught via trolling hardware or traditional streamers, or still fishing with bait), but with the fish concentrated in spring and fall, casting to them can be very productive. The traditional northern New England methods—either anchoring a boat at the fringes of the feeders and casting into them or drifting with the wind and casting—are effective here, especially early in the day when the fish are most active and receptive to flies. In addition, biologists have identified a significant segment of the smelt population that are shoal-water spawners, so casting to the slopes leading up onto the shoals can be productive in spring.

Of the two arms that form Quabbin, the west side is the more noted for its cold-water fishery. Try any of the feeder streams that flow in from the west side, or motor up to where the West Branch of the Swift (see below) enters the reservoir at the very top of the west arm. The eastern arm is much larger, but not as deep. Landlocked salmon, however, can be found anywhere in spring where there are smelt, and the smelt use both the feeders and the shoals on the east arm to spawn.

Access to the western arm is via US 202 in Belchertown at Gate 8, Boat Launch Area 1. The eastern arm has access at Gate 31, Boat Launch Area 2, at its northern tip. Find it via MA 122, which turns east from US 202 on the north end of the reservoir. Gate 43, Boat Launch Area 3, is about midway down the eastern shore. Travel north from Ware on MA 32 to MA 32A and into Hardwick center. Turn west on Greenwich Road and follow the signs to Gate 43.

Bring your own boat (remember the horsepower restriction), or rent a boat and motor at the water's edge. No, canoes are not allowed, but neither are speedboats, sailboats, personal water craft, or any other type of vessel—it's V-bottom fishing boats or nothing (they can be as large as you like, but if they have larger than 20-horsepower motors mounted, the propeller must be removed). Quabbin, Wachusett (see chapter 4), and Sudbury Reservoirs are the only waters in the commonwealth that have closed fishing seasons. Generally, they open on the third Saturday in April, if the ice is entirely gone, and they close exactly 6 months later, generally on the second Saturday in October. These dates are not written in stone, so call the Visitor Information Center at Quabbin (413-323-7221) to be sure that the season is open.

West Branch of the Swift River

The West Branch of the Swift River is notable because of the wild, nearly untouched woodlands through which it flows. It is the main tributary to the west arm of the Quabbin Reservoir, entering right at the north end, and you can fish it within the confines of the protected watershed if the reservoir itself is open to fishing. This can be important early and late in the season, because landlocked salmon are often available in the stream as they spawn or chase smelt.

But the West Branch is open year-round outside of the Quabbin lands. There is good angling for landlocks, especially in the fall as they head farther upstream, and for stocked and holdover trout throughout the year. And look for stream-born brook trout, especially above US 202.

Find the West Branch on US 202 at the Shutesbury–New Salem boundary. The stream flows through a culvert, so its run under the highway is not terribly obvious. Downstream from the highway is Quabbin land, with its seasonal restrictions, but upstream is open year-round. New Boston Road, a dirt road, parallels the upper stretch of the West Branch. Find it by turning west onto Cooleyville Road from US 202 just north of the stream. The second right turn from here is New Boston Road.

East Branch of the Swift River

The East Branch of the Swift River flows out of the Popple Camp State Wildlife Management Area (WMA) in Petersham and Phillipston and empties into the Pottapaug Pond section of Quabbin Reservoir's east arm. It's notable because high-quality cold water flows in it and because it runs through some of the region's most beautiful forests. In addition, it is more fertile than many of the other Quabbin tributaries and has stronger insect hatches. And it receives stocked trout and holds them well throughout the season. It does not, however, get the spring and fall runs of landlocked salmon from Quabbin Reservoir, because Pottapaug Pond is backed up behind a dam at the reservoir and the salmon cannot get to the East Branch.

Find the lower East Branch by traveling north on MA 32A from Hardwick center into Petersham. The stream flows under the road a mile north of the boundary. Downstream from the highway is Quabbin land, with its seasonal restrictions, but upstream is open year-round. Just beyond the bridge, turn east onto Glen Valley Road, which parallels the stream to the Harvard Forest. Continue on Glen Valley Road after the stream runs north away from it, and turn north on MA 32 and 122, which follows along upstream to Connor Pond. To find the headwaters, turn east on East Street in Petersham center, travel 1 mile to the stream, and fish downstream.

MILLERS RIVER

Maps *USGS:* Orange (Connecticut River to Orange), Athol (Orange to South Royalston), Winchendon (South Royalston to Winchendon), Ashburnham (Winchendon to Ashburnham).

Description The Millers River is a lovely, fertile, freestone stream that runs across the top of Worcester County and into Franklin County from east to west. It encompasses both remote runs of river and easily accessible flows that provide a wide variety of angling opportunities. PCB and mercury pollution have made the lower river de facto catch-and-release water, and, in addition, the state has established two formal fly-and-artificial-lure-only, catch-and-release-only sections that include the best examples of the river's qualities.

Historically, the Millers River was the top trout-angling river in the state, but industrial pollution wiped out its insect and fish life earlier in the century. With the passage of the Clean Water Act in the early 1970s, the abuse was largely stopped, and slowly but surely the high qualities the river once

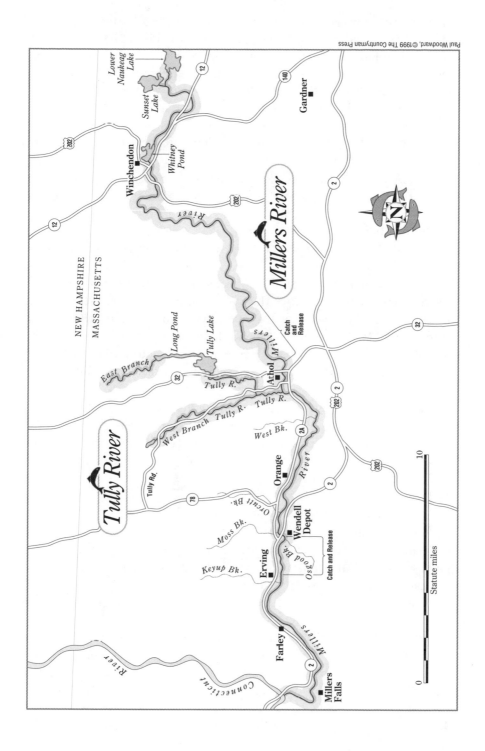

Lower
Naukeag
Lake

Sunset
Lake

202

12

Winchendon

Whitney
Pond

140

Gardner

River

202

Millers River

2

NEW HAMPSHIRE

MASSACHUSETTS

Long Pond

East Branch

Tully Lake

32

Tully R.

Catch
and
Release

Millers

Athol

32

Tully River

West Branch Tully R.

Tully R.

Tully Rd.

West Bk.

2A

78

Orange

River

2

202

Orcutt Bk.

Wendell
Depot

202

Moss Bk.

Keyup Bk.

Erving

Osgood Bk.

Catch and Release

Millers

Farley

2

Millers
Falls

Connecticut

River

0   10

Statute miles

enjoyed have returned. Yet its popularity as a fishing destination has not. This creates a good news/bad news situation for anglers. The good news is that the river rarely sees much angling pressure, aside from the early season. The bad news is that it has not received the attention it deserves, from the public at large or from the authorities, to remove the remaining pollution and to regain its old place as a top-quality, destination-type trout resource. As awareness of the river's fine qualities returns, however, so too may the respect that it deserves. Before long, anglers throughout the region may again flock to its shores.

Access MA 2 closely parallels the best runs of the lower Millers River from its mouth upstream into Orange. Turnouts and parking along the river are numerous, but a short hike down steep banks is often necessary. In Orange, MA 2A continues along the river into Athol, where the highway becomes Main Street, but upstream from the Starret factory dam, the river has only remote, hike-in access for better than 6 miles to South Royalston. River Road follows the river out of South Royalston, but another remote section is accessible only from the Birch Hill dam flood-control project. Northeast of the project, US 202 picks up the river and follows it into Winchendon Center, where MA 12 parallels it into Ashburnham. Find its headwaters by turning north onto Depot Road and west onto Sherbert Road, which crosses the outlets from both Lower Naukeag Lake and Sunset Lake, the headwaters of the Millers.

Regulations The Otter River joins the Millers River in western Winchendon and is the source of the PCB and mercury pollution. Downstream, the official advisory states that no brown trout should be consumed, but practically, this section of river is catch-and-release only for all species. Legally, the entire river is designated as a major river, with a three-fish-a-day limit. In the two catch-and-release areas, only artificial lures and flies may be used, and all fish must be released unharmed back into the river.

Don't miss The upper catch-and-release section on the Millers River is scenic, fertile, and remote, and it stretches for better than 6 miles from the South Royalston/Athol railroad trestle bridge downstream to Athol center. You can drive only to its upper end in South Royalston, its lower end in Athol, or to its middle via Gulf Road and Bearsden Road, both of which are gravel byways. The entire section is protected from development by an array of public land ownership. The most extensive of these owners is the Athol Conservation Commission, which controls all river frontage on the south side in its Bearsden Forest Conservation Area. On the opposite bank, most of the land is a state-owned WMA. Numerous hiking trails lead to the river through all of this public land, and the Boston and Maine Railroad follows close by the entire stretch. You can get into the river here, but it takes effort.

The Millers River below Farley Flats is fertile and productive.

What you'll find, however, are remote pools, strong hatches, holdover trout, and solitude.

Best asset The Millers River is fertile in its own right, but the numerous sewage treatment plants along it return water to the river that is technically clean but that includes even more nutrients. The result is a veritable insect factory that includes clouds of mayflies and caddis and astounding populations of stonefly nymphs and hellgrammites (the dobsonfly larva). The trout in the Millers, which are mostly browns, quickly grow fat and large.

Biggest drawback The pollution sources have been identified and stopped, but the long-term effects of both PCBs and mercury remain. The stigma attached to these deadly chemicals casts a pall on an otherwise outstanding river.

Necessary patterns *Underwater:* Pheasant Tail Nymph (#14–20), Hare's Ear Nymph (#12–16), Hendrickson Nymph (#12–16), Leadwing Coachman (#12–14), Caddis Larva (#14–18), Caddis Emerger (#12–18), Woolly Bugger (#4–12), Giant Black Stonefly Nymph (#2–8), Golden Stonefly Nymph (#4–10), White Stonefly Nymph (#4–8), Black-Nosed Dace (#4–10), Muddler Minnow (#2–12), Mickey Finn (#4–12). *Dry flies:* Quill Gordon (#12–16); Hendrickson (#12–16); Red Quill (#12–16); Rusty Spinner (#12–16); March Brown (#12–14); Gray Fox (#12–14); Mahogany Dun (#12–16); Mahogany Spinner (#10–16); Sulphur Dun (#14–16); Light Cahill (#14–16); Green Drake (#6–10); Brown Drake (#10–12); Golden Drake (#8–12); White Mayfly (#12–14); Natural or Olive Usual (#12–16); Humpy (#8–14); Stimulator (#10–14); Tan, Yellow, Brown, Green, or Black Caddis (#12–18); Blue-Winged Olive (#12–20); Cream Midge (#18–22); Trico (#18–24); Alder (#16–18); Cricket (#10–14); Hopper (#4–12); Black or Cinnamon Ant (#10–20).

Stocked feeder streams worth a look Tully River (see below). Also, from downstream to upstream, Lyons Brook, Mormon Hollow Brook, Keyup Brook, Osgood Brook, Moss Brook, Orcutt Brook, West Brook, Otter River, Priest Brook, Tarbell Brook.

Other feeders Schoolhouse Brook, Briggs Brook, Packard Brook, Whetstone Brook, North Pond Brook, Fall Hill Brook, Gulf Brook, Red Brook, Shingle Swamp Brook, Ice Company Brook, West Gulf Brook, Buckman Brook, Rich Brook, Thousand Acre Brook, Beaver Brook, Kenny Brook, Stockwell Brook, North Branch.

The Millers River runs from the headlands of northern Worcester County in the lake country of Ashburnham southwest and west for 50 miles through Winchendon, Royalston, Athol, Orange, Erving, and Millers Falls

The upper catch-and-release area of the Millers River can only be accessed from its top or bottom, or in the middle, shown here.

before draining into the Connecticut River just above Barton's Cove. It is of particular note because it offers excellent angling over strong hatches of insects for nearly its entire length, because it was once the premier trout-destination stream in the state of Massachusetts, and because, once again, industrial pollution killed it early this century. It has been cleaned up since that pollution desecrated it, and the hatches and the good fishing have returned, but persistent problems with PCBs and mercury remain. Those particular pollutants do not flush from a river as others do, and they infest the food chain, ultimately concentrating in the fatty tissues of fish. This makes much of the lower river, from where the Otter River flows into the Millers in Winchendon downstream, a de facto catch-and-release river.

Fortunately, the state has declared two long runs of the river as catch-and-release areas where only flies and artificial lures are allowed. The formality of the designation allows the state to stock these stretches and adds the weight of the law to the practical necessity of returning all fish to the river.

The river itself is an amalgam of wild beauty and manufacturing utility. The communities through which it runs depended on its water power in years past, and while the industrial revolution has waned and other sources of power become more convenient, the towns that grew up along the Millers still exist and in most cases thrive. The towns center on the river, but the wild gaps between the towns are numerous.

The best way to learn about and enjoy the variety of the river is to fish in the two catch-and-release areas. The lower area runs from the Wendell/Erving Road bridge at the western fringe of the town of Orange to the breached dam 2½ miles downstream in Erving Center. Find the upper limit just west of where MA 2A exits MA 2. You can park right at the Wendell Road bridge or just below the MA 2 overpass. Wendell State Forest abuts much of the southern bank of the river here, so access is never a problem. You can also fish the river off MA 2, but you'll need to hike down over the railroad tracks to do so.

Better yet, go to Erving Center and drive into the now-abandoned administrative offices of Erving Paper. Park there and fish the river right behind the offices, or cross the bridge and fish upstream in the catch-and-release area. You'll need to hike a little way upstream because there is still a backwater to the breached dam.

Downstream from the bridge the Massachusetts Division of Fisheries and Wildlife has recently purchased the frontage on the south bank for a Wildlife Management Area (WMA). There's a dirt road following along the river, and the angling along this stretch of river is superb, with some deep pools harboring trophy-sized browns. Downstream from the WMA the river enters a famous area called Farley Flats, which is best accessed from MA 2 on the north bank. It's the best-known section of the river because it is entirely in view from the highway. In the area known as Farley, at the bottom of this stretch, there is another steel bridge that offers access to the opposite bank. And downstream from Farley, you can hike down to the river from a number of parking areas on MA 2.

The second, upstream catch-and-release area is as remote as any prime fishing water gets in southern New England. Starting at the Starret factory dam right at the east end of downtown Athol, the river upstream for 6 miles flows through protected, undeveloped forest land to South Royalston. Only a well-used railroad line disturbs the feeling of remote wilderness, but the track also offers the best access to the river, up- or downstream, because it follows the flow very closely.

Get to the lower end of the catch-and-release area by traveling to the east end of Main Street, Athol, which is also MA 2A and 32, to Green Street. Turn onto Green Street and travel to its end, which looks like a driveway as it bears left and down a steep hill. Drive just past the garage and onto a dirt road, and park adjacent to the garage. The dirt road continues on along the river, but is permanently gated and has become just a broad hiking trail. The river quickly comes into view, and its banks are entirely undeveloped. You can hike upstream for as far as you like.

The upstream boundary of the catch-and-release area is found by traveling into South Royalston. Exit 20 on MA 2 leads to Highland Avenue, which is east of the exit and runs north into South Royalston. Don't be tempted to take Royalston Road, just west of Highland, because it dead-ends short of your destination. Fish downstream from the bridge in South Royalston, or hike down a half mile to the railroad trestle, the start of the catch-and-release area.

The only other vehicular access to this upper area is via a pair of dirt roads that lead to the very top of the oxbow formed by the river here. In South Royalston, travel north through the center of town on MA 68 to Prospect Street. Bear left, and near the top of the hill turn left (west) onto Bearsden Road, which quickly becomes Gulf Road as it crosses back into Athol. It soon turns to dirt. Travel along this beautiful country lane for 2 miles to the only left (south) turn. Take it, and soon you'll find yourself in what appears to be the yard of the only home on the river in this area. It is. The home is private, but a sign next to it announces that this is a formal fishing access to the Millers River. Park near the sign and hike down to the river in front of you.

Don't be tempted to go past the left turn, as the road soon becomes impassable, even though many maps show that it connects back to a highway near Athol center. The fire department won't even attempt the road with their four-wheel drive brush truck.

There are many more miles of the Millers River to explore, particularly in the Birch Hill Wildlife Management Area behind the flood control dam all the way upstream into Winchendon and beyond. You could easily spend an entire season, or a lifetime, exploring the river and finding new and exciting places to fish.

Tully River

The Tully River flows into the Millers River just west of Athol center. Its short main stem runs for just a mile from the juncture of its West and East Branches just north of Sportsmans Pond, which sits on top of Athol's downtown area. These three reaches of the Tully all offer good angling for stocked and holdover browns and rainbows, and, in the headwaters, native brook trout, and all of them have high-quality water and strong hatches.

The best access to the main stem is via North Orange Road. Turn north onto it from MA 2A just west of where MA 2A crosses the Millers River on the west edge of Athol. The Tully runs right next to the road, or you can fish it upstream from the 2A bridge, but it is urban here. For the West Branch, turn north onto Exchange Street from Main Street, Athol, and bear left on Pequoig Avenue, which shortly becomes Pinedale Avenue. Sportsmans Pond is on the right and Pinedale turns right across the top of the lake and connects with MA 32, West Royalston Road. Continue straight when Pinedale turns right, and the road becomes Tully Road just past the Orange town line.

It parallels the West Branch all the way to Tully Pond. Do take the Pinedale turn to MA 32, turn north on it, and this road parallels the East Branch to Tully Lake. Fish either of the branches all along these roads as there is plenty of access and good water.

SMALLER CONNECTICUT RIVER FEEDERS

Fort River

The Fort River is the longest undammed tributary to the Connecticut River in Massachusetts. That in itself would make it noteworthy, but it also contains some very fine trout water that is largely overshadowed by a number of other regional streams that receive much more attention (see above).

The Fort River runs from where four cold-water tributary brooks come together in East Village, Amherst, southward through Amherst and then westward through Hadley to the Connecticut River. While the lower reaches are meandering meadow-type water, getting into them and fishing the undercut banks and deep pools often surprises anglers with big, strong holdover browns. In its upstream stretches, the Fort receives stocked trout and holds them well throughout the season. And in the four headwater brooks—namely Hawley, Adams, Heatherstone, and Amethyst—brook trout thrive, often not seeing anglers for the entire season. As a plus, Adams Brook receives a spring stocking of trout.

Access to the Fort River is decent if not extensive. The best angling—and access—is near its headwaters where Pelham Road, an easterly extension of Main Street, Amherst, crosses the river. Hike upstream from the bridge for some excellent main-stem fishing. Amethyst Brook enters from the east a quarter mile upstream, while Heatherstone comes in from the east another quarter mile beyond, and Adams and Hawley Brooks join just upstream from Heatherstone. For the lower river, several crossroads provide access: MA 9, Southeast Street, and MA 116 in Amherst; and South Maple Street and MA 47 in Hadley.

Sawmill River

The Sawmill River is a pretty mountain stream that originates at the outflow of Lake Wyola and tumbles down out of the hills of Shutesbury and Leverett, flowing roughly from east to west until it turns due north and flows into the small community of Montague Center. Downstream of Montague Center, the Sawmill enters the Connecticut River flood plain and slows and meanders until it meets the big river.

Because it flows through mostly mature woodlands, the Sawmill stays cool all year and holds trout well, even during the dog days of summer when its flows are adequate. In addition, stream-born brookies are available, especially in the more remote pools and in the many small feeder streams. Hatches of mayflies and caddis are strong, especially on its lower half.

Access to the Sawmill River is exceptional all along its length. From Lake Wyola, follow North Leverett Road westbound all the way down out of the hills. The river is never more than a short, easy hike from the road. Where North Leverett Road meets MA 63, cross the highway onto MA 47, which shortly turns south. Turn north instead, onto Main Street, which leads into Montague Center. Again, the river parallels Main Street.

Other Stocked Streams that Flow from the Midstate Highlands toward the West and the Connecticut River

Franklin County *Leverett:* Doolittle Brook, Roaring Brook; *Montague:* Goddard Brook; *Northfield:* Four Mile Brook, Mill Brook, Pauchaug Brook; *Shutesbury:* Dean Brook; *Sunderland:* Dug Brook, Mohawk Brook; *Warwick:* Mill Brook.

Hampshire County *Amherst:* Adams Brook, Mill River, Cushman Brook; *Belchertown:* Broad Brook, Scarboro Brook; *Granby:* Bachelor Brook; *Hadley:* Harts Brook, Russellville Brook, Mill River; *Pelham:* Amethyst Brook; *Ware:* Flat Brook, Muddy Brook.

Hampden County *Chicopee:* Fuller Brook; *East Longmeadow:* South Branch of the Mill River; *Hampden:* Scantic River; *Holland:* Stevens Brook; *Springfield:* North Branch of the Mill River; *Wales:* Wales Brook.

Worcester County *Athol:* Ellinwood Brook, West Brook; *Barre:* Burnshirt River, Canesto Brook, Prince River; *Hardwick:* Moose Brook, Danforth Brook; *Hubbardston:* Natty Pond Brook, Joslin Brook; *New Braintree:* Winimusset Brook, Meadow Brook; *North Brookfield:* Five Mile River; *Oakham:* Parker Brook; *Petersham:* West Branch of the Fever Brook; *Phillipston:* Beaver Brook; *Royalston:* Lawrence Brook, Scott Brook; *Spencer:* Cranberry River.

Important Stocked Lakes and Ponds

Franklin County (stocked spring and fall) *Erving:* Laurel Lake; *Orange:* Lake Mattawa; *Shutesbury:* Lake Wyola; *Warwick:* Sheomet Pond. **(Stocked only in spring)** *Montague:* West Pond; *Sunderland:* Cranberry Pond; *Warwick:* Moore Pond.

Hampshire County (stocked spring and fall) *Amherst:* Factory Hollow Pond; *Belchertown:* Metacomet Lake; *Granby:* DuFresne Pond; *Ware:* Peppermill Pond. **(Stocked only in spring)** Quabbin Reservoir.

Hampden County (stocked spring and fall) *Chicopee:* Chicopee Reservoir; *Holland:* Hamilton Reservoir; *Ludlow:* Chapin Pond; *Palmer:* Forest Lake; *Springfield:* Five Mile Pond, Watershops Pond, Loon Pond. **(Stocked only in spring)** *Brimfield:* Woodman Pond, Dean Pond; *Holland:* Holland Pond; *Springfield:* Lake Lorraine.

Worcester County (stocked spring and fall) *Hubbardston:* Asnacomet Pond; *Rutland:* Long Pond; *Spencer:* Browning Pond; *Winchendon:* Lake Dennison. **(Stocked only in spring)** *Athol:* Silver Lake; *Gardner:* Kendall Pond, Dunn Pond; *Hardwick:* Hardwick Pond; *Petersham:* Connor Pond; *Rutland:* Demond Pond, Whitehall Pond; *Spencer:* Sugden Reservoir.

4 | Central Massachusetts Waters: From North to South

Nashua River

The Nashua River is important to trout fly-fishermen for two reasons. First, even though the state does not stock the river with trout, a few impressive fish are taken each year—migrants downstream from the streams that the state does stock. Second, two of Massachusetts' most impressive trout streams—the Nissitisset and Squannacook Rivers (see below)—feed into the Nashua in the north-central part of the state between Fitchburg and Lowell.

Much of the Nashua River is slow moving and bass filled, best accessed with canoes or johnboats. That there are fish at all is a tribute to the efforts of many people and environmentally aware organizations. Like too many rivers in the Northeast, the Nashua was degraded and polluted for years, but enlightened laws and awareness have now made it a true pleasure to explore.

Trout can be found at the mouths of stocked rivers and streams, especially when water levels or temperatures have forced the fish downstream to the Nashua. Both the mouths of Mulpus Brook and the Squannacook River can produce surprising catches, but they are best accessed by canoe. The ¾-mile reach of river below the Pepperell Paper Company dam in East Pepperell can be waded at normal or low water levels and can hold trout, which probably originate from the Nissitisset. Access the river via MA 113 (Main Street) in Pepperell. Turn north on Groton Street to the covered bridge and fish up- or downstream. The Nissitisset River marks the start of the downstream area where the Nashua again broadens out and requires a boat or canoe for its remaining 2-mile run into New Hampshire.

Nissitisset River

The Massachusetts section of the Nissitisset River runs from the New Hampshire border to the Nashua River in the town of Pepperell. It includes

The Nissitisset River catch-and- release area is well marked and accessible.

one of Massachusetts' first fly-fishing-only areas, originally only a mile long and with no catch-and-release restrictions. Now it's nearly 2 miles long, still fly-fishing only, but with the added benefit of a full catch-and-release regulation.

The Nissitisset State Wildlife Management Area (WMA) borders nearly the entire fly-fishing-only area, which starts at the state line and runs to the first downstream bridge at Prospect Street. Access to the river is excellent from the Prospect Street bridge, from North Street on the north side of the river for the lower reach, or from Brookline Road on the south bank for the upper section. Brookline Road runs north (left) from MA 111 just above Pepperell center, and Prospect Street turns right about a mile along. North Street turns west off Prospect Street just north of the bridge. You can wade right into the river at the bridge, off both North and Brookline Streets, where the hike is a few hundred easy yards.

The most popular access is along Brookline Street to just above the middle of the fly-fishing-only area. A sign identifies the area as the Henry Colombo WMA, and a gate beside it leads down a wide path that divides. Both trails lead down to the river, and bankside trails lead up- and downstream.

Below the fly-fishing-only area, the Nissitisset remains an excellent trout stream, but with limited access. The Town of Pepperell Conservation Commission owns an access trail to the river near Twin Valley Farm on Brookline Street, downstream from the fly-fishing-only area. Look for the labeled parking lot on the west side of the road and for a gate and trail on the opposite side that leads to the river. An old railroad bed runs along the river, providing easy walking up- and downstream. Be sure to fish under the trestle bridge upstream from where the trail meets the river. Other downstream accesses can be found at the MA 111 (Hollis Street) bridge and at the Mill Street bridge.

The Nissitissit River enjoys a full complement of hatches, but match the water type to the insects you would expect to find. In the upstream reaches, and in a few downstream runs, stoneflies are available, with their imitations productive for taking some very big holdover browns, especially at dusk or after dark. These riffles are complemented by a few other sections throughout the river where mayflies are predominant, but they are never present in overwhelming numbers. The caddis hatches are truly impressive, however, with a wide variety of sizes and colors hatching throughout the year.

SQUANNACOOK RIVER

Maps *USGS:* Ayer (Nashua River to West Groton), Townsend (West Groton to West Townsend), Ashburnham (West Townsend to Ash Swamp).

Description The Squannacook River is a perfect example of a transition river. It includes within its 14-mile run the best assets of freestone hill streams, as well as the lower gradient meanders of meadow or limestonelike reaches. It has waters best suited for headland brook trout, others that are ideal for holding fast-water-loving rainbows, and slow-water runs with undercut bankings that attract and hold lunker brown trout. And all of these water types are blessed with abundant hatches of caddis, mayflies, and, where appropriate, stoneflies.

In addition, the Squannacook has plenty of publicly owned land, in the form of state forests and game management areas, that provides an attractive variety of angling experiences. Seclusion and good angling are available to energetic anglers not afraid of hiking, but there is also plenty of productive water near the bridges and roads to keep less energetic anglers content. The river is very deserving of its regional, and growing, fame.

Access The Squannacook River provides the full array of trout fishing access, from easy by-the-bridge pools, to access roads that parallel productive runs, to short hikes through state lands, to bushwhacking through bogs and swamps. Take your pick.

The run of river from the Vose dam in West Groton upstream to Harbor Pond in Townsend is one of the most popular stretches on the entire river, mainly because it is easy to get to and because much of both sides of the river are owned by the state in its Squannacook River Wildlife Management Area (WMA). Access to the lower section is via Townsend Road on the east

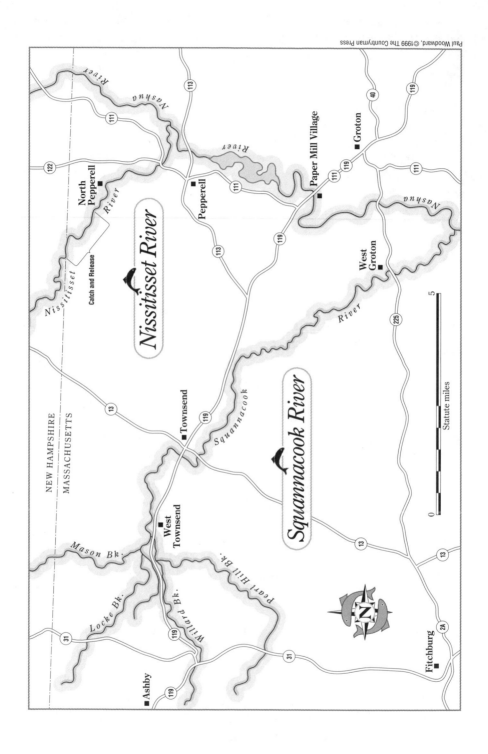

Nissitisset River

Squannacook River

Catch and Release

NEW HAMPSHIRE
MASSACHUSETTS

North
Pepperell

Pepperell

Paper Mill Village

Groton

West
Groton

Townsend

West
Townsend

Ashby

Fitchburg

Nashua River

Nissitisset River

Squannacook River

Mason Bk.

Locke Bk.

Willard Bk.

Pearl Hill Bk.

Nashua

River

Statute miles

0   5

122   111   113   111   119   40   119   111   13   119   225   31   2A

bank in Groton, and via another Townsend Road in Shirley on the west bank. This Townsend Road becomes Shirley Road in Townsend, and on this west side, it's about a quarter-mile hike through the WMA down to the river.

From Townsend Harbor upstream to Townsend, access is along MA 119. Turn south onto Meetinghouse Road, a one-lane dirt road that is passable right to the river where it dead-ends. Fish upstream from here, or park behind the Sterilite factory, and hike out behind it to the river. Follow the most heavily used paths, as there are many all-terrain vehicle (ATV) trails.

Between Townsend center and the headwaters of the Squannacook, access to the river near the center of town is via a trail behind the new elementary school off MA 13, Brookline Street, just north of the center, or by turning west onto Dudley Street just beyond the school and hiking through the Townsend State Forest. The upper reaches can be found by turning west onto MA 119 in Townsend center and bearing right onto Turnpike Road. Fish up- or downstream from the bridge that crosses the river about a mile from the center. To fish the section just downstream from where several attractive brooks meet to form the Squannacook, park at the VFW parking lot on MA 119 west of the center and walk to the river, just north of the lot. Fish downstream on the main stem or upstream toward the feeder streams.

Regulations The Squannacook is classified as a major river, making the daily limit three fish. There are no tackle restrictions and no closed season.

Don't miss Black Rock is a famous reach of the river, dominated by a huge overhanging boulder. It produces some of the very best hatches and contains some of the best trout water and trout in the Squannacook. It's famous, but it's lightly fished because of the effort needed to get to it. This reach is a long walk in from nearly any access point, and few anglers are willing to make the pilgrimage. You can get to it by hiking upstream from the trails behind the elementary school in Townsend.

Best asset The Squannacook River drainage is largely protected by public ownership of many miles of its shores. The Squannacook River State WMA is a patchwork of properties up and down the river that keeps its banks from being further developed. The Townsend State Forest protects habitat that is closer to the center of Townsend. And the Willard Brook State Forest protects the watershed of that major tributary in the Squannacook's headwaters. Not only does this public ownership provide access to the river and its headwaters, it also helps keep the waters shaded, cooled, productive, and protected as a trout fishery.

Biggest drawback Because of the abundance of public land, bridges, access, and indeed, the quality of the water, the Squannacook is fast becoming a well-known and popular trout river. Unfortunately, with this popularity comes the inevitable problems of too many people. Where the easiest accesses draw the most anglers, trash and disrespect for the property becomes evident. And even when you do get away from the crowds, ATVs have chewed up some of the countryside, or thoughtless campers have left fire rings full of cans and trash.

Necessary patterns *Underwater:* Pheasant Tail Nymph (#14–20), Hare's Ear Nymph (#12–16), Hendrickson Nymph (#12–16), Tellico (#10–16), Leadwing Coachman (#12–14), Caddis Larva (#14–18), Caddis Emerger (#12–18), Black-Nosed Dace (#4–10), Mickey Finn (#4–12), Muddler Minnow (#8–12). *Dry flies:* Adams (#10–22); Quill Gordon (#12–16); Hendrickson (#12–16); Red Quill (#12–16); Rusty Spinner (#12–16); March Brown (#12–14); Gray Fox (#12–14); Mahogany Dun (#12–16); Mahogany Spinner (#10–16); Sulphur Dun (#14–16); Light Cahill (#14–16); Pale Evening Dun (#12–18); White Mayfly (#12–14); Tan, Yellow, Brown, Green, or Black Caddis (#12–18); Blue-Winged Olive (#12–20); Cream Midge (#18–22); Trico (#18–24); Alder (#16–18); Cricket (#10–14); Hopper (#4–12); Black or Cinnamon Ant (#10–20).

Stocked feeder streams worth a look (from downstream to upstream) Witch Brook, Bixby Brook, Mason Brook, Walker Brook, Locke Brook, Willard Brook, Trapfall Brook.

The last five brooks listed here come together in and around Ash Swamp and just south of it to form the Squannacook River. They all receive ample trout stockings and all (plus Pearl Hill Brook) support brook trout populations, a quite amazing turnaround from a mere 10 years ago when their acidity prevented trout from surviving in them.

Other feeders Trap Swamp Brook, Pumpkin Brook, Trout Brook, Bayberry Hill Brook, Pearl Hill Brook.

The Squannacook River in Townsend, and downstream where it forms a boundary between Shirley and Groton, is a first-class trout stream that is finally receiving the accord it deserves. Its waters are pure and fertile, supporting year-round trout and ample insect life. Access to it is superb, which is due in large part to the wise purchase by the state of wildlands along its shores. And it offers a full complement of fishing opportunities to suit the tastes of most anglers—bridge and roadside or deep woods and swamp. In addition, its headwater feeder streams are cold enough—and often remote enough—to support strong populations of stream-born brook trout.

It has other assets, too; namely, a variety of water types that offer slow meandering corner pools and quick freestone runs, along with riffles and pocket water. Because of the extensive publicly owned forests along it, trees and blowdowns regularly form deep-water hiding holds for trout that can be measured in pounds, not inches. It even has a pair of millponds, Harbor

Pond and Thompson's Mill Pond, that provide good still-water trout fishing.

It's a distinct help that the Squannacook does not flow through any of the larger manufacturing centers, like Fitchburg or Lowell, that are nearby. Outside of a persistent acidic tinge to the headwaters that has since disappeared, these waters have not suffered the degradation that so many waterways did in New England. And because of this and the extensive state-land ownership, you can get the vivid impression that you're fishing in a river untouched by the ravages of the Industrial Revolution. You might even envision the river, in places, as it must have looked in colonial times.

Adding to this charm is the presence of several small towns along the river that have guarded their colonial aura and maintained their rural roots. Sure, there are grinder shops and gas stations, but there are also colonial homes, farms, and picturesque back roads worth investigating.

But it's the fine trout fishing that draws us back to the Squannacook. The river deserves its regional renown, so early-season trips will usually find plenty of anglers around the stocking sites and near the easiest access points. But hike away from these areas at almost any time of year, and the quality of the angling will improve.

Because the state stocks only downstream to the dam in the Vose section of West Groton, few anglers fish for trout below this point. Some rainbows and browns, however, do migrate there and can grow to very good sizes. The best access is at the MA 225 bridge in West Groton, then hike downstream. Upstream from Vose, the variety of water and access is immediately obvious (see "Access," above), and the angling holds up well for almost the entire year.

Wachusett Reservoir and Its Feeders

The Wachusett Reservoir is the state's second-largest lake, a drinking-water source within the Metropolitan District Commission's (MDC's) extensive watershed grid, which was created in the 1930s and '40s to slake Boston's thirst. The 4,100-acre reservoir sits amid a 68,000-acre protected watershed, and it also receives a major supply of water from Quabbin Reservoir (see chapter 3) via an underground bedrock tunnel that empties into the lower Quinapoxet River (see below).

Wachusett is important to anglers for several reasons. Primary among them are the facts that the reservoir lies only 10 miles north of Worcester, the second-largest city in Massachusetts, and that it literally teems with lake trout, landlocked salmon, bass, and smelt. In addition, Wachusett's two major tributaries, the Quinapoxet and the Stillwater Rivers (see below), offer superb trout angling for much of the year and good landlocked salmon angling in both spring and fall.

Fishing regulations on Wachusett differ substantially from those on

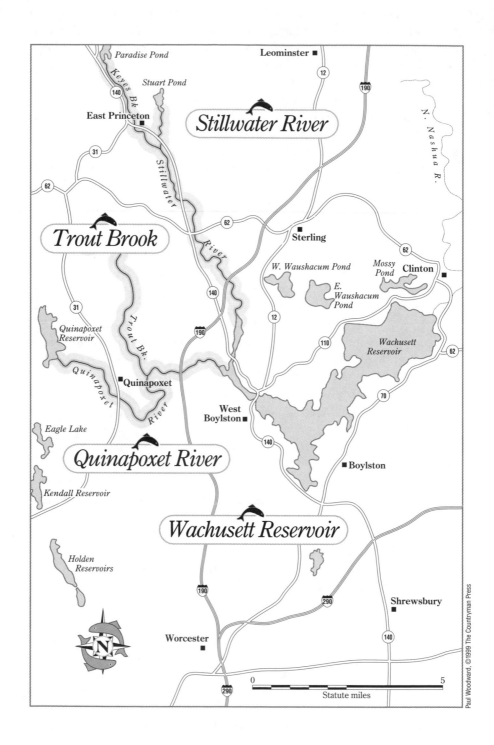

Paul Woodward, ©1999 The Countryman Press

Quabbin in that no boats are allowed, but the angling season runs longer, from April 1 to November 30 annually. As in Quabbin, no wading whatsoever is allowed. And bear in mind that the watershed rangers, the environmental police, and the state police are dead serious about enforcing the rules that govern the MDC's property. They will find you if you are not observing the rules, and they will ticket you.

The no-boating restriction has raised some interesting problems for fisheries biologists on Wachusett and some unique opportunities for anglers. The problems center on the fact that most of the fish population is out of reach of anglers for much of the year, particularly during the summer months when it seeks out more comfortable temperatures in deep water. This has led to something of an overpopulation of lake trout, famous deep-water denizens. They have become so numerous that length restrictions have been eliminated, with a three-fish-a-day limit, and biologists are asking that anglers do indeed take their three lake trout and not return them to the water.

By lowering the lake trout numbers, forage for landlocks and the other game species will become more abundant, allowing them to grow bigger and more enticing to anglers. That Wachusett has the capacity to raise large fish is illustrated by the fact that it currently holds the state records for smallmouth bass (8 pounds, 2 ounces), brown trout (19 pounds, 10 ounces), rainbow trout (13 pounds, 13 ounces, caught April 19, 1999), and landlocked salmon (10 pounds, 2 ounces). Folks, those are big fish.

For fly-fishermen, Wachusett Reservoir is largely an untapped resource. True, in recent years, the watershed management practices along the shores have made casting a fly difficult by allowing brush and saplings to grow unchecked. But within the last 2 years, new thoughts on shoreline management have called for the removal of vegetation. Call the MDC Watershed Rangers (978-365-3800) to find out exactly where the brush is being cut, and fish there. The Rangers can also provide you with a map of the area.

In addition, according to Joe Bergin, the state fisheries biologist in charge of Wachusett, fish the windward shores where feed fish and game fish pile up. You'll be casting into the wind, but you don't need to throw 80 feet of line when the fish are within 30 feet of shore. And concentrate your efforts during spring and fall, when water temperatures bring the fish in close.

The landlocked salmon are a self-sustaining species in Wachusett, with extensive spawning runs up the Stillwater River. And the Stillwater is such an excellent nursery that it annually produces, on its own, double the salmon smolt escapement needed to maintain optimum levels of mature salmon in the reservoir. Brown trout, most from the self-sustaining population in the Quinapoxet River, are available, but not abundant. And the state also stocks rainbows in both the Quinapoxet and Stillwater Rivers that make their way down into the reservoir.

The Wachusett Reservoir is encircled with highways that offer easy access to it. MA 140 on the west, MA 70 on the southeast, and MA 110 on the northwest get you to nearly all of the access gates. Then hike down the trails to the reservoir and fish nearly anywhere. There is no fishing on the east end, where the water is drawn off near the dam to be sent along to Boston, but it is clearly posted.

Use smelt pattern streamer flies, like the Gray, Black, and Pink Ghosts; Nine-Threes; Joe's and Jerry's Smelt; and Ballou Specials, especially in spring when shoal and shore spawning smelt are close. In addition, white perch fry and yearlings make up a substantial portion of the forage that all game species use in Wachusett, so use broader-bodied streamers to imitate them, like Hornbergs, Threadfin Shad, or Erskines.

QUINAPOXET RIVER

Maps *USGS:* Sterling (mouth to Canada Mills), Worcester North (Canada Mills to Quinapoxet), Sterling (Quinapoxet to Quinapoxet Reservoir).

Description The Quinapoxet River flows for a brief 7 miles from the Quinapoxet Reservoir in Holden to the Wachusett Reservoir in West Boylston. It is a protected river, owned entirely by the Metropolitan District Commission (MDC), and it is fertile, cold, and popular.

The river's charm includes its semblance of wilderness (as there is virtually no development along its shores) and its proximity to the Wachusett Reservoir watershed, an oasis of wilderness in the midst of the highly developed and growing sprawl of the nearby city of Worcester. It is truly a relief to have this high-quality stream (it's not really large enough to be called a river) so close to so many enthusiastic anglers and to have it open to all and easily accessible. The Quinapoxet deserves its reputation because of its strong population of stream-born brown and brook trout and its strong, steady hatches of mayflies, caddis, and stoneflies. The state does its part by stocking it heavily with rainbows.

Access Access to the Quinapoxet is excellent for its entire short run. All of the river and its banks are owned by the MDC, and hiking and stream access are allowed up and down the river. There are a few smatterings of private property that you might want to cross, but most are not posted. Just respect landowner rights.

You can access the lower river, from where the Quabbin Aqueduct enters through an MDC power station to the mouth, from the junction of River Street and Thomas Street, just south of the triple-arched stone bridge in the

The Quinapoxet River feeds into Wachusett Reservoir under the triple-arched bridge of MA 140.

Oakdale section of West Boylston. River Street continues upstream through mostly MDC property, under I-190, and then bends away from a big oxbow in the river, but the road parallels the shores again at Canada Mills and on to Lovellville. Watch carefully for the first upstream bridge, because River Street takes a sharp north (right) turn over it. If you're not right next to the river on River Street, then it is only a short easy hike to the water. Laurel Street in Oakdale becomes Manning Street in West Boylston on the north side of the river, and this road provides the best access to the top of the oxbow on the river.

The upstream areas are accessed via MA 31, Wachusett Street, in Holden. Turn north onto MA 31 at the west end of River Street or Manning Street. Turn west (left) onto Mill Street for a bridge access or a bit farther north onto Elmwood Street, which parallels the river to the Quinapoxet Reservoir. Hike downhill to the river.

Regulations From the MDC power station downstream, the Quinapoxet is governed by the same rules that govern the Wachusett Reservoir: The season runs from April 1 to November 30, and no wading is allowed. There is a no-fishing zone just below the power station outlet and for 200 feet above the settlement dam at the power station. Above that, the Quinapoxet is governed by major-river state fishing rules. It has no closed season, and only three fish a day may be taken. All methods of angling are allowed.

Don't miss Because the river is so close to the access roads for much of its run, the few remote sections of it are largely ignored. Hike into the upper river above Mill Street, or try the west side of the oxbow on the river between River Street and Manning Street. There is a marked trail off River Street.

Best asset The Quinapoxet River stays cool enough even in the summer to support strong populations of stream-born brown and brook trout that stay active all year. The river runs entirely through protected watershed that has grown a canopy of forest over it, and a cold-water mountain stream, Trout Brook (see below), contributes chilled water and essential nutrients to the Quinapoxet. In addition, there are numerous springs that feed into the riverbed.

Biggest drawback Because angling pressure on the Quinapoxet has grown substantially over the years, a catch-and-release section would be a boon. Sportsmen approached the MDC with a catch-and-release proposal for the downstream side of the power station, but the idea was never pursued. More logical would be the protection of a section of the river upstream from the power station, where the river's natural cold-water flow and high fertility could be used to maximum advantage.

Necessary patterns *Underwater:* Pheasant Tail Nymph (#14–20), Hare's Ear Nymph (#12–16), Hendrickson Nymph (#12–16), Montana Stonefly (#2–12), Leadwing Coachman (#12–14), Caddis Larva (#14–18), Caddis Emerger (#12–18), Black-Nosed Dace (#4–10), Mickey Finn (#4–12), Muddler Minnow (#2–10), Hornberg (#8–14). *Dry flies:* Quill Gordon (#12–16); Hendrickson (#12–16); Red Quill (#12–16); Rusty Spinner (#12–16); March Brown (#12–14); Gray Fox (#12–14); Sulphur Dun (#14–16); Light Cahill (#14–16); White Mayfly (#12–14); Picket Pin (#8–14); Yellow Stonefly (#8–14); Tan, Yellow, Brown, Green, Black, or Gray Caddis (#12–18); Blue-Winged Olive (#12–20); Cream Midge (#18–22); Trico (#18–24); Alder (#16–18); Cricket (#10–14); Hopper (#4–12); Black or Cinnamon Ant (#10-20).

Feeder streams worth a look Trout Brook (see below). Also, from downstream to upstream, Chaffins Brook (not stocked), Asnebumskit Brook (stocked).

The Quinapoxet River is a popular dream of a stream that flows close enough to the urban sprawl of Worcester to attract much attention, yet it is resilient and fertile enough to maintain good populations of stream-born brook and brown trout. In addition, the state supplements these native trout with regular annual stockings of rainbow trout and a few browns. The river's cool waters hold up well throughout the season, and many veterans of the stream advocate summer angling for solitude.

The Quinapoxet feeds southeast out of Quinapoxet Reservoir in Holden, turns due east in Lovellville, and flows into Wachusett Reservoir in West Boylston. A distinct stone bridge with three arches is located just off

MA 140 in the Oakdale section of West Boylston and marks the river's merger with the Thomas Basin of Wachusett.

The lower river, a 1,500-foot-long reach from the power station to the bridge, often bulges and roars with the added water from the Quabbin Reservoir, but it attracts much angling pressure early and late in the season because of the strong run of landlocked salmon that push up into it. And just below the bridge is where the state record brown trout—a 19-pound, 10-ounce monster—was taken. Be aware that this section is governed by Wachusett Reservoir rules, and the authorities take these rules very seriously. There is no wading, and the season is open from April 1 to November 30, if there is no ice on the reservoir. Check with the MDC Watershed Rangers (978-365-3800) to be sure that the season is indeed open.

The joy of the Quinapoxet is its protected watershed. Its shores and streambed are owned by the MDC, who have realized the recreational values of their lands and have improved their public relations throughout their large land holdings. The Quinapoxet has the aura of a remote backwoods trout stream, but make no mistake—you are still in Massachusetts, and the river is sometimes overrun with anglers. Still, it's a joy to be able to meander a pretty stream's banks, knowing that it holds good populations of trout, and to fish over trout accustomed to seeing the strong natural hatches that occur here throughout the year.

Access to the Quinapoxet is superb, and you can either step off a road and into the water or enjoy a leisurely stroll through unspoiled forests to the river's edge. A catch-and-release section on the stream would be a welcome addition; with the angling pressure that the river receives, the native browns are largely nocturnal, and the brookies often retreat into and up the feeders. But all in all, the Quinapoxet is a sweet stream that can charm you into staying on it for an extra day or two.

Trout Brook

Trout Brook is formed at the junction of Governor Brook and the outflow of Cournoyer Pond, itself fed by the aptly named Cold Brook, in the hills north of the community of Quinapoxet. Trout Brook flows due south for almost 2 miles into the Quinapoxet River, where its cold and fertile waters aid that river's ability to hold trout. However, it is an excellent native brook trout stream in its own right.

Find access to Trout Brook along Laurel Street and Manning Road, which parallel the north bank of the Quinapoxet between Oakdale and Quinapoxet. The brook flows under the road just west of the MDC's picnic area access road. Fish downstream to the Quinapoxet from Manning Street, or park in the picnic area and fish upstream.

The brook's cold-water flow and excellent fertility keep the trout happy

The Stillwater River's main claim to fame is its excellent angling for landlocked salmon in the spring and fall, but it holds trout, too.

and the insect hatches strong, but it is a small brook, so a 7-foot, 3-weight rod would be better than your standard 9-foot, 6-weight.

Stillwater River

Visit the Stillwater River in late summer, as I did, and you might not be terribly impressed. Yes, it's a pretty little trout stream with a variety of fast-water pools and slow meadow-type runs, but it can suffer from low-water flows and temperatures that warm to the near-lethal level for trout. In spring, when the water levels are up, the trout angling for stockers can be good, and there are some decent hatches. In addition, the river does have excellent access, as MA 140 closely follows its flow from Wachusett Reservoir in Oakdale north to its headwaters in East Princeton. You can fish at any of a number of crossroads or right along MA 140.

But the Stillwater's claim to fame is the quite astounding run of land-locked salmon that zooms up its waters from Wachusett Reservoir in spring and fall. In a river where you'd be happy with a 9-inch brookie, a 5-pound salmon can certainly grab your attention.

And we're not talking an occasional fish here. According to Joe Bergin, the state fisheries specialist whose beat includes Wachusett and its feeders, the Stillwater River produces nearly twice the salmon smolt escapement each year that is needed to keep Wachusett stocked with an optimal level of mature landlocks. And the big spawning adults have been found more than 6½ miles upstream from the Stillwater Basin of Wachusett.

As Bergin explains it, the Stillwater has nearly ideal spawning gravel, and with the Wachusett population of adults finding the Quinapoxet blocked by the sedimentary dam, the Stillwater attracts nearly all of the spawners. So when the big adult salmon are chasing the smelt into the river in spring, and again when they run up in fall, bring the 8-weight fly rod and the reel with the good drag. You'll probably need it.

Time your spring trip to the Stillwater River with the smelt run. It usually occurs just as the roiled runoff water begins to clear. And in the autumn, look for that first good rainfall in late September and through October. If there's a half inch or more of rain, the river will rise and draw the fish in. Big smelt streamers work well for the salmon, like the Gray Ghost, the Nine-Three, or the Black Ghost.

Remember, too, that downstream from where Waushacum Brook enters, the Stillwater Basin is governed by Wachusett Reservoir rules. There is no wading (or boats like canoes) allowed. But upstream is governed by general state laws for major trout streams, with no closed season and a three-trout-a-day limit. For the salmon, the minimum length is 18 inches, with a two-fish-a-day limit. But please realize how special and rare a salmon run is in southern New England, and release the majority of the fish you take.

Seven Mile River

Seven Mile River is an interesting and varied flow, although not extensive, that originates at Browning Pond in north Spencer and south Oakham and runs due south into East Brookfield and the East Brookfield River, meeting the river just south of its outlet from Lake Lashaway. Seven Mile River is stocked heavily by the state, with much of it a put-and-take fishery, but there are some holdover brown trout, especially in the more remote, swampy reaches adjacent to Meadow Road, just north of MA 9. It's listed as a major river by the state, making the daily trout limit three fish.

Find access to the lower river, below MA 9, by turning south onto Bridge Street near the Lake Lashaway outlet, via Cove Street a half mile east on MA 9, or by taking MA 49 south from MA 9 in Spencer near the East Brookfield line. This lower river section has plenty of runs and pools and much good holding water. Be sure to try the railroad trestle pool just downstream from the Cove Street bridge.

Just east of the MA 49 turnoff and west of Spencer center, Meadow Road runs north along the river. A sign on MA 9 points toward MA 31. While fly-fishing this stretch of river is difficult because of the brush and marshland, it can be accomplished with a small canoe or johnboat, and there are some very nice holdover brown trout if you can get to them. Access this area just south of where Meadow Road meets MA 31 by turning west onto Smithville Road and parking in the field on the west side of the bridge. The field serves as a parking lot for the Spencer fair and is adjacent to the fairgrounds.

The upper river is small but productive and can be waded. Get to it via an east turn off MA 31 onto Cooney Road. Park at the gauging station gravel turnaround and fish up- or downstream. Or hike into the river upstream by walking in east from MA 31.

Quinebaug River

The Quinebaug River begins its long run through Massachusetts and Connecticut to Long Island Sound at Hamilton Reservoir in Holland, Massachusetts. It flows northward through Holland Pond and into East Brimfield Reservoir, a favorite bass and northern pike water. The water immediately downstream and into Old Sturbridge Village is relatively inaccessible, although you can get onto it behind some of the stores along US 20. In Old Sturbridge Village itself, and the land the village owns along the river, there is decent access, and anglers are invited to use the private access road that turns south just inside Leadmine Road, the road to the entrance to the village. There are many warm-water species here, however, including large- and smallmouth bass and a few northern pike that spill downstream from East Brimfield.

The best trout angling is found downstream from Old Sturbridge Village, where the flood plain of the Army Corps of Engineers flood-control dam at Westville Lake occurs. Access this area by traveling south from Sturbridge center about a mile on MA 15 (it parallels I-84) to River Road, a south (left) turn opposite Interchange 2 of I-84. Farquhar Road is the first left turn off River Road and shortly crosses the Quinebaug, providing access up- and downstream.

Farther south, River Road meets Mashapaug Road. Turn east (left) on it, and north onto Breakneck Road. Breakneck Road leads directly downhill to the Westville Lake Recreation Area of the Corps of Engineers, where there is plenty of parking right at the river. Hike and fish upstream from here, and enjoy the fact that the Corps has preserved this area for all comers, including anglers. Just upstream, you'll find yourself in the middle of the woods and along the shores of one of the best trout areas of the entire, long Quinebaug River.

West River

The West River is a high-quality trout fishery that maintains excellent water levels and temperatures year-round, holds fish exceptionally well, enjoys some of the best mayfly hatches in the region, and has ample access. It originates out of Wildwood Lake on the west side of Upton near MA 140 and flows for nearly 10 miles due south to its confluence with the Blackstone River in Uxbridge.

The upper two-thirds of the West is part of the Army Corps of Engineers flood-control project behind the West Hill dam in Uxbridge. Upstream from the dam, nearly all of the land (and access) along the West River is either under easement to the Corps or owned outright. This is the most attractive fishing area of the river. Although it does flow through some marshy areas and is often brush lined, much of the river in this reach has a fertile, sandy bottom, making wading relatively easy. And for those anglers willing to hike up and away from the access road bridges, the angling can be exceptional.

If there is a problem on the West River, it is political, not natural. Unfortunately, the Corps' dam is situated near where the towns of Upton, Mendon, Northbridge, and Uxbridge all come together, and the Upton State Forest lies in Upton, Northbridge, and Uxbridge. Of course, each of the towns names its roads according to old usage: Mendon Road in Northbridge is Miscoe Road in Mendon; Wolf Hill Road in Northbridge becomes Upton Road in Uxbridge; and there's a West River Road in Upton and another in Uxbridge, but they don't connect. Luckily, the Corps has erected signs throughout its domain here directing visitors to its most important sites. But be patient near the West River, and you will find good angling.

Find the main office of the Corps by traveling east on West Hartford Avenue from MA 122 in North Uxbridge or west from MA 16 in Mendon onto East Hartford Avenue. At their headquarters by the dam, they have plenty of information, maps, and parking, and you can fish the river upstream from here.

West Hill Park was developed by the Corps for recreation and includes the famous Harrington Pool (a popular swimming area in the summer), picnic and bath facilities, and parking. An entrance fee is charged. The area is formally closed from the second Sunday in September to the third Saturday in May, but there is a parking lot just outside the gate to allow anglers to hike down to the river at any time (and hunters to ply the uplands of the wildlife management area there). Find this parking lot and the park by turning north onto Upton Road just west of the dam road. Upton Road becomes Wolf Hill Road in Northbridge and leads to Quaker Street. West Hill Road turns east (right) and leads to West Hill Park. The route is also marked by Corps of Engineers signs. By continuing north on Quaker Road and turning east onto Mendon Road, another access is available where the road crosses over the river.

Downstream from the West Hill Dam, there is also some decent water, and it is accessible from East Hartford Avenue, from MA 16 below West River Pond, and from Hecla Street, which turns south from MA 16 just west of Wheelockville.

Other Stocked Waters that Flow in the Midstate Highlands

Worcester County *Ashburnham:* Phillips Brook, Whitman River; *Blackstone:* Fox Stream, Mill River; *Charlton:* Little River, South Fork of the Little River; *Douglas:* Mumford River; *East Brookfield:* Five Mile River; *Fitchburg:* Fallulah Brook, Wyman Pond Brook; *Grafton:* Miscoe Brook, Quinsigamond River; *Harvard:* Bowers Brook; *Mendon:* Muddy Brook, Mill River; *Oxford:* Lowes Brook, Little River, French River; *Southbridge:* McKinstry Brook, Keenan Brook, Lebanon Brook; *Sterling:* Justice Brook; *Upton:* Center Brook, Warren Brook; *Uxbridge:* Emerson Brook; *Westminster:* Burnt Mill Pond Brook.
Middlesex County *Ashby:* South Branch of the Sowhegan River; *Pepperell:* Gulf Brook, Sucker Brook.

Important Stocked Lakes and Ponds

Worcester County (stocked spring and fall) *Douglas:* Wallum Lake; *Lancaster:* Fort Pond; *Lunenburg:* Whalom Lake; *Shrewsbury:* Lake Quinsigamond; *Sturbridge:* Big Alum Pond; *Webster:* Webster Lake. **(Stocked only in spring)** *Clinton:* Mossy Pond, Lancaster Mill Pond; *Harvard:* Mirror Lake; *Lancaster:* Spectacle Pond; *Leominster:* Barretts Pond; *Milford:* Louisa Lake; *Millbury:* Singletary Lake; *Oxford:* Carbuncle Pond; *Shrewsbury:* Jordon Pond; *Sterling:* West Waushaccum Pond; *Sturbridge:* East Brimfield Reservoir; *Upton:* Pratt Pond; *Westminster:* Crow Hill Pond; *Worcester:* Coes Pond, Bell Pond.

5 | The Northeast: From North to South

Merrimack River

The Merrimack River dominates the northeastern corner of Massachusetts. Flowing southerly out of New Hampshire, it enters Massachusetts in Tyngsborough and quickly turns northeast, flowing for better than 50 miles to the sea, which it reaches in Newburyport at the top of Plum Island. Although the Merrimack Valley was settled in the 17th century and was always envisioned as a nearby source of cheap waterpower by Boston investors, it wasn't until the mid-19th century that dam-making technology had advanced far enough to tap the big, heavy flows of the river. In 1822 in Lowell, the first dam was erected across the river, and in 1845, Lawrence's dam was added. They remain the only two impediments to the river in Massachusetts.

The Merrimack is important to trout and other anglers for several reasons. Primarily, it is recognized as the dominant watershed for nearly a quarter of the state, receiving the flows from major tributaries like the Nashua (see chapter 4) and the Concord and draining most of northern Worcester County and much of Middlesex and Essex Counties. Trout waters play an important part in the watershed in its headlands, particularly with the Squannacook and Nissitisset Rivers (see chapter 4) feeding into the Nashua River, which itself originates at Wachusett Reservoir (see chapter 4). And as water quality and respect improves for rivers like the Assabet, Concord, and the main stem of the Nashua, trout may become important additions to already thriving populations of large and smallmouth bass, northern pike, and pickerel—but they aren't yet.

That the Merrimack can sustain and support cold-water species like trout is illustrated by the attempt to restore Atlantic salmon to the river, an effort that has seen slow but steady progress. The overall water quality of the Merrimack has improved to the point that salmon are returning, and it has become a major smallmouth bass fishery in both New Hampshire and Massachusetts.

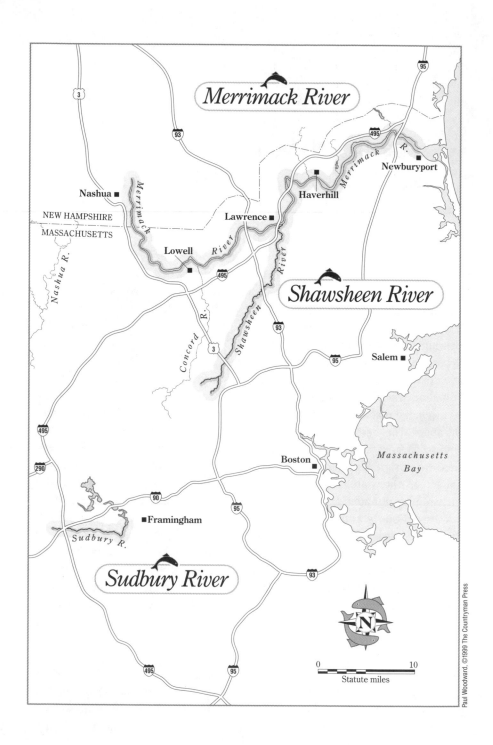

Merrimack River

Shawsheen River

Sudbury River

3

93

95

495

Newburyport

Nashua

NEW HAMPSHIRE

MASSACHUSETTS

Merrimack

River

Lawrence

Haverhill

Merrimack R.

Lowell

Nashua R.

495

Concord R.

Shawsheen River

3

93

95

Salem

495

290

90

95

Boston

Massachusetts Bay

Framingham

Sudbury R.

93

N

0   10

Statute miles

495

95

For trout anglers, the Merrimack does hold fish that have migrated down the feeder streams and directly into the river. Not counting the fish that find their way into it from the bigger tributaries, there are two dozen streams that receive stocked trout that often end up in the Merrimack. From downstream to upstream they are the Powow River in Amesbury, Little River and East Meadow River in Haverhill, Spickett River in Methuen and Lawrence, Shawsheen River (see below) in Andover and Tewksbury, Bartlett Brook in Methuen, Richardson Brook in Dracut, Beaver Brook in Dracut and Lowell, Stony Brook and Deep Brook in Chelmsford, and Bridge Meadow Brook in Tyngsborough. While each of these brooks and streams has access and decent angling on their main stems, they can and do provide welcome surprises for trout anglers on the Merrimack, particularly when the fish sweep downstream in spring freshets or seek more suitable water during the heat and low flows of summer. If you are targeting Merrimack River trout, find them at the mouths of these feeders, especially when the low water levels of summer have concentrated the fish in the best holding pools at or just below the feeder mouths.

And don't ignore the Atlantic salmon. Although targeting Atlantic salmon downstream from the Essex Dam in Lawrence is illegal, the river upstream from the dam can provide some exciting angling. Remember that all fish that are returning to the Merrimack directly from the sea are fully protected and must be immediately returned, unharmed, to the water throughout the river. But New Hampshire brood-stock fish are stocked into the river in that state, an average of 2,500 of them annually, and they do migrate downstream. These fish have tags that identify them as New Hampshire stocked fish, and Massachusetts law allows anglers to keep two brood-stock salmon a day if they're more than 15 inches long. And all of the New Hampshire fish are at least that long, with a few pushing 20 pounds. Releasing them back into the river unharmed might be the best action, as they could return from the sea again as second- or third-time spawners. A major hot spot for the salmon is below the Pawtucket Dam in Lowell.

Access to the Merrimack River is easy and abundant. There are numerous formal boat-launching facilities, innumerable informal car-top canoe and boat launches, and miles and miles of riverbank open to anglers. Just remember that this is big water, that its currents can be swift and deceptive, and that flows can change dramatically because of dam water releases. Respect the Merrimack River but enjoy its bounties.

Shawsheen River

The Shawsheen River originates near the Hanscom Air Force Base landing strip in Bedford and meanders for 23½ miles toward the northeast and its meeting with the Merrimack River in North Andover. Along the way it travels through the suburban sprawl of both Boston and Lawrence in the towns of Billerica, Tewksbury, and Andover. Yet the Shawsheen provides some very exciting angling, both for early-season fishermen near the many bridges and stocking sites, and during the later season for those willing to explore those areas of the river protected by marshes and sometimes difficult access.

While the Division of Fisheries and Wildlife officially designates the Shawsheen River as a put-and-take fishery, local anglers know that there are not only plenty of deep holding pools and spring seeps along it, but also a few cold-water tributaries that keep many sections of the river attractive to trout year-round. And the hatches are strong and abundant, if not as varied in the numbers of different insects as many other regional rivers. In fact, one of the most attractive hatches in the Shawsheen is the *Hexagenia* hatch, an early-summer event that brings the very biggest trout to the surface.

The Shawsheen can be divided roughly in two, with Boston Road (MA 3A) in Billerica as the marker. Upstream, the river holds some surprisingly fertile and relatively remote angling over a sandy bottom in a small stream setting. Adventuring into it is like discovering a stream that few people know, even though it runs right through their backyard. You can get onto the river at its headwaters, via Bridge Street, a dead-end dirt road off Pine Street just south of MA 225 and 4. A bit farther downstream (north), access is via Page Road, off MA 62—be sure to fish upstream to the junction of Elm Brook, which is a stocked stream. You can wade downstream for some distance from the MA 62 bridge, getting off the river either at US 3 or farther downstream at the Middlesex Turnpike, or best yet at MA 3A, Boston Road. You can even wade downstream some from Boston Road, but a canoe is probably a better idea.

Below MA 3A, there are numerous spots to explore and a number of places to launch a canoe, particularly at the power lines behind Shawsheen Technical School, at MA 129, at Brown Street, at MA 38, at Strong Water Brook on Shawsheen Road in Tewksbury, and at Mill Street off Shawsheen Road down to Ballardvale Coves, which are just downstream from I-93 in Tewksbury. Many short stretches through this area can be waded. The river has become big enough here to make fly casting easy, and there are decent, even exceptional, trout lurking beyond the immediate areas of the accesses.

The Ballardvale Coves in Andover slow the river and warm the water, making it more fertile for warm-water species, but there are a number of runs downstream where trout can be found. Fish the quick water near the Central Street bridge and the stone railroad trestle just below it. And try below the breached dam just upstream from the Essex Street bridge and again below the Stevens Street dam. Much of the rest of the river to the Merrimack is too urban and warm to hold trout, but you might find a local-ized pocket or two of water that attract downstream migrants.

Sudbury River

The Sudbury River joins the Assabet River in Concord to form the Concord River, which itself is a major tributary of the Merrimack to the north. Would that we could make a long discussion of the trout angling in the Sudbury, for it has many miles of what could be prime fishing water. Unfortunately, it has severe mercury pollution from the Pleasant Street–Cordaville Road bridge in Ashland on downstream. In fact, this pollution is so severe that it not only precludes consumption of any fish in the Sudbury but also in the Concord River.

Upstream from Ashland, the state stocks trout in about a half-dozen locations, and this area does have some small-stream delights. Access is good, with bridges at Howe Street in Ashland, and at MA 85, Cedar Street, and Fruit Street in Hopkinton. As with any stream that flows through populated areas, hiking up- or downstream from these bridges and finding the more remote flows and holding water will produce better catches throughout the season. In Hopkinton, hike into the section of river downstream from MA 85. It holds some of the river's best riffle water and pools.

Parker River

The Parker River is one of northeastern Massachusetts' best trout rivers, but it sometimes gets lost in the praise that is accumulated by the other nearby rivers that are bigger and better known. The mighty Merrimack (see above) flows directly to the north of the Parker, and the more extensive Ipswich River (see below) runs just due south. But the Parker River needs not take a backseat to either of these other rivers because it has a charm and a productivity for anglers to which the others cannot lay claim. It flows through much protected and accessible state- and locally owned land, supports abundant and varied insect life, and has plenty of cold-water feeder streams and springs to keep trout content and growing year-round.

As with most other coastal-plain rivers, the Parker has a leisurely, meandering flow to it, traveling for nearly 22 river miles from its origins at Sperry's Pond in Boxford to Plum Island Sound in Newbury. In its upstream areas, you can wade much of its riverbed, but you always need to be watchful for deep holding pools and bottom makeup. The deep pools can harbor surprisingly large holdover trout, and some may reach 3–4 pounds in the more remote and hard-to-get-to areas.

The best of these upstream areas can be delineated as running roughly from Pentucket Pond in Georgetown to Main Street in the Byfield section of Newbury. Upstream of Pentucket Pond the river is small, but it does get stocked with brook trout and a few browns and can be accessed via Willow Road in Boxford. Note that Main Street, Byfield, is the extension of North

The lower Parker River is tidal and holds stocked and sea-run trout.

Street out of Georgetown, and that this road neatly touches the start of the good upstream angling, then crosses the Parker, where wading ends and floating in a canoe begins.

The Crane Pond Wildlife Management Area (WMA) encloses most of this lovely upstream section, and you can access the stream from either end of North Street. To find the midpoint of this area, however, turn west onto Thurlow Street from North Street in Georgetown to where Thurlow crosses the river. Thurlow Street is Byfield Road coming out of Groveland. From the Thurlow Street crossing, you can hike and wade up- or downstream and find plenty of good holding water.

Be sure to ply the waters of Crane Pond, the namesake of the wildlife management area, if you get downstream from Thurlow Street far enough. It is a bit of a hike, especially if you are fishing along the river, but there are reports of impressive browns in Crane and of an excellent *Hexagenia* hatch in June. You can also target the pond by following the trail to it through the WMA. This run of the river from the bridge to Crane Pond can get brush choked in places, boggy in others, and it can be deep, so allow plenty of time to explore and learn it. You can also hike in the power line trail off Thurlow Road to the pretty section of river below Crane Pond. The power line takes you to a mill pond, but upstream the river runs through a section of hemlock forest and offers good runs and pocket-water angling.

From Main Street, Byfield downstream, the river becomes noticeably larger. While there are spots that can be waded, experience in this section is essential, and a better plan is to float the river here in a canoe or johnboat. Yes, there are excellent trout here, an abundance of forage, and plenty of room for backcasting. Just be wary of every footstep, or you might be in the river up to your neck.

If you float this section, you can take out at any number of downstream crossroads—Larkin Street, Central Street, Middle Road, or US 1. And note that below the Central Street bridge, the river becomes tidally influenced. The bad news is that unless you know that the tide is going out, you'll be paddling against it, but the good news is that even if you're targeting trout, you just might find yourself on the fighting end of a 20-pound striped bass.

IPSWICH RIVER

Maps *USGS* (from downstream to upstream): Ipswich (Little Neck to Topsfield), Salem (Wenham Swamp and Boxford to Danvers), Reading (Danvers to Wilmington).

Description The Ipswich River is a coastal plain river that flows for 34 miles, originating in Wilmington and traveling downstream through North Reading, Lynnfield, Peabody, Middleton, Danvers, Topsfield, Boxford, Hamilton, and Ipswich before emptying into Ipswich Bay at the southern tip of Plum Island. The river holds a wide variety of trout habitat, which includes good pool-riffle-run types of water as well as long stretches of slick, slow water. There's even an expansive swamp, Wenham Swamp, that provides more trout hideouts than one angler could ever investigate in two lifetimes.

Although there are a few sections of the river that resemble classic trout water and should certainly be investigated and waded, many of the most productive areas of the river are best fished from a canoe or johnboat. And although there are several reaches of the river that are publicly owned and accessible, floating downstream into some of the more inaccessible private areas will produce some very good angling over large holdover and stream-born trout.

Water quality in the Ipswich is good, with some cold-water tributaries and spring seeps, and fertility is exceptional. Mayflies are prolific, as are caddis, and there is an abundance of feed fish.

Access The Ipswich River flows through some very populated areas with numerous roads and bridges from which to get onto the river. In addition, there are a number of state- and locally owned public areas along the river where a canoe can be launched, and the Essex County Greenbelt Association and the Ipswich River Watershed Association have worked diligently to preserve the shores of the river. Willowdale State Forest in Ipswich and the

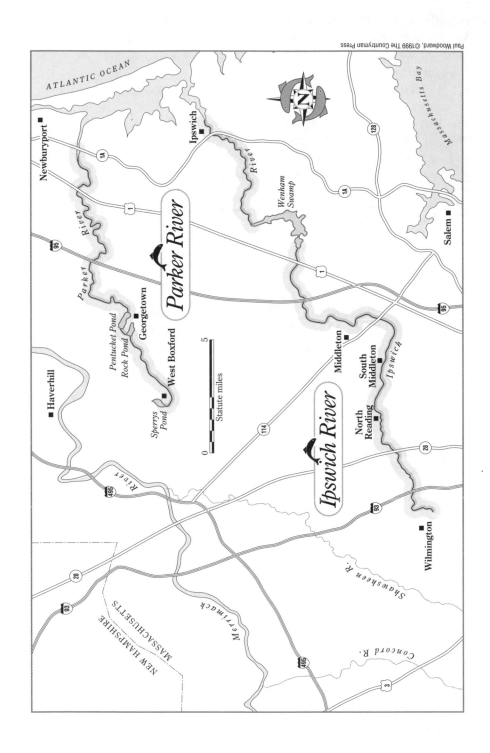

Bradley Palmer State Park in Topsfield abut the river on opposite sides and provide full access to one of the more productive angling reaches.

Regulations The Ipswich River is a major Massachusetts trout stream and as such, the daily limit is three trout year-round. All methods of angling are legal.

Don't miss A new river park and canoe access has recently been completed in North Reading that opens up a long stretch of the Ipswich River in its upper reaches. Find it by turning south onto Central Street from MA 62 just west of the center of North Reading. The canoe access and parking lot are located right on Central Street and were created by the Massachusetts Public Access Board specifically for anglers. It's an easy haul down a wide set of steps to the river. The adjacent park is gated, but is open from dawn until 10 PM, providing shore anglers not only with access but also with plenty of productive fishing hours at dawn and dusk. The river immediately downstream is broad but has plenty of current and cover to hold trout.

Best asset The Ipswich River has gathered attention from a large number of conservationists and organizations. Led by the Ipswich River Watershed Association, but also including the Essex County Greenbelt Association, the Audubon Society, Massachusetts Department of Environmental Protection, and local communities, awareness of both the value and the susceptibility of the river and its shorelines has remained high.

Many sections of the river now prosper under the stewardship of these groups, including large tracts of land in the Bradley Palmer State Park in Topsfield and Hamilton, the Willowdale State Forest in Ipswich, the Willowdale Dam Reservation in Hamilton, and Audubon's Ipswich River Wildlife Sanctuary in Topsfield. There are many other smaller holdings that are no less important, and a map of them is available from the Essex County Greenbelt Association by calling them at 978-768-7241 or dropping them a note at Essex Greenbelt Headquarters, Cox Reservation, #80R, Route 133, Essex, MA 01944. A small donation would be nice, too.

Biggest drawback It isn't so much a drawback as it is a draw*down*. Fourteen communities and a half-million people draw their drinking water from the Ipswich River watershed. The effect can be dramatic, as certain stretches, particularly upstream from Topsfield, can become de-watered during hot, dry spells in the summer. One of the avowed purposes of the conservation groups is to protect the river from such drastic drawdowns, and they are making progress in getting water users to be more aware of the problem. But it does still exist.

Necessary patterns *Underwater:* Pheasant Tail Nymph (#14–20), Hare's Ear Nymph (#12–16), Hendrickson Nymph (#12–16), Zug Bug (#10–14), Leadwing Coachman (#12–14), Caddis Larva (#14–18), Caddis Emerger

(#12–18), Black–Nosed Dace (#4–10), Mickey Finn (#4–12), Muddler Minnow (#4–12), Woolly Worm and Bugger (#4–12). *Dry flies:* Black Quill (#10–16); Adams (#12–20); Quill Gordon (#12–16); Hendrickson (#12–16); Red Quill (#12–16); Rusty Spinner (#12–16); March Brown (#12–14); Gray Fox (#12–14); Mahogany Dun (#12–16); Mahogany Spinner (#10–16); Sulphur Dun (#14–16); Light Cahill (#14–16); Ginger Quill (#12–18); Green Drake (#6–10); Brown Drake (#10–12); White Mayfly (#12–14); Tan, Yellow, Brown, Green, or Black Caddis (#12–18); Blue-Winged Olive (#12–20); Cream Midge (#18–22); Trico (#18–24); Alder (#16–18); Cricket (#10–14); Hopper (#4–12); Black or Cinnamon Ant (#10-20).

Stocked feeder streams worth a look (downstream to upstream from above tidewater in Ipswich): Howlett Brook, Pye Brook, Fish Brook, Boston Brook.

Other feeders Miles River, Black Brook, Gravelly Brook, Mile Brook, Idlewild Brook, School Brook, Nichols Brook, Norris Brook, Wills Brook, Martins Brook, Bear Meadow Brook, Lubbers Brook, Maple Meadows Brook.

If the Merrimack River is the dominant watershed in the northeastern corner of Massachusetts, and it is, then the Ipswich River is the dominant trout stream. Blessed with pure waters and a largely protected watershed, the Ipswich River long ago was flagged as the main source of drinking water for large numbers of communities and people. As such, it gained protection from pollution before the value of pure water was universally recognized, even if some of the river's waterpower was tapped.

The Ipswich's meandering nature and extensive swamps, bogs, and backwaters are the reason that it can sustain so many people as a water source and why it holds trout year-round and from season to season. It is like a vast natural reservoir. Certainly there are stretches that resemble classic trout water, with runs and riffles, pools and pocket water. But angling for the best and biggest holdover and stream-born trout is found away from the classic flows, which although heavily stocked are extremely popular and heavily fished. A canoe is indispensable for finding the very best trout angling.

The headwaters of the Ipswich—and the trout angling—start just west of Interchange 39 of I-93 at the bridge on Woburn Street in Wilmington. Immediately, the character of the Ipswich is evident as the slow-flowing Lubbers and Maple Meadow Brooks join just upstream to form the Ipswich in a marsh known locally as 100-Acre Swamp. The channel is slow but deep and holds good trout, especially downstream from the bridge, away from where anglers on foot or in waders can go.

You can float and fish the river in similar surroundings all the way downstream to the Ipswich River Park in North Reading, a distance of just less than 5 miles. You can take out at a pair of bridges just upstream of the park, at Mill Street or Chestnut Street, but the Massachusetts Public Access Board has created a perfect takeout at the edge of the park on Central Street. It has a sandy beach landing area just a few steps from the eight-car parking lot on the street.

The park itself is very well done, providing a fine place to picnic or watch a soccer game, and it's open for the convenience of shore fishermen who can ply the waters of the river where they broaden out to form a small but tempting pond. Park your car at the far end of the park, hike down the well-marked trail to the downstream end of the pond, and fish your way back up to the sandy beach takeout. The park itself is open from dawn to 10 PM.

If you're canoeing, take note of the memorial to Michael James Mitton, a young 19-year-old who drowned here in 1996 for lack of a life vest. If you don't have one, borrow one at the memorial. And also note that by Massachusetts law, from September 15 to May 15, all canoe occupants must wear a U.S. Coast Guard–approved personal flotation device. That, of course, is only logical during cold-water seasons because hypothermia can render a person unconscious in less than a minute. But it's also essential, in my opinion, when canoeing any river at any time. Lazy-looking flows can have surprising and dangerous power, and unsuspecting anglers can be vulnerable any time of year if they take a plunge. Wear a vest!

A good stretch of productive trout water runs from the Ipswich River Park downstream to the Peabody dam, a distance of about 2½ miles. There is bridge access in this section at Haverhill Street and at the MA 62 bridge, but most of this run is fertile, productive, and canoeable.

The most remote and attractive reach of the river is found below the Peabody dam and Peabody proper downstream for another 4 miles all the way to the Howe Station section of Middleton. An interesting access is found just beyond the Thompson Country Club along MA 62 and below the Peabody dam. Turn south onto Boston Road just east of the town line for North Reading and Middleton. At the bridge there's a dirt road running upstream, with parking and access to the river, where decent wading is available below the mill dam.

Another good access point is found about midway along this stretch at the MA 114 bridge. Park in the abandoned and fenced parking lot on the upstream side. Log Bridge Road provides some bank fishing in this area. It's just opposite River Road, across MA 114, and is the entrance road to the North Shore Technical High School. Now there is no log bridge, just the old abutments, and the end of the road belongs to the Danvers Fish and Game Club. There's a good takeout farther along on MA 62 at Howe Station and some bank and wade fishing.

From Howe Station downstream to Bradley Palmer State Park, you may have the company of other canoeists in warm weather, for this 10-mile-long run down to and through Wenham Swamp is very popular. There are several bridges before you enter Wenham Swamp where you can take out and/or fish the banks, including at Peabody Street, Thunder bridge on East Street, Rowley Bridge Road, Salem Road, US 1, and MA 97. You might enjoy stopping at the Topsfield fairgrounds, near the US 1 bridge, before the river enters the swamp to fish the meadowlike undercut banks where some very large brown trout lurk.

But once you're in the swamp, you'll need to travel its entire length, a distance of about 4 miles—to the bridge at Asbury Street at the edge of Bradley Palmer State Park—before you can take out. Some knowledge of the riverbed is needed during high water, because when the swamp is flooded it can be difficult to stay on the river channel. And don't be tempted by the channel that flows southeast shortly after entering the swamp. That's the Salem Beverly Waterway canal.

The Bradley Palmer State Park on the south bank and the Willowdale State Forest on the north bank flank the river downstream to the Willowdale Dam Reservation of the Essex County Greenbelt Association. Ipswich Road in Topsfield, which becomes Topsfield Road in Ipswich, also parallels the river. This section has several very attractive areas for wade or bank fishing. Park along the Topsfield/Ipswich Road, or use the parking lot in the Bradley Palmer State Park, where you can picnic, hike, and use the facilities.

From the Willowdale dam downstream to Ipswich center and the head of tide at the Ipswich dam is a canoe run of about 5 miles, and it is well worth exploring. Many trout that escape the onslaught of spring anglers upstream find this area to be well suited for holing up. The area is largely tree lined and easily canoed, and there are several places where you can get out of the boat and wade the stream. Not too many anglers do, so the action here can be steady.

Because of its local renown, the Ipswich River is a well-used trout stream, but its meandering, swampy character gives many trout the chance to live long, idle lives, and some wise old fish in the more remote sections hardly ever see the shadow of a fly line. Get away from the easy accesses at almost any time of year, and you'll hardly think that you're within a half hour of Boston.

Charles River

The Charles River needs to be included in any book on rivers, because it is one of the most dramatic success stories of the reclamation of rivers from the ravages of civilization. An open sewer and worse for much of its history since European contact, the Charles epitomized the neglect and abuse that

There are some surprising and interesting runs of trout water in the upper Ipswich River.

our waterways suffered for so many decades. Yet this river, once deemed by many as beyond hope, now runs clean and has become a beacon of the success that is possible when citizens, industry, and government join forces to renew a resource.

True, it does still have a fish consumption advisory on largemouth bass where it runs from the Medway dam to the South Natick dam, and on carp downstream to the Museum of Science dam in Boston, because of mercury contamination. But all other fish in the river, including stocked trout above the South Natick dam, are deemed safe to eat.

For trout anglers, the state stocks fish at a half-dozen sites between Myrtle Street in Norfolk and the South Natick dam in Natick. The most attractive area for fly casters is the stretch of river than runs along MA 16 in South Natick and upstream at the Farm Road bridge area in Dover. Angling for trout can also be good at the MA 115 bridge (Baltimore Street) in Millis and downstream for about a half mile. And there are trout at the Myrtle Street bridge in Norfolk.

But by and large, the Charles River is a warm-water stream. The trout are a put-and-take proposition for spring anglers. But that doesn't diminish the accomplishments of cleaning the river, because it now has a very good reputation for its largemouth bass, for bragging-sized pickerel and carp, for northern pike, and for oversized panfish. And because it covers 79 meandering river miles, it might just tempt a trout fisherman to try these other game fish from a canoe. There's absolutely nothing wrong with a 5-pound largemouth on a fly rod.

Other Stocked Streams in the Northeast:

Essex County *Essex:* Alewife Brook; *Georgetown:* Penn Brook; *Ipswich:* Bull Brook, Dow's Brook; *Newbury:* Mill River; *North Andover:* Mosquito Brook; *Rowley:* Batchelder Brook, Mill River.

Middlesex County *Acton:* Nashoba Brook, Fort Pond Brook; *Ayer:* Bennett Brook; *Boxboro:* Beaver Brook, Guggins Brook; *Carlisle:* River Meadow Brook; *Chelmsford:* Crooked Spring Brook; *Dracut:* Richardson Brook; *Dunstable:* Unkety Brook, Salmon Brook; *Groton:* Cow Pond Brook; *Holliston:* Boggastow Brook; *Hopkinton:* Whitehall Brook; *Hudson:* Hog Brook, Danforth Brook; *Littleton:* Beaver Brook; *Stow:* Assabet Brook; *Tewksbury:* Strong Water Brook; *Westford:* Nashoba Brook, Stony Brook, Keys Brook; *Weston:* Cherry Brook.

Worcester County *Berlin:* North Brook; *Bolton:* Great Brook, Danforth Brook; *Northboro:* Cold Harbor Brook.

Norfolk County: *Bellingham:* Peters River; *Canton:* Ponkapoag Brook, Massapoag Brook; *Dover:* Trout Brook; *Foxboro:* Wading River; *Franklin:* Miscoe Brook, Dix Brook; *Medfield:* Vine Brook, Mine Brook; *Medway:* Hopping Brook; *Milton:* Pine Tree Brook; *Norfolk:* Mill River; *Norwood:*

Traphole Brook; *Plainville:* Ten Mile River; *Sharon:* Beaver Brook; *Weymouth:* Old Swamp River; *Wrentham:* Eagle Brook.

Important Stocked Lakes and Ponds

Essex County (stocked spring and fall) *Boxford:* Stiles Pond; *Haverhill:* Saltonstall (Plug) Pond; *Lynn:* Sluice Pond; *Saugus:* Griswald Pond; *Wenham:* Pleasant Pond. **(Stocked only in spring)** *Boxford:* Baldpate Pond; *Georgetown:* Pentucket Pond, Rock Pond; *Gloucester:* Cape Ann Club Pond; *Haverhill:* Lake Pentucket, Millvale Reservoir; *Methuen:* Forest Lake; *North Andover:* Berry Pond; *Wenham:* Idlewood Lake.

Middlesex County (stocked spring and fall) *Ashland:* Ashland Reservoir; *Concord:* Walden Pond, White Pond; *Framingham:* Lake Cochituate; *Groton:* Baddacook Pond, Knops Pond; *Hopkinton:* Hopkinton Reservoir; *Newton:* Crystal Lake; *Westford:* Long Sought For Pond; *Wilmington:* Silver Lake; *Winchester:* Wedge Pond; *Woburn:* Horn Pond. **(Stocked only in spring)** *Ayer:* Sandy Pond; *Brookline:* Brookline Reservoir; *Dunstable:* Lake Masappoag; *Hopkinton:* Whitehall Reservoir; *Lexington:* Lexington Reservoir; *Natick:* Dug Pond.

Suffolk County (stocked spring and fall) *Boston:* Jamaica Pond.

Norfolk County (stocked spring and fall) *Milton:* Houghton's Pond; *Wrentham:* Lake Pearl. **(Stocked only in spring)** *Franklin:* Uncas Pond; *Sharon:* Lake Massapoag; *Westwood:* Buckmaster Pond; *Weymouth:* Whitman Pond.

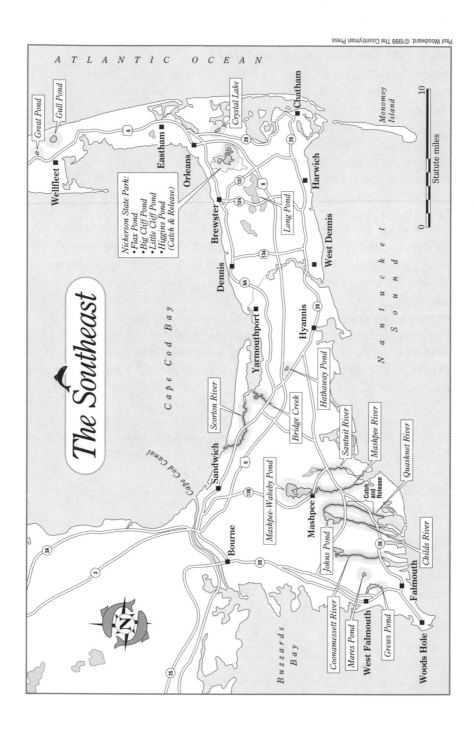

The Southeast

ATLANTIC OCEAN

Great Pond
Gull Pond
Wellfleet
Eastham
Orleans
Crystal Lake
Chatham

Nickerson State Park:
• Flax Pond
• Big Cliff Pond
• Little Cliff Pond
• Higgins Pond
  (Catch & Release)

Brewster
Harwich
Long Pond
West Dennis
Dennis
Monomoy Island

Cape Cod Bay

Yarmouthport
Scorton River
Hyannis
Hathaway Pond
Bridge Creek
Santuit River
Mashpee River
Quashnet River

Nantucket Sound

Sandwich
Mashpee-Wakeby Pond
Mashpee
Catch and Release
Johns Pond
Childs River
Falmouth

Bourne

Cape Cod Canal

Buzzards Bay

Coonamessett River
Mares Pond
West Falmouth
Grews Pond
Woods Hole

10

Statute miles

0

6 | The Southeast: From West to East

Southeastern Massachusetts is tacked onto the bedrock of the mainland as a sandy appendage, formed when the last ice sheet retreated. As such, it is unique to southern New England, not only in its geology, but also in the type of angling for trout that it offers. Fly-fishing for trout here demands new approaches in flowing water and in lakes and ponds alike, but the effort to relearn the lessons of the more typical inland waters will be rewarded with opportunities to land sea-run and freshwater trout that are big, wild, and exciting.

While there are scattered ponds that do offer good trout angling typical of the rest of the state—notably Fulton and Cabots Ponds in Mansfield and Falls Pond in North Attleboro—most of the best trout fishing occurs in the town of Plymouth and across the Cape Cod Canal on the Cape proper. Here, the glacial action gouged out deep, spring-fed kettle holes that are cold and pure, that have the full complement of still-water insect forage, and that often add anadromous feed, like alewives and blueback herring, to help trout grow large quickly.

The streams that flow to the sea originally supported teeming masses of sea-run brook trout, fish that moved easily in and out of salt and fresh water and that grew large in the brackish waters of the estuaries and at sea. But as the cranberry industry tapped the freshwater flows of these streams and dammed them to form controlled-water bogs, the natural access to perfect spawning habitat was blocked and the habitat itself degraded. The runs of salters, as they're known, dwindled to precious few fish.

Yet in the mid-1970s, as awareness of the value of clean, free-flowing waterways grew throughout the country, the fate of these streams took a turn for the better. By identifying them as valuable, fertile, natural resources and rediscovering their potential for producing sea-run trout, their importance to anglers was reestablished and new attention was paid to them.

Today, restoration efforts by a large number of individuals and organizations, particularly the Cape Cod chapter of Trout Unlimited and the Division of Fisheries and Wildlife, have brought many of these streams back to productivity and prominence.

Although much has been accomplished, more remains to be done. As has been proven time and again, undoing Nature's good work is easy—build a dam or dump in pollution. It's the restoration that's hard. Vigilance and the difficult effort to return streams to their natural banks and habitat must continue. We all must get involved, with our wallets and with our backs.

Sea-Run Trout Tactics

While most of the angling in Cape Cod's sea-run trout streams in the 1970s and '80s was for brown trout, in the '90s biologists have placed increased emphasis on restoring salters—sea-run brookies—to appropriate streams to supplement remnant populations. Salters are the primary game fish now in several streams that no longer receive stocked trout, particularly in the Quashnet River, but also in the Mashpee and the Santuit Rivers. Brown trout stocking still occurs in Scorton River, Bridge Creek, Childs River, and Coonamessett River, and good angling in them is available. Because these fish—both brookies and browns—move easily between salt, brackish, and fresh water, knowledge of techniques specific to each of these types of water is necessary.

Accurate imitation and careful presentation are a must, but the details vary considerably depending on the water you're fishing. The small freshwater flows of the headlands demand light tackle and stealth, because the streams are crystal clear and cold, and the fish are aware of their vulnerability in them. In the estuaries, the terrain is more open, but the fish are most active and available during the 2 hours on either side of a low tide, when forage is most concentrated. Again, stealth, careful approach, and accurate imitation are essential.

For sea-run brown trout, the angling season begins as the fish gather at the mouths of the streams and enter the estuaries in midsummer. There, they feed heavily on the ample forage of these fertile nurseries, but they are often difficult to approach. As summer days shorten and autumn arrives, the fish push up into the streams, their spawning drive increasing. Luckily, the fish remain voracious feeders throughout their spawning cycle. Unlike Atlantic salmon, which cease feeding as they encounter brackish and fresh water, sea-run trout retain their taste for anything foodlike.

November and December see the fish pushing all the way upstream, into the pure fresh water, still feeding, but also accomplishing their spawning. Because they become concentrated in the smaller headwaters of the streams, they are easily spotted, but they are more difficult to approach as they'll spook at even the gentlest footfall. And with the onset of cold weather and water, they tend to hold close to the bottom, and that's where your fly needs to find them. In midwinter, generally by the end of January, they have returned to the estuaries and the sea.

In recent years, the Division of Fisheries and Wildlife has been stocking 12- to 14-inch browns, which are larger than the 7-inch smolts they used initially. The division is certain they are getting as many mature fish back into the streams as they did with the smolts, and they feel that mortality has been reduced with the larger fish. One of the interesting side effects of the striped bass boom of recent years is that the stripers often congregate at the mouths of the sea-run trout streams, even in January, to feast on the forage that is coming down the streams—including the sea-run trout.

Salters are much less disciplined in their migrations. Certainly by the time they have reached 3 years old, they've made at least one foray downstream, gaining the silvery sides typical of time spent in the salt. This coloration, however, fades quickly in fresh water. Generally, they return to the brackish estuary and salt water after spawning in fall in October. They come back to the cooler waters of the freshwater streams in the heat of summer or later, as spawning urges arise, in September. And some even stay in fresh water for an entire year before making another trip to the salt. Suffice it to say that if you find a brook trout in the fresh water of one these Cape streams that exceeds 2 pounds, he's certainly a salter.

These sea-run trout, both browns and brookies, feast on the abundant smorgasbord of the brackish and salt water in the estuaries. Grass shrimp, mummichogs, silversides (smelt), killifish, and sand eels are all relished. And in fresh water they'll vacuum up alewife and herring fry as well as the natural insects and nymphs found there, like mayflies and caddis. As with any trout, however, these fish are selective, feeding on mummichogs when they are available, for instance, to the exclusion of all else. You need to know what the fish are focused on and then imitate it accurately.

In spite of the obvious difficulties in approaching and presenting accurate imitations, the rewards of sea-run trout fishing are impressive, with brook trout pushing 4 pounds and a few browns each year tipping the scales at 10 pounds. The still-water fish are impressive, too, with sea-run trout sometimes migrating up into the ponds to chase alewives, but with the stocked trout, mostly rainbows, also holding over exceptionally well and growing very large. The former state record rainbow trout, in fact, came from Johns Pond in Mashpee. It weighed 13 pounds, 7 ounces, and had been stocked as a 1-pounder.

Sea-Run Trout Streams

The following listing of sea-run trout streams gives an overview of where to find the streams and how to get onto them. Learning their subtle secrets is up to you.

Note that when fishing these streams in fresh water, a state fishing license is required. When fishing them in their tidal zones, no license is required. Also note that in most of the following streams, there is a closed trout season, from March 15 to May 30, generally in the seaward, brackish, and saltwater areas, and that the daily limit on sea-run brown trout is two fish.

These are the nuts and bolts of fishing for sea-run trout, but do not despair if your success rate is, at first, modest. The fish are there, the streams are improving, and once you've encountered this type of angling, you may well find it fascinating and addictive.

Scorton River

Note that many maps, as well as the Division of Fisheries and Wildlife, label this Scorton Creek, but another stream flows east from the headwaters here and it's also labeled Scorton Creek. Fish this one, Scorton River, which flows toward the west, and note that Scorton Creek flows east into Great Marshes. It is not stocked with trout.

Scorton River and Bridge Creek (see below) are the only two sea-run brown trout streams that flow into Cape Cod Bay, rather than to the open sea on the south side of the Cape. Scorton River is the primary destination here, being larger and better established than Bridge Creek, and most veteran sea-run trout anglers consider it the most consistent producer of trout on the Cape.

Find Scorton River in East Sandwich, along MA 6A and adjacent to the Fisheries and Wildlife Game Farm and the East Sandwich trout hatchery, which produces most of the browns that are stocked into the Cape's streams. Use 6A as a dividing point for fishing—the upstream side of 6A is best late in the year when the fish are spawning, and the downstream side is better earlier in the year.

Find Scorton Harbor, where the river enters the sea, by turning north from MA 6A onto Ploughed Neck Road, which leads to North Shore Boulevard. Make a right (east) turn onto it and park at the end. The mouth of Scorton River is directly in front of you, and you can fish there or upstream as the season dictates. This is a marshy and boggy river. Indeed, it's almost entirely tidally influenced, so pick and choose your footing carefully.

To fish above the MA 6A bridge, park just inside the Game Farm road and walk to the river. Fish the pool below the MA 6A bridge and upstream. Be courteous of private property once you're above the state property. The river from Jones Lane seaward to Cape Cod Bay is closed to trout fishing from March 15 to May 30.

Bridge Creek

Bridge Creek is a little-known gem of a stream that flows into Great Marshes in West Barnstable, just east of the center of town. It lies about 4 miles east

Scorton River on the bay side of Cape Cod produces the very best fly-fishing for sea-run brown trout.

of the State Game Farm on MA 6A and passes under the highway. Park near the bridge and fish downstream. Pay particular attention to the railroad trestle bridge just below the highway where there's a decent pool, but fish the stream down through its tidal section. Wherever it cuts under the banking, good trout can be hiding. Again, depending on the time of year, the fish can found all along it to where it joins Spring Creek near Slough Point. You can also fish a short way upstream from 6A, but it's a very small flow here.

The Division of Fisheries and Wildlife does not list Bridge Creek as one of its special regulation sea-run trout streams in its regulations booklet, but they have been stocking 300–500 browns a year in the 12- to 14-inch range for some time. They now feel there is a decent return of mature trout, which may become excellent in the future. Pay attention in years to come, because Bridge Creek soon may come under sea-run trout regulations. And in the meantime, release the trout you catch here, for they may help establish an even better run of fish.

Coonamessett River

The Coonamessett River originates at Coonamessett Pond in Falmouth and flows due south for 3.5 miles into the Great Pond estuary just below MA 28. It's a crystal-clear stream that supports large numbers of herring and alewives that run up it and into the pond, with the young fry providing excellent forage for the sea-run browns. These fry draw the fish up into the river much sooner than in other rivers, and the fishing above MA 28 can be good from midsummer right through early winter. In addition, there is no tidal effect from the pool at the MA 28 dam upstream. This makes the stream much more attractive to anglers throughout the day, because they aren't slaves to the tidal charts.

If there is a problem with the Coonamesset, it's the extensive cranberry bogs that are present on it. Anglers can fish through the bogs as long as they stay in the streambed and do not walk on the bogs themselves, but the effect on the water is to warm it to sometimes uncomfortable levels for the trout. The warm water also promotes the presence of warm-water species, so you might find yourself on the fighting end of a smallmouth bass instead of a trout, especially in the bog ponds just south of the Sandwich Road. When the water is warm, the trout are often found in the pool just below MA 28, which is still above tidewater and is cooled by underground springs.

During the autumn and into the early winter, the trout will run up the river, and even into the pond, so they can be found almost anywhere. It's best in this case to sight fish for the trout, finding individual trout and casting to them. The heavy brush along the banks of the stream above the Sandwich Road can make casting a fly difficult at best, but rest assured, you won't be bothered by other anglers. Most anglers concentrate on the river downstream from the Sandwich Road right into the estuary.

A benefit of the cranberry bogs is that when they are releasing water, the alewives and herring fry will run downstream in good numbers, which gets the trout running upstream to meet them. Find spots where they converge, and you can enjoy some truly outstanding angling. And as in other streams, the trout will feed on the abundant insect life when they aren't focused on feed fish or grass shrimp.

Find the Coonamessett River a mile west of East Falmouth on MA 28. There is parking adjacent to the bridge. The John Parker Road provides upstream access, crossing from the east side to the west about halfway to the Sandwich Road. Above there, Turner Road parallels the west bank to the pond. Coonamessett River, from where John Parker Road crosses it to Vineyard Sound, is closed to trout fishing from March 15 to May 30.

Childs River

The Childs River originates out of the south end of Johns Pond in Mashpee and flows due south through Falmouth, under MA 28, and into the Eel Pond estuary. While there are access problems because of private property in its head-waters, good angling for sea-run browns is available in its lower reaches and into Eel Pond, and there are decent numbers of salters to be had along its entire length.

Find the Childs just east of East Falmouth on MA 28, and fish right at the bridge near the town public boat landing. The fishing can be exceptional throughout Eel Pond, but a boat is usually needed. Veteran anglers also con-centrate on the Narrows, just past the point of the mainland where the Seapit River comes in from the northeast.

Upstream from MA 28, most anglers fish the brackish waters below Barrows Road. Find this spot from the west by turning north onto Fresh Pond Road from MA 28, then east onto Barrows Road. It crosses the Childs about ¾ mile along and then connects back onto MA 28 just east of the river.

The Childs has some cranberry bogs along it, and the browns move up into the river when water is released from the bogs in October, pushing the alewives and herring downstream. Later in the year the trout are up in the headwaters, often moving into Johns Pond, while earlier they'll be found south of MA 28. The Childs River, from Barrows Road seaward to Vineyard Sound, is closed to trout fishing from March 15 to May 30.

Quashnet River

The Quashnet River originates in the northeastern corner of Johns Pond and quickly buttonhooks toward the south and to the sea. It's a notable flow for several reasons. Primary among them is the catch-and-release regulation that is in force from MA 151 downstream to MA 28. While sea-run browns had been the main attraction of Quashnet in years past, in 1994 the state fisheries biologists determined that there was a strong population of salters—sea-run brookies—in the Quashnet that could, with protection, become self-sustaining. With the catch-and-release regulation in place, the state stopped stocking brown trout to encourage the growth of the salters. Yes, there are still a few sea-run browns using the Quashnet, but the experiment with the salters has worked well.

The Quashnet is also of note because of its length, which at 5¾ miles is the longest trout stream on the Cape, and because the access to some of its best waters is owned by the Division of Fisheries and Wildlife. Find this sec-tion, roughly a mile of streamside, just east of the Waquoit section of Falmouth along MA 28. Hike up from the highway or turn north onto Martin Road, which loops quickly back to the highway. At the top of the loop, there's

The Quashnet River is now being managed exclusively for salters, sea-run brook trout.

a trail on the west bank that parallels the river upstream for the entire length of the public property to a low dam and fish ladder. There is also a dirt trail along the east bank that runs south from MA 151 to the dam and fishway.

This length of stream has been restored to its former productivity by Trout Unlimited in conjunction with the Division of Fisheries and Wildlife.

Brush has been cleaned out, banks stabilized, deflectors installed, and pool and riffle water recreated. Thousands of hours and dollars have been donated, and the success of the project will be immediately evident to anyone walking the stream. The fishing for native brookies and salters has improved significantly, too.

The angling can also be good below MA 28, in the estuary just below the highway and also below the neck of land formed where Meadow Neck Road crosses the marshlands. Find this road by turning south onto Metoxit Road in Waquoit. Meadow Neck Road is the second left (east) turn. The Quashnet River, from MA 28 to Vineyard Sound, is closed to trout fishing from March 15 to May 30.

Mashpee River and Santuit River

Both the Mashpee and Santuit Rivers need to be mentioned here because they were formerly heavily stocked with brown trout to support a sea-run fishery. That stocking has been stopped by the state. There are some remnant browns still running into these streams, but not many. Instead, there is a population of native brook trout that are clinging to existence. Their numbers are growing, and there are a few salters running into the estuaries, but the state biologists emphasize that this is a fragile fishery now. If you do fish these rivers, please return any brook trout—especially breeding-sized salters—back into the stream unharmed. The future of these fish and streams is uncertain, but they may someday provide decent angling. Both the Santuit and Mashpee Rivers are closed to trout fishing from March 15 to May 30.

Other Sea-Run Trout Rivers

Several other streams flowing to the sea in the Southeast Wildlife District have begun to turn up sea-run brown trout, mainly from the standard stocking of browns that the state accomplishes on a regular basis, and/or salters. They have not, as yet, become noted for their regular returns of fish, but that may change as the trout become better established and as the streams and their historic habitat improve. They include:

Bristol County *Rehobeth:* Palmer River and tributaries; Westport River tributaries; Taunton River tributaries.

Plymouth County *Wareham:* Agawam River; *Mattapoisett:* Mattapoisset River; *Plymouth:* Beaver Dam Brook, Eel River, and Town Brook; *Hanover:* Indian Head River and its tributaries; *Kingston:* Jones River; *Marshfield:* South River.

Barnstable County (in addition to the streams discussed above) *Truro:* Pamet River; *Brewster:* Stony Brook.

Dukes County *Oak Bluffs:* Upper Lagoon Pond.

Other Stocked Trout Streams in the Southeast

Barnstable County *Barnstable:* Marston Mills River.

Bristol County *Acushnet:* Acushnet River; *Attleboro:* Bungay River; *Dartmouth:* Shingle Island River; *Dighton and Taunton:* Segregansett River; *Freetown:* Rattlesnake Brook; *Mansfield and Norton:* Canoe River, Wading River; *Rehobeth:* Rocky Run; *Swansea:* Cole River, Lewin Brook; *Westport:* Bread and Cheese Brook.

Plymouth County *East Bridgwater:* Beaver Brook; *Halifax:* Winnetuxet River; *Hanover:* Third Herring Brook; *Hanson:* Shumatuscacant River, Indian Head River, Poor Meadow Brook; *Hingham:* Plymouth River, Weir River; *Kingston:* Furnace Brook; *Norwell:* Second Herring Brook; *Pembroke:* Herring Brook, Indian Head River; *Plympton:* Barrows Brook, Winnetuxet River; *Rochester:* Doggetts Brook, Mattapoiset River; Scituate: Bound Brook, First Herring Brook.

Trout Lakes and Ponds

Cape Cod's freshwater ponds may be the most fertile still-water trout resource in the state. They are deep kettle holes that enjoy ample cold, spring-water inflows. Most of them are nurseries for anadromous river herring, both bluebacks and alewives, on which the trout feast. The pure, cold waters of these ponds also support most of the standard invertebrate insects, especially mayflies and midges. Stocked trout hold over easily from season to season and grow large quickly. Most of the ponds have easy, public access. And these waters are largely overlooked as the recent phenomenal saltwater angling for stripers and bluefish draws fly casters away from the fresh water. While you'll never mistake Cape Cod angling for fishing in the wilds of the great north woods of Maine, you are likely to find trout in these ponds that rival Maine's best brookies.

The comparison to Maine's ponds is appropriate here because many of the tactics used in those fine trout waters are appropriate in the Cape Cod ponds as well. The depth of the Cape's ponds and their cold-water springs help keep these waters productive during the entire year. In spring, insects, crustaceans (particularly grass shrimp), and feed fish mass in shallow water. In summer, the deep, cold waters prevent the ponds from becoming too warm to support active trout, as is often the case throughout southern New England. And in fall, the trout chase the fry of the river herrings—as well as young yellow perch, killifish, and shiners—like demons possessed.

Therefore, the fly-fishing pattern on the Cape parallels that in the north. In spring and early summer, fish the strong hatches of mayflies and use big streamers to find cruising trout along the shores, shoals, and drop-offs. In summer, identify cold-water upwellings by studying the surface for smaller fish rises, then use a sinking fly line to get down to the big trout below. In autumn, pay particular attention to the outlets where big trout will hold as the feed fish start to migrate downstream. And always keep an eye out for the mayfly hatches of the extreme-sized bugs—huge *Hexagenia* mayflies in June and July and tiny chironomids at almost any time. The biggest trout in the water cannot ignore them and will come to the surface.

The ponds discussed below are a sampling of the Cape's best waters, listed from west tot east, but they are gleaned from an array of waters too extensive to detail here. Suffice it to say that if you're near a cold-water body of water on the Cape, you're near good fly-fishing for trout.

Grews Pond

Grews Pond (13 acres, 35 feet deep), is a little gem of a pond in Goodwill Park. The park entirely surrounds the pond and is owned by the town of Falmouth, making the pond fully accessible. It is located just south of the much larger Long Pond, a public water supply with no fishing, along MA 28, just north of the center of town. Turn into the park, where access is from the beach. You can launch a canoe if you like, but the pond is easily covered with a belly boat. No motors of any kind, even electrics, are allowed.

The pond is stocked only in the spring, but the real attraction here is how well the fish carry over and grow, some to 5 pounds. Yes, there are plenty of feed fish, although there is no access for river herring. Instead, there are plenty of shiners and dace and an abundance of mayflics. The midge hatches are surprisingly abundant, so fish the tiny flies dead drift when no obvious hatch is in progress if you're seeing big fish cruising, their dorsals bulging the surface.

Mares Pond

Mares Pond (28 acres, 55 feet deep) in Falmouth is very similar to Grews Pond, its close neighbor, in that it is small, deep, and fertile. It is landlocked, with no inlet or outlet streams, but it has an abundance of cold, spring-fed water that helps keep trout active throughout the year. In addition, Mares Pond has more of the feel of being out in the woods, with the stunted pitch pine and oak forests typical of the Cape that surround it.

Mares Pond is stocked in the spring with rainbows and browns, which can both grow to impressive sizes. But it is the browns that have been documented as reaching 8 pounds. To target these big fish, use big streamers and fish the shallows, particularly in the south end, in spring. Later in the year the fish will suspend in the 20–30 foot depths, so density-compensated, full-sink lines are called for. In autumn, especially October, the fish are quite active and the pond all but abandoned.

Find the Mares Pond access at the town landing on the west side of the pond on Locustfield Road, which turns north off Brick Kiln Road. Brick Kiln

Road runs between MA 28A on the west and the Sandwich Road on the east. The ramp is steep but can accommodate car-top boats and canoes. No gasoline-powered outboards are allowed, but electric motors are fine.

Johns Pond

Johns Pond (317 acres, 62 feet deep) in Mashpee may well be the best trout producer among the entire excellent array of Cape Cod waters. It has the ideal qualities required to produce large trout and plenty of them: ample cold, pure, well-oxygenated water; a forage base of invertebrates, shiners, perch, and river-run herrings; enough size to prevent the concentration of the fish in any one spot; and access to the sea via two outlet streams, the Quashnet and Childs Rivers. Add to this the fact that the former state record rainbow trout was caught in Johns Pond—a 13-pound, 7-ounce monster—and you have proof of its quality.

The pond has a variety of interesting water for the fly-fisherman to ply. In spring, as in most other Cape waters, concentrate on the shallows along the shore where insect hatches and feed fish will be available to the trout. The shallows in Johns Pond are extensive, with all of the edges gradually declining to 10-foot depths, except in the northern end where the water quickly drops to its 62-foot maximum near the Quashnet River outlet.

In addition, in the southern basin, the water gradually drops to 30-foot depths but then rises to a shoal that's only 10 feet deep. Fish the shoal early and the drop-offs around it later. In the heat of the summer, the fish can be found in the southern basin, in the middle of the lake where there's a 30-foot hole, or especially in the northeastern corner where the deepest hole occurs. The fish, particularly the browns, will suspend in the 20–35-foot depths during hot weather, so a density-compensated, full-sinking line will get you to them.

Late in the year, the blueback herrings and alewife fry will migrate out of the lake via the two outlets, and large trout will stage near the mouths of the streams. And don't be surprised if big brookies turn up in your catch, because the Quashnet River is now being managed for salters, and they have access right up into the lake.

Access to Johns Pond is via a Town of Mashpee boat-launch ramp on Hooppole Road on the northwest corner of the lake. Find it by turning onto Ashumet Road from MA 151. Ashumet Road loops off and back onto MA 151, with Hooppole Road turning north about midway along. There are no outboard motor restrictions on Johns Pond and it is a favorite recreational spot, so use belly boats wisely or stick to canoes and boats.

Mashpee-Wakeby Pond

Mashpee-Wakeby Pond (769 acres, 87 feet deep) in Mashpee rivals its close neighbor, Johns Pond, for accolades as the best trout destination on the

Cape. It's really two large basins connected by a neck of water that share the same qualities of cold water, ample forage (including herring), and oversized trout. And at a total of 769 acres, it's the largest lake on the Cape. But don't let the combined size of Mashpee-Wakeby put you off. The basins are equal sized, both have deep holes and upwelling spring water, and both produce very well.

Of the two, the north basin, Wakeby Pond, has the largest variety of water, with three islands offering good springtime opportunities. The deepest hole in Wakeby is just north of Cleveland Island, which is found in the southeastern bay of the pond. It's 60 feet deep with close access to shallows, which makes it a prime spot throughout the year. Unfortunately, it's also the farthest spot from the state launch ramp, which is on the south end of Mashpee Pond. Jefferson Island is just off the north shore, and Keith Island is just west of Conaumet Point.

Mashpee Pond is the southern basin, and it has a more uniform drop-off to its 87-foot-deep hole, which is just south of the center of the pond. Many locals consider the slot of water between the western shore and Conaumet Neck (the peninsula of land that separates the two basins) to be particularly productive. In addition, Conaumet Neck is entirely open to the public as a major part of the Lowell Holly Reservation, so shore fishing all along it is allowed. Pay particular attention to Conaumet Point, which juts out into Wakeby and separates Cleveland and Keith Islands.

Find the launch ramp on the eastern edge of Attaquin Park, which lies between MA 130 and the southern shore of the lake. MA 130 connects Sandwich to the north and Cotuit to the southeast, with the lake about halfway between the two. For shore fishing, find the Lowell Holly Reservation by turning north onto South Sandwich Road just a few hundred yards east of the boat-launch-ramp road. The entrance to the park is on the west side of the road, a left turn, about ¾ mile along.

Hathaway Pond

Hathaway Pond (20 acres, 57 feet deep) in Barnstable is another of those small landlocked Cape ponds that doesn't look to promise much but produces excellent catches—in this case, big brookies. The brookies are holdover fish from Division of Fisheries and Wildlife stockings, which also include a mix of browns and rainbows.

The pond's depth and its excellent and extensive springs mean that there is plenty of good holding water to keep the fish actively feeding year-round. And even though it is landlocked, there is a population of herring in it, perhaps the product of angler releases. Regardless of where they came from, there are also plenty of dace, crustaceans (both crawfish and grass shrimp), and insects.

The Mashpee-Wakeby Ponds rarely freeze over, providing good cold weather angling.

Find the town-owned and -maintained access to the pond about 1½ miles east of MA 132 and MA 6, Exit 6. Take MA 132 east and turn north (left) onto Phinney's Lane, then onto the access road. Note that there is another Hathaway Pond just south of this one, but it does not have access. The Town of Barnstable uses the pond for its town beach, but that's because of the extreme purity of the water, and they do guard its quality—no outboard motors allowed. That's okay, because this pond was made for belly boats or small canoes anyway.

Nickerson State Park

Nickerson State Park in Brewster includes Flax Pond (48 acres, 75 feet deep), Big Cliff Pond (193 acres, 88 feet deep), Little Cliff Pond (33 acres, 33 feet deep), and Higgins Pond (25 acres, 67 feet deep).

Nickerson State Park is an oasis—if not of wilderness, then of undeveloped woodlands—in the midst of Cape Cod's vacation-home and suburban sprawl. It consists of almost 1,800 acres of scrub pine and oak forests, has campsites numbering more than 400, and contains four of the most attractive trout-pond kettle holes you'd ever like to find.

All four of these ponds are attractive because of the way they grow trout. An abundance of insects, crustaceans, and feed-fish bases allow stocked trout to put on inches quickly, and the water quality and depth keep the fish feeding and growing all year. In addition to the standard mayfly dry and nymph imitations, be sure that you have some Grass Shrimp Flies (#

14–18) and plenty of streamers to imitate the dace, perch, and herring that constitute the bulk of the diets of the biggest fish.

Big Cliff Pond attracts the most attention from anglers, especially from boats, because of its size. There are also boat launches on the smaller Little Cliff and Higgins Ponds, but Flax is a wade or belly-boat proposition. In addition, Higgins Pond is an artificial-lure-only, catch-and-release affair that has responded well to the restriction, with plenty of big trout. It's also worth noting that shore fishing and wading along the edges is productive, especially early and late in the season when the fish cruise the shallows.

Find the main entrance to Nickerson State Park in East Brewster along MA 6A. The park entrance is on the south side and obvious. Make your camping reservations early—this is a very popular spot from Memorial Day to Labor Day.

Crystal Lake

Crystal Lake (36 acres, 44 feet deep) is worth noting because it is farther out on the Cape in Orleans, because it carries trout well from season to season, and because it has excellent access. Like other typical kettle holes, Crystal Lake is surprisingly deep for its size at 44 feet and is spring fed with high-quality, well-oxygenated water.

Although the lake has historically suffered from inconsistent angling success, especially before the 1960s, it now appears that its forage base has stabilized to the point that trout feed on it and grow very well all year. Holdovers of impressive size are reported annually. That forage base consists mainly of smelt, grass shrimp, and mayflies, with some heavy spring hatches and consistent midge rises.

Work the shores and shallows early in the season, and don't miss the shoal just east of the north launch area. Later in the year, the trout will suspend over the deep water, which runs from the northwest corner right down through the middle of the pond.

Find one town landing on the southern tip of the lake via Monument Road, which turns east off MA 28, or find the other on the northern end of the lake adjacent to MA 28.

Gull Pond

If you get far enough out onto the Cape, say to Wellfleet, the last thing you'd expect is a good—no, a *great*—trout pond. Wellfleet Harbor pinches into the Cape's forearm from the southwest, and the Cape Cod National Seashore protects the open ocean beaches, yet here sits Gull Pond (109 acres, 61 feet deep) inside the National Seashore lands. It's a large freshwater pond that has been flagged by state biologists as one of the best holdover trout waters in the entire state.

Gull Pond's success stems from that familiar Cape Cod freshwater formula. It's a kettle hole with exceptionally high-quality cold water. It's deep. It has an abundance of mayflies and caddis. It has crawfish, shrimp, and shiners. And it supports a strong run of blueback herring and alewives that come into it via the Herring River. This combination of factors keeps the trout in the pond fat and happy, and they grow as fast as anywhere in New England.

Gull Pond has an abundance of wade fishing, especially on its western and southern shores, but a canoe or belly boat helps you reach its best waters. Note that no gasoline outboard motors are allowed on the pond, but that electric motors are okay. Also fish along the neck of land on the north shore that separates Gull Pond from Higgins Pond (a second Higgins Pond, different from the one in Nickerson State Park), especially in the fall when the river herring fry are migrating. The trout will hold near the outlet and feed heavily on them.

In spring and early summer, fish the weed edges and drop-offs, and don't ignore the hump of cover on the east side directly across from the town landing. Mayfly Nymphs and Emergers work well when there aren't any duns showing. And use big streamers, as well as Matukas, Zonkers, and Woolly Worms and Buggers. Bulging fish can be feeding on midges or grass shrimp.

The deepest water runs diagonally across the pond from the northwest toward the southeast, and the oversized brown trout will suspend over it during the heat of the summer. Use a density-compensated, full-sinking line to get to them.

Find Gull Pond and its landing via Gull Pond Road, which turns east from US 6 about a half mile north of Wellfleet center. Gull Pond Road runs about 1½ miles to the town landing access road, a left (north) turn.

Great Pond

Great Pond (17 acres, 35 feet deep) is found about a mile north of Gull Pond, the second pond on the east side of US 6 just over the Truro town line (the first is Snow Pond). It's smaller and is often overlooked because of its size, but if it's big brook trout you're after, Great Pond is, well, great. It has a small but devoted following of anglers who know that trophy brookies—fed by abundant insects, shrimp, and forage fish—inhabit this pond.

It too lies within the borders of the Cape Cod National Seashore, and although there are a few cottages on its shores, plenty of wade fishing is available. The access is via a town right-of-way on its southern tip located on Great Pond Road, an east turn off US 6. Wading is easy, a belly boat is better, or you can drag a canoe to the water.

Other Stocked Lakes and Ponds

Plymouth County (stocked spring and fall) *Plymouth:* Big Sandy Pond, Fearings Pond, Little Pond, Long Pond; *Rochester:* Mary's Pond. **(Stocked only in spring)** *Norwell:* Norris Reservation Pond; *Plymouth:* Fresh Pond, Lout Pond, Russell Pond, Sawmill Pond; *Scituate:* Tack Factory Pond.

Barnstable County (stocked spring and fall) *Barnstable:* Hamblin Pond, Shubael Pond; *Brewster:* Sheep Pond; *Chatham:* Goose Pond; *Dennis:* Scargo Lake; *Eastham:* Herring Pond; *Falmouth:* Ashumet Pond; *Orleans:* Baker Pond; *Sandwich:* Peters Pond, Spectacle Pond. **(Stocked only in spring)** *Barnstable:* Lovell's Pond; *Chatham:* Schoolhouse Pond; *Falmouth:* Deep Pond; *Sandwich:* Hoxie Pond, Pimlico Pond; *Yarmouth:* Long Pond.

Dukes County (Martha's Vineyard) (stocked only in spring) *Oak Bluffs:* Upper Lagoon Pond; *West Tisbury:* Old Mill Pond, Seths Pond.

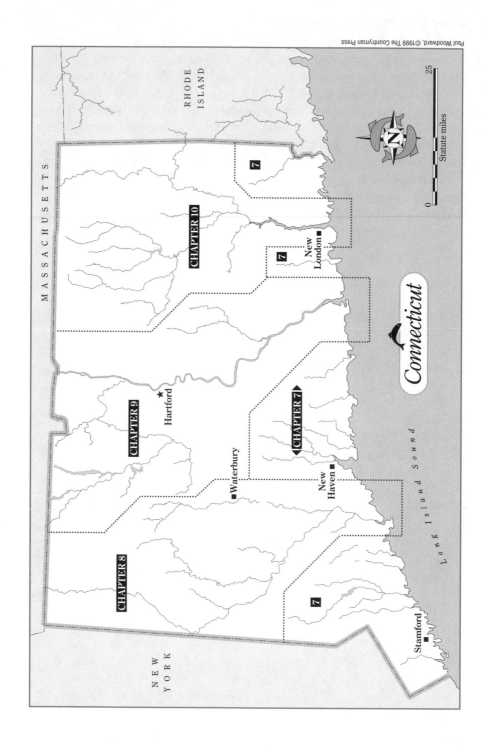

RHODE ISLAND

MASSACHUSETTS

NEW YORK

CHAPTER 10

CHAPTER 9

★ Hartford

CHAPTER 8

■ Waterbury

CHAPTER 7

New Haven ■

New London ■

7

7

7

Stamford ■

Long Island Sound

Connecticut

N

Statute miles

0   25

II | CONNECTICUT

Fly-fishing for trout in Connecticut is the well-kept secret of anglers who regularly ply the wide variety of waters that occur throughout the state. They know how good the fishing can get, and they're often reluctant to sing the state's praises too loudly lest too many folks find out. But make no mistake. This state—with an image centered on urban wonders, suburban luxury, technological marvels, and the general idea that there are too many people cramped into too few acres—has good fly-fishing, and plenty of it.

To illustrate this, according to the Department of Environmental Protection's Fisheries Division *Report on Connecticut Streams and Rivers*, more than 4,000 out of 6,587 miles of flowing water were found to contain wild, reproducing trout, in a state that ranks forty-eighth in size and is one-sixth the size of Maine! Not bad.

In addition, a huge variety of water is available to explore. From the big strong rivers in the north—the Housatonic and the Farmington—to the small intimate freshwater streams of the coast, to the interesting and varied waters of the Connecticut River Valley, to the surprisingly overlooked regions of the eastern half of the state, Connecticut has plenty of options for anglers of every persuasion. An abundance of the state's best waters are also governed as Trout Management Areas (TMA), where a variety of more stringent restrictions apply—from fly-fishing-only and catch-and-release waters to sections of streams with reduced daily creel limits.

And Connecticut has an active trout stocking program that annually produces and releases more than 600,000 catchable-sized trout, almost 2,000 surplus brood-stock trout, and even 1,600 surplus brood-stock Atlantic salmon. These Atlantic salmon are available in their natural habitat, running fresh water, which is virtually the only place in southern New England where they can be sought after using traditional fly-fishing techniques.

Fly anglers new to the state, or residents of the state looking for new waters to investigate, would do well to look to any of Connecticut's 12 TMAs and/or fly-fishing-only areas and its one Wild Trout Management Area (WTMA), the Tankerhoosen. These sections of streams have been flagged as some of the best water in the state. They hold trout well, have excellent hatches, and include easy access. Each of them is detailed in the chapters that follow.

And if you've never had an Atlantic salmon on the end of your fly rod, you really should try either the Shetucket River salmon area or either of the two reaches of water on the Naugatuck River that receive salmon. Both are stocked with surplus salmon late in autumn and into winter, and these fish are big, well fed, and as energetic as any in the world. Details on the rivers are given below.

Although the general trout fishing season in Connecticut is closed from March 1 to 6 AM on the third Saturday in April, devoted anglers should note that in most of the TMAs, the season remains open for the entire year. And there are a number of waters listed in the state's annual publication, *Connecticut Anglers Guide,* that are also open year-round. There is simply no reason in Connecticut not to fish any time you want to.

Be sure to pore over the *Anglers Guide.* It is issued anew each year and includes a wealth of information, including any new regulations and designations. Be watchful for new restrictions on additional streams that may soon receive more protected status. Several are being considered for inclusion as WTMAs. In addition, the Fisheries Division *Report on Connecticut Streams and Rivers* was put together with the specific purpose of improving the management of the state's rivers. In the near future, the information in the report should lead to better stocking practices, as well as to wiser use of Connecticut's premier trout waters.

In all, 50 Connecticut waters are discussed in detail in the chapters that follow. Details are given on the trout that are available in the rivers and streams, the forage in them, the flies needed to cover most angling situations, and where the best accesses can be found. Also included at the end of each chapter is a full listing of all the remaining stocked waters in the state, flowing and still, that are not specifically discussed.

With this information, no angler need stay at home during any season for lack of a place to fish in Connecticut. So gear up and get out.

7 | Trout Streams Flowing South to the Sea: From West to East

Mianus River

The Mianus River flows out of New York State and into Connecticut's Fairfield County appendage before it drains into Long Island Sound. For running in and out of such enriched real estate, the river is surprisingly wild, with three separate swaths of state parks and an active grassroots group, the Mianus River Coalition, working hard to preserve the natural beauty of its riverbank.

With this preservation of the watershed has also come a retention of high water quality and good trout habitat. In fact, the state has created a Trout Management Area (TMA) on the Mianus, which runs from Merribrook Lane in Stamford upstream for a mile to an old breached mill dam. And even above this TMA, the water is largely open to the public and available for anglers.

Using the Merritt Parkway as a dividing line, find the TMA by traveling south on Westover Road to Merribrook Lane. The turnoff to the road, to the west, is on a dangerous curve that is marked by blinking yellow lights. Travel up Merribrook Lane to the river where parking for four to six vehicles is available. Be sure not to park anywhere else, as this is an exclusive neighborhood where cars will be towed. The hiking trail is on the west side of the river, is maintained by the coalition, and is well marked.

Above the Merritt Parkway, access is via the west-leading crossroads off Riverbank Road, which is the northern extension of Westover Road. Good fishing is available upstream to Farms Road, which crosses the river at the base of the Mianus Reservoir.

On the TMA, there is no closed season, and it is restricted to single-hook artificial lures and catch and release only from March 1 to the third Saturday in April. During the remainder of the year, the daily limit is three

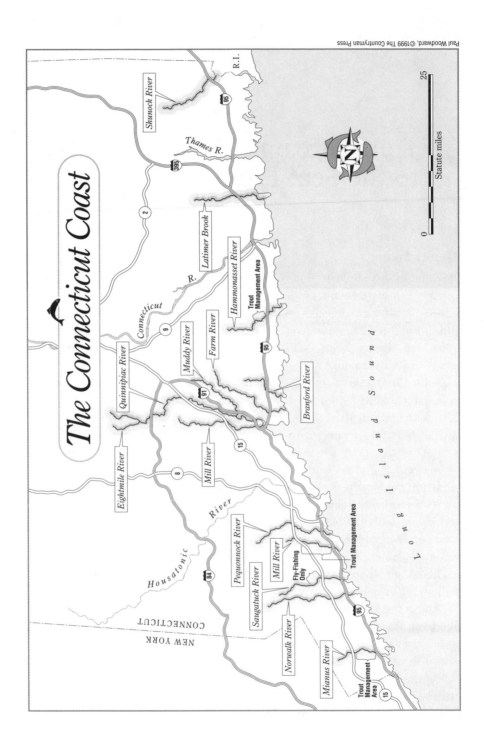

The Connecticut Coast

Shunock River

R.I.

Thames R.

Latimer Brook

Connecticut R.

Hammonasset River

Trout Management Area

Muddy River

Farm River

Quinnipiac River

Branford River

Eightmile River

Mill River

Long Island Sound

Housatonic River

Pequonnock River

Saugatuck River

Mill River

Fly-Fishing Only

Trout Management Area

Norwalk River

Mianus River

Trout Management Area

NEW YORK
CONNECTICUT

0   25
Statute miles

fish with a minimum length of 9 inches. The rest of the river falls under general regulations.

Norwalk River

The Norwalk River is a medium-sized river that provides more than 14 miles of trout water on its run from Seth Lowe Pierrepont State Park south to the city of Norwalk and Long Island Sound. It is one of Connecticut's more urban flows, running as it does through a number of developed communities and along a major road, CT 7. But it is a credit to the efforts of all of these communities and to the state that the water in the Norwalk is high-quality trout water, producing good hatches—especially caddis—and holding trout in parts of it throughout the year.

In addition, the Norwalk is a very public river, with plenty of pullouts and parking along it; flows through a number of parks that offer nice settings for angling; and fosters a general attitude that the river belongs to everybody. No exclusivity here.

Because of its length and highly developed watershed, the Norwalk provides a broad array of water types to ply. There are a number of mill ponds, some of them still maintained and used, that back up water and can be fished from shore or with a small boat. There are also many places where the water rushes along and drops through sloughs, providing good fast-water angling and plunge pools. And the river meanders in many other spots, revealing classic riffle-pool-run water.

Find the Norwalk River at Exit 40 of the Merritt Parkway, CT 15, and turn north onto CT 7 to travel along it upstream. At any number of crossroads there is parking, and in almost all cases you can walk down- or upstream from the bridges. In addition, there are many commercial establishments, retail and industrial, that allow parking along the lower Norwalk. It's pretty much a "take your pick" situation, and the water is high quality and well stocked.

Farther upstream you enter the town of Wilton, where two municipal parks provide good access and fishing. The first is Schenck's Island Park. It is located on the west side of the river south of CT 33 and 106, which cross the river in Wilton. Turn south (left) just after the bridge, and the park is on your left, opposite a grocery store. The second is Merwin Meadows Park, which is on the same (west) side of the river, but upstream from the bridge. It has ample parking and a nice hiking and bike trail upstream along the river.

Farther north on CT 7, after it crosses to the west side of the river, a Little League baseball park and a Kiwanis family park provide more good access and ample parking, with the river nearby. And once you enter Ridgefield, after the highway has crossed the river a couple of times,

The author reads the notices at the lower access to the Mianus River hiking trail.

Riverside Park lies between the highway and the river to the west. Continuing upstream, where the river becomes smaller and more intimate, there is good access and angling at the state's flood-control project, which includes Miller's Pond, and, for headwater type angling, at Martin Park, adjacent to Haviland Road.

And these are just the most obvious and easiest places to get onto the river. It's easy to see that the Norwalk is something of an everyman's river, that even though it is popular, there is enough of it open to the public to make finding your own little niche not only possible, but probable. And its clean waters, ample stocked trout, and steady hatches make it very attractive, even if it is quite urban. General regulations apply along the Norwalk's entire run.

SAUGATUCK RIVER

Maps *USGS (from Long Island Sound upstream):* Sherwood Point (mouth to Saugatuck), Westport (Saugatuck to Saugatuck Reservoir), Botsford (Saugatuck Reservoir), Bethel (Saugatuck Reservoir to headwaters in Bethel).

Description The Saugatuck River is a very respectable, midsized stream that holds trout well, has high-quality water, and has decent access for its location. From its headwaters in West Redding, the river cuts due south to the town of Westport on Long Island Sound, interrupted midway by the large

Saugatuck Reservoir impoundment and by several smaller dams near its mouth.

Above the reservoir, the Saugatuck is a small rural river that receives a good supply of stocked trout and also holds some decent native brookies. Directly below the reservoir the river is fast flowing and difficult to wade, but farther downstream, where the gradient is not as steep, the fly-fishing is more challenging as the variety of forage and insects broadens. And there is an excellent, if abbreviated, fly-fishing-only area that has been nurtured and improved over the years.

Access The Saugatuck Reservoir in Weston neatly divides the Saugatuck River in two. Upstream the river is rural and wood lined, often requiring a short hike through pleasant surroundings to get to the small flow. Downstream is suburban becoming urban, and you need to know precisely where you can get onto the water. But this is Fairfield County in southern Connecticut, so the river is never very far from a highway or paved road upstream or down, and you can explore most of the Saugatuck's best water in an easy day.

Regulations General regulations apply to the entire length of the Saugatuck River, open season running from the third Saturday in April to the last day in February, with a five-fish-a-day limit. From the Dorr's Milo dam to the Merritt Parkway bridge, fly-fishing only is allowed. Special regulations apply to the reservoir (see "Best asset" below).

Don't miss The fly-fishing-only area of the Saugatuck is not extensive, but it is one of the best the state has to offer. It wasn't always this way, however. The Nutmeg Chapter of Trout Unlimited has done extensive work here to make this not only water capable of holding trout, but also one of the most attractive areas on the entire river—to the trout. They hold well because of the stream structure and channels that have been improved by the chapter. Because of this and the state's stocking practices, this area provides excellent angling throughout the season.

Best asset It's not often that southern New England anglers get the chance to cast over brown trout that consistently run more than 10 pounds. However, in the early 1990s a unique state program on the Saugatuck Reservoir was initiated that introduced young Seaforellen brown trout into the reservoir to take advantage of an overabundance of alewives. The trout have grown fat and large in the years that have passed, and each year many exceeding 10 pounds are caught. The state has wisely continued the annual stocking.

That's the good news. For fly-fishermen, the bad news is that angling is limited to fishing from the west shore of the reservoir, with no boats, canoes, flotation devices, or wading allowed. And this is a protected watershed, so the forest does grow down to the shore in most places. But the allure of the big trout may help overcome the drawbacks, and the idea of hooking and landing trout of this dimension is certainly intriguing.

The Bridgeport Hydraulic Company owns the Saugatuck Reservoir, and in addition to a regular Connecticut fishing license, all anglers must also have in their possession a fishing permit from the company. It costs $20 for the year or $5 for one specific day. Senior citizens and handicapped anglers receive the permit for free, and there is a handicapped-accessible fishing pier near the dam. Call the company at 203-336-7788 for details.

Biggest drawback The fly-fishing-only area extends for less than ¾ mile on the lower Saugatuck River, and the five-fish-a-day limit prevails. Both of these facts are something of a shock. The Saugatuck is the longest river in southwestern Connecticut this side of the Housatonic, and it has the high-quality water to sustain a good—bordering on great—fishery. When coupled with this kind of angling pressure, a fishery this good deserves better. Maybe the state's new cold-water fisheries management plan—promised for within 2 years but probably more like 4 years away—will address this problem.

Necessary patterns *Underwater:* Pheasant Tail Nymph (#14–20), Hare's Ear Nymph (#12–16), Hendrickson Nymph (#12–16), Stonefly Nymph (#4–10), Caddis Larva (#14–18), Caddis Emerger (#12–18), Black–Nosed Dace (#4–10), Mickey Finn (#4–12). *Dry flies:* Quill Gordon (#12–16); Hendrickson (#12–16); Red Quill (#12–16); Rusty Spinner (#12–16); March Brown (#12–14); Gray Fox (#12–14); Mahogany Dun (#12–16); Mahogany Spinner (#10–16); Sulphur Dun (#14–16); Light Cahill (#14–16); Green Drake (#6–10); Brown Drake (#10–12); Golden Drake (#8–12); White Mayfly (#12–14); Tan, Yellow, Brown, Green or Black Caddis (#12–18); Blue-Winged Olive (#12–20); Cream Midge (#18–22); Trico (#18–24); Alder (#16–18); Cricket (#10–14); Hopper (#4–12); Black or Cinnamon Ant (#10-20).

Stocked feeder streams worth a look Aspetuck River, West Branch of the Saugatuck River.

Other feeders (from downstream to upstream) Ivy Brook, Stony Brook, Deadman Brook, Willow Brook, Poplar Plains Brook, Silver Brook, Kettle Creek, Beaver Brook, Jennings Brook, Hawley's Brook, Moffit's Brook, Mountain Brook, Sympaug Brook.

The Saugatuck River, in its long run from West Redding to Long Island Sound, encompasses all that can be good about a Connecticut trout stream, and yet it also epitomizes some of the long-term problems that face all southern New England waters and their anglers.

The good is very good. Largely because the river provides drinking water from the Saugatuck Reservoir, the entire watershed, especially above

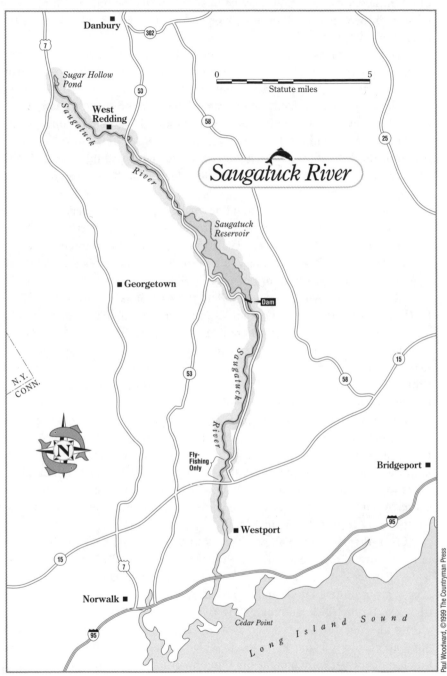

Danbury

7

302

Sugar Hollow
Pond

53

Saugatuck

West
Redding

58

25

0   5
Statute miles

Saugatuck River

*Saugatuck
Reservoir*

Georgetown

River

Dam

N.Y.
CONN.

Saugatuck

53

58

15

N

River

Fly-
Fishing
Only

Bridgeport

15

7

95

Westport

Norwalk

95

Cedar Point

Long Island Sound

Paul Woodward, ©1999 The Countryman Press

and along the reservoir, is carefully guarded to maintain purity. This habit of cleanliness extends all the way downstream to the Sound, and it provides trout with the opportunity to hold over and grow large. Thank goodness the Saugatuck is pure.

The bad involves access and state protection of the fishery. In too many places, average Joe anglers can't get onto the best runs of the stream. You hear too often that you need to know some property owner to get to the good angling. And the state offers no protection for the trout anywhere along the river to allow the fish at least to be caught more than once, if not to grow large and enticing.

Still, the Saugatuck offers good fishing to those willing to seek it out, and the discussion below is more detailed than usual because getting onto the river can be difficult.

Most of the best fishing is found downstream from the reservoir because this is bigger water than upstream, but there are some very pretty and accessible runs of river above the reservoir that shouldn't be ignored. So enjoy the Saugatuck, explore it where you can, and be a river steward to keep it pure and to help open up more of it to anglers.

Above the reservoir, CT 53 parallels the east bank of the river to West Redding. Take note, however, that from the reservoir upstream to 1 mile above the Mark Twain Library there is no fishing. Above this, the Saugatuck is a delightful, small mountain stream. From West Redding, take the West Redding Road all the way upstream to the river's headwaters at Sugar Hollow Pond to where the road meets CT 7. Wooster Mountain State Park is just to the west and is undeveloped.

Follow CT 53 downstream and you find yourself cruising along what may be the most pleasant road in the state. It borders the west shore of the reservoir, where the watershed is entirely undeveloped—meaning that there aren't any power lines, passing lanes, or frenetic traffic jams. When CT 53 veers to the west, turn east onto Valley Forge Road, which stays along the shore. When you emerge at the Samuel Senior dam you'll see where the best trout fishing begins, below the dam.

Cross the river on Valley Forge Road, park here, and you've got a mile or more of excellent fishing, although it is a bit of a hike down to the water. Farther downstream, along Valley Forge Road, there are intermittent accesses, but quite a bit of land is posted. About 1½ miles downstream, from the west, Davis Hill Road crosses the river to meet Valley Forge Road, providing up- and downstream access at the bridge. And downstream there is good access along Lyons Plain Road, which is the extension of Valley Forge Road, on the east shore both at the Church Pool and the Firehouse Pool. Yes, there are both a church and firehouse.

There is another bridge, a wooden one, at Cartbridge Road, a mile below the Church Pool. Cross it and fish the nice pool at the bridge and the good pocket water downstream, but stay on the west shore. Then recross back to the east shore and travel downstream to River Road, a west (right) turn, which leads to Keene's Park, a Town of Weston facility. It has ample parking and there are plenty of good riffles, pocket water, and pools all along the town's reach of stream.

River Road continues downstream to another bridge. Park on the west end of the bridge and hike upstream on the trail there. Fishing downstream from the bridge, you should use the access along the east bank. Just past the bridge River Road intersects with Good Hill Road, which leads south (left) to CT 57, Weston Road. Turn left again, and within ¾ mile you'll find a pair of bridges that cross back to the east shore, first over the Saugatuck and then almost immediately over the Aspetuck. (Note: The East Aspetuck River is a different bird altogether, flowing north of here and into the Housatonic River. It's not even in the same watershed. Go figure.)

The Twin Bridges, as they're known, do have some angling above and below them, but they also help to identify the limited, but excellent, fly-fishing-only area of the Saugatuck, which is just downstream, starting at the dam a few hundred yards below. To fish it, turn south onto Ford Road just east of the Twin Bridges. You'll parallel Glendenning Pond, the still water above the Dorr's Milo dam (also known more familiarly as the Glendenning dam), and see the river just below the dam. Park along the road, and appreciate the work done on this short run of river by the local TU chapter. They've made it a very decent fly-fishing area with the addition of low diversion dams and carefully placed stream structures.

The fly-fishing-only area extends for less than ¾ mile to the Merritt Parkway bridge, which is just upstream from Lee's Pond, which itself is quickly followed by Wood's Pond. These are essentially warm-water ponds, but some trout are stocked. They are best fished from a small canoe or a car-top boat, which can be launched just above the Merritt Parkway bridge.

Below Wood's Pond dam, the river turns brackish, and while there is excellent angling to be had for a variety of fresh- and saltwater fish all the way downriver to Hendricks and Cedar Points, it's beyond the scope of this book to detail this stretch. Suffice it to say, if you're in a mood for stripers, blues, herring, and the like, the lower Saugatuck is as good as any Connecticut water.

Mill River (Fairfield)

The Mill River in Fairfield is a pretty stream that has benefited from the insistence of the citizens of that town to maintain open space along it. Largely because of this preservation and the access it provides to anglers, the state has created a very attractive Trout Management Area (TMA), which runs from the Merritt Parkway bridge downstream to Mohegan Lake. Mohegan Lake is the first downstream impoundment, and it is not always labeled on maps.

Find the TMA by taking Exit 46 off the parkway and turning south onto CT 59. Turn right (south) almost immediately, and this little side road will lead down to the river near the bridge. You can fish the water downstream and back easily in an afternoon.

In addition, you can fish the water above the TMA by turning north onto CT 59 from Exit 46 and almost immediately turning left (south) onto Congress Street, which parallels and crosses the river. And downstream, below the Samp Mortar Reservoir, you can fish the river along Brookside Drive and can access its lower reaches via the Duck Farm Road bridge.

On the TMA, there is no closed season on trout and char, and from March 1 to the third Saturday in April all fish must be released. During the rest of the year, the daily limit is three fish, and they must be at least 9 inches long. There are no tackle restrictions. Outside of the TMA, general regulations apply.

It's nice to know that even though the Mill River is not a major river or trout fishery, it has been respected and appreciated by the people who surround it, with access for all. It is attractive, clean, and holds trout surprisingly well.

Pequonnock River

The Pequonnock River in Trumbull is typical of several streams that flow through the southern part of Connecticut to the sea in essentially urban areas, yet retain much of their feeling of country remoteness. This is possible because the terrain the streams have created is usually steep banked where it is virtually impossible to develop the land, thank goodness. And the Pequonnock is a prime example of this phenomenon.

The river's good trout angling begins just north of Long Hill at Spring Hill Road, where it crosses the river just east of CT 25. Downstream, the river cuts under the four-lane highway that CT 25 becomes and runs along the base of a very steep western shore. Access to this section, which is the best along the entire river and is locally known as the Trumbull Basin, is via an old railroad-grade trail on the west shore that can be reached off Whitney Road. Bear right onto an unimproved road that leads to the railroad grade, and fish downstream for 2 miles.

You'll almost always be alone, and the water holds trout well throughout the year. In addition, you'll often be surprised with the strength and size of the good holdover fish, as well as the possibility of hooking one of the brood-stock rainbows the state adds to the mix. They'll often travel downstream to this section, hold over, and grow even bigger. You'll know you are at the end of this good water when the residential houses crowd the river. You can walk up through the development to Farm Road on the east side of the river, or spend the entire day by fishing back upstream. Below here, the river is urban, with crossroad access in several spots and a nice swath of larger, slower-moving water to fish in Beardsley Park in Bridgeport.

The entire Pequonnock is governed by general regulations, opening to angling on the third Saturday of April and closing on the last day of February. All legal methods of angling are allowed, with a daily limit of five fish.

Quinnipiac River

The Quinnipiac River runs down nearly half of the state—from its head-waters near New Britain to Long Island Sound at New Haven—but in spite of its long run, there's only one relatively short stretch that attracts anglers. That stretch is the Quinnipiac Gorge in Cheshire, and it is only 2 miles long. But it is a nice piece of water, and the state stocks it well with brown trout, many of which hold well throughout the season.

Find this stretch by traveling west down Main Street, South Meriden, to where it blends into River Road, which shortly crosses Cheshire Street. Turn north (right) on Cheshire; soon a bridge crosses the river. Fish downstream. You can also walk down into the gorge from River Road. Turn right instead of merging onto it at Main Street. The good fishing runs between the Cheshire Street bridge through the gorge to the Oregon Road bridge, which is just upstream from Hanover Pond.

Below Hanover Pond the river warms beyond the ability to hold trout, and its pollution becomes more condensed, especially with PCBs. But above the Quinnipiac Gorge there is a slug of cooler water, largely from Eightmile River (see below), and there are some naturally reproducing browns in the river. The fly-fishing for these trout is really better in nearby Eightmile, but if pollution sources are identified and eliminated and the upstream sewage treatment improves, this entire run of the Quinnipiac could become very attractive trout water.

The Quinnipiac is also of note because it receives the waters from three very good trout streams—the Mill and the Muddy Rivers (see below), both of which join it near its mouth, and Eightmile River (see below), which joins it upstream from the Gorge in Southington.

Mill River (Hamden)

The Mill River in Hamden, just north of New Haven, is another of those southern Connecticut urban flows that can be quite surprising in the angling opportunities it provides. In this case, the Mill River has the added attraction that no boats or canoes are allowed on it or on the three small ponds along it, which can also hold good fish.

The river's headwaters rise up in the hills north of Sleeping Giant State Park in Cheshire, but the first good angling is found in Sleeping Giant,

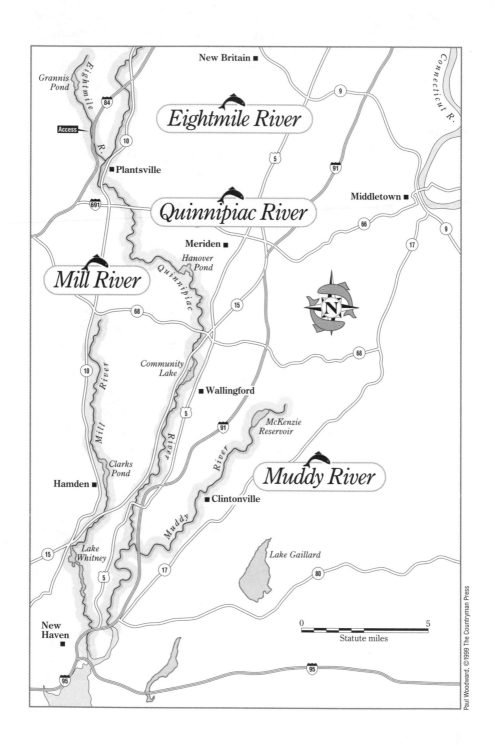

New Britain ■

Grannis Pond

84

Access

10

■ Plantsville

691

Eightmile R.

Eightmile River

9

5

91

Middletown ■

Quinnipiac River

66

9

Meriden ■

Hanover Pond

17

Mill River

68

Quinnipiac

15

N

68

10

Community Lake

■ Wallingford

5

McKenzie Reservoir

91

Mill River

Muddy River

Clarks Pond

Hamden ■

■ Clintonville

15

Lake Whitney

5

17

Lake Gaillard

80

Muddy River

New Haven ■

0   5

Statute miles

95

95

Paul Woodward, ©1999 The Countryman Press

which has ample parking, good facilities, and the aura of remoteness. The water here is very high quality, holding stocked trout well throughout the season and supporting a strong native population of brook trout. Find the park off CT 10, the main route that parallels the entire river from West Haven to Cheshire, by turning east onto Mount Carmel Road. The entrance to the park is opposite the campus of Quinnipiac College. Axle Shop Pond is in the park and is also heavily stocked.

You can also fish the river downstream and along New Road to where it crosses under Sherman Avenue, which connects back out, west, to CT 10. Just above Sherman Avenue is tiny Clark's Pond, where you can fish along the shore and where there is a handicap-access pier for fishing.

New Road continues along the river on its east side, crosses to the west bank, and soon meets Ives Road, CT 22. Turn east, park near the bridge, and fish up- or downstream. This is a protected watershed area, is posted as such, and requires that you be off the water by dark. There is limited access below here. Only two crossroads at Dixwell Avenue and Skiff Street allow fishing—only near the bridges because of private land problems—and no fishing is allowed below Skiff Street.

The Mill River does have some pleasant surprises if you are willing to walk its banks. There are places where light swampy areas keep most of the anglers away, but this is high-quality water with the capability of holding trout year-round. It does get fished hard early in the season, as do most Connecticut streams, but later in the year, and especially in autumn, the angling and the surroundings can be especially rewarding. General regulations apply.

Muddy River

The Muddy River is a rural stream that flows near some highly populated areas. As such, it's a stream that beckons to those anglers willing to get off the beaten path, to hike down its waters, and to find both good stocked and holdover trout plus some native brookies. Even so, access to the river is fairly easy, as far as getting within its vicinity.

The good angling on the Muddy begins just below McKenzie Reservoir in East Wallingford. Northford Road runs east from Exit 14 of I-91, but beware Exit 14. If you are traveling southbound, Exit 14 drops you onto East Center Street, which becomes Northford Road east of the highway (a left turn). But if you're traveling north on I-91, Exit 14 drops you onto Woodhouse Avenue, and you must turn left (north), travel to South Airline Road, turn right, then turn right onto East Center Street, which as above becomes Northford Road. Only in the skewed planning of the federal road-masters could one full exit really be two half-exits.

Regardless, the Muddy River soon crosses under Northford Road, and just before the bridge, Tylers Mill Road turns south (right) and follows the river downstream for 1½ miles to another bridge. The reach of river between the two bridges is productive, especially for native brookies, although a few stockers and holdovers do show up.

Below the Tylers Mill Road bridge, the river heads out and away from civilization until it reaches Woodhouse Avenue (of Exit 14 fame), and this stretch, a distance of about a mile, is pleasant and productive. Below Woodhouse Avenue, you can fish downstream to Dayton Pond, but below here it becomes more of a meandering meadow stream. Yes, there are some good holdover trout that hide under the bankings, but once you get into Clintonville, suburbia begins to take over and access is restricted. There are a few pools along Mill Road, which connects to Woodhouse Avenue via CT 22, but the good angling pretty much ends at the south end of Mill Road where it meets Spring Road in North Haven.

General regulations apply along the entire length of the Muddy River.

Eightmile River (Southington)

Eightmile River in Southington (not to be confused with Eightmile River in Lyme) is a high-quality trout stream that feeds into the Quinnipiac River near Exit 30 of I-84. Several groundwater seeps keep the water cold throughout the season, and the state has recently identified the river as an excellent spawning ground for stream-born brown trout. The downside is that these browns contain high levels of PCBs, making them dangerous to eat, but in the near future the state may create a Wild Trout Management Area (WTMA) here to protect the trout and provide some excellent angling.

In spite of the close proximity and noise of I-84, Eightmile has excellent access and good hatches, and can provide an interesting day of angling. From Exit 30, turn east onto Marion Avenue and then quickly north (left) onto West Street. Turn west (left) onto Prospect Street to the bridge, or continue past Prospect to West Center Street. Turn west (left), find the Eightmile River State Access Area, and fish up- and downstream from here. At its headwaters near Grannis Pond, there is access via Churchill Road. Find Churchill Road by continuing west on West Center Street to Mt. Vernon Road, turn north (right), and then west (right) on Churchill after about 1½ miles. Churchill soon crosses the river.

Currently, Eightmile River is governed by general regulations, but do not eat the fish because of PCB contamination. Let's hope that soon the state makes this river a WTMA, preserving its wild populations of trout.

Farm River

The Farm River is another of southern Connecticut's surprises that has exceptionally high-quality water, receives a decent planting of stocked trout, and has been proven to hold native and stream-born trout as well. The river rises up in North Branford and quickly receives high-quality water from Pistapaug Pond from the west and the mountain brooks draining off Totoket Mountain from the east. It is a meandering meadow stream in many places, but occasional swaths of woodlands help keep the water cool in summer, keeping the trout active and available.

The good angling starts just south of the town of Northford along Forest Road, CT 22. The river is sandwiched between this road on its east and Totoket Road on its west, with several cross roads, like Village Street and Augur Road, providing access. Farther downstream Mill Road crosses between Totoket Road and CT 22, just at the outlet of Pages Mill Pond, itself worth a few casts.

Because of its high quality of water and proven ability to produce trout, some of the best angling occurs later in the year, after the stocked trout have either been caught near the bridges or have migrated away from them. In fact, hiking only a few hundred yards away from these popular spots in June can produce good angling over trout that may not have seen a fly for a year or more.

Currently, general angling regulations prevail on the Farm River.

Branford River

The Branford River is a good early-season stream with decent riffles and runs, good access, and a decent supply of stocked trout. Unfortunately, the Branford suffers from extremely low water during the summer months, largely because of the siphoning of its water from Lake Gaillard. But when it's fishing well in spring, it is worth a trip.

The Branford originates at the dam on Lake Gaillard and flows due south through the town of North Branford until it crosses under Valley Road, CT 139, the start of the good fishing. Hike downstream from here for some decent meadow runs and a few riffles, until the stream finds School Ground Road. Shortly below this bridge, the Branford curls into a wooded, boggy stretch, but there can be some excellent trout here, as well as at the good-angling and easy-access end at North Branford Road, about a half mile farther along. North Branford Road intersects with the Boston Post Road a scant quarter mile north from Exit 55 of I-95, the Connecticut Turnpike.

The Branford has good potential as a southern Connecticut trout stream, but until it receives its due portion of water, which is not going to happen anytime soon, it will remain interesting to anglers for only a short period early in the season.

Hammonasset River

The Hammonasset River flows directly into Long Island Sound some 10 miles west of the Connecticut River in the towns of Clinton and Madison. At its mouth lies the Hammonasset Beach State Park, a popular seaside spot in summer. For all of the fame of the beach, the river itself is relatively small, but it does have a delightful 2½-mile-long TMA that resembles a small mountain stream with good pocket and plunge-pool water. And this upper river section flows through the midst of a mature forest, is fully canopied, and holds trout well, often right through summer. In addition, there is good access with a well-maintained trail along the TMA, in addition to some posted private land access.

Find the upper end of the TMA at the bridge on CT 80 west of Killingworth. Park off the road, hike down under the bridge, and fish the entire length of the TMA to Chestnut Hill Road, which connects to the west with CT 79, which itself leads south to Exit 61 of I-95. You can also get onto the river by traveling east on Chestnut Hill Road (the river runs along it for a half mile), turning right on River Road, right again on Papermill Road, and finding the bridge on Green Hill Road just south of the intersection. Green Hill Road then returns to CT 79.

The special regulations of the Hammonasset TMA make it a catch-and-release-only water in autumn, and with good reason. It is particularly enjoyable at this time of year as the water cools and the trout become active. In addition, the setting is very enjoyable, with trees turning, biting insects nearly nonexistent, and the area nearly abandoned. Fish the Hammonasset anytime, but be sure to get there in autumn.

There is no closed season on the Hammonasset River TMA, but from the third Saturday in April to the last day in August the daily limit on trout and char is three, with a minimum length of 9 inches; during the rest of the year, the area is strictly catch-and-release.

Latimer Brook

In spite of its small size, Latimer Brook in East Lyme is of interest to anglers because it has some very high-quality water, good access, and decent holdover trout. In addition, an angler might find himself attached to a decent sea-run brown, the product of a restoration effort in the 1950s and '60s that was not altogether unsuccessful.

Latimer Brook, or Latimer's Brook as some maps identify it, offers good angling all along its length, but particularly from Silver Falls Road to the Boston Post Road right near Exit 75 of I-95, the Connecticut Turnpike. Travel west on the Post Road to Chesterfield Road, CT 161, and turn north (right). This road parallels the river all the way upstream to Silver Falls and Silver Falls Road. For about a mile, the river runs right alongside the road. The area here is growing quickly, with a number of new subdivisions offering access down to the riverbank, but be sure to ask for permission to cross private property. In many places, the Latimer hugs the base of the far ridge,

The Hammonasset River Trout Management Area begins under the CT 80 bridge.

a short walk across open meadows, but again, gain permission before trudging across the fields.

Upstream from Silver Falls, Latimer Brook is a headwater stream surrounded by heavy undergrowth and boggy footing, but some anglers will appreciate the challenge of getting to the water and finding the native brook trout that thrive there. Find this section by turning north onto CT 85 just above Silver Falls, traveling through Chesterfield, and turning right onto Beckwith Road, which becomes a dirt road past Beckwith Pond.

Latimer Brook is governed by general regulations.

Shunock River

The Shunock River in North Stonington is, for Connecticut, a very rural stream that contains a variety of water that will interest fly-fishermen. Its very high-quality waters head up above Hewitt Pond near CT 2, the Westerly Norwich Road, but the good angling begins just below Hewitt Pond, south of the roadway. Shortly, the river enters Gallup Pond, and the outflow quickly passes under the highway before entering a broad boggy area where the river is not well defined. Still, you can venture into this area and find some trout in the few exposed river areas. A better idea, however, is to fish it just above the center of the town of North Stonington proper.

Hewitt Pond Road crosses the Shunock just below Lower Hewitt Pond, a good place to sample the waters here, which resemble a limestone creek. They are clear, weed laden, and full of forage and trout. The angling is not easy—it never is when the trout are hiding under the weeds and along undercut banks—but the trout are mostly holdover or stream-born, making the effort well worth it. Find Hewitt Pond Road on CT 201, just south of the intersection of CT 2 and CT 201. Turn right (east).

Downstream from the town, the good angling continues along Babcock Road, which travels east out of North Stonington off Rocky Hollow Road, just north of town. The river is adjacent to the road near town; farther downstream, you can hike down the feeder streams that cross under Babcock Road.

When Babcock Road ends at Voluntown Road, turn south (right) and then west (right) on the New London Turnpike, CT 189, to where the Shunock passes under it, about a quarter mile along. Fish up- or downstream. And there is good access and angling where the river passes under Voluntown Road south of I-95.

The Shunock River is governed by general law regulations, but with its high-quality waters, its fertility, and its good accessibility, it would make an excellent candidate for more protection from the state.

Other Stocked Streams in the Southwestern Corner of the State

Fairfield County *Bethel and Danbury:* East Swamp Brook; *Greenwich:* Byram River; *New Canaan:* Silvermine Brook; *New Field:* Ball Pond Brook;

Newtown: Pond Brook and Pootatuck River; *Ridgefield:* Ridgefield Brook and Titicus Brook; *Shelton:* Indian Hole Brook; *Sherman:* Sawmill Brook; *Stamford:* Rippowam River.

New Haven County *Bethany:* Hopp Brook; *Bethany and Naugatuck:* Beacon Hill Brook; *Cheshire and Hamden:* West River; *Cheshire and Southington:* Ten Mile River; *Guilford:* East River and West River; *Guilford and Madison:* Iron Stream; *Madison:* Neck River; *Middlebury:* Eight Mile Brook, Hop Brook, and Long Swamp Brook; *Milford and Orange:* Wepawaug Brook; *Naugatuck:* Long Meadow Pond Brook; *Orange:* Race Brook; *Oxford:* Little River; *Seymour:* Bladens Brook; *Southbury:* Kettletown Brook, Transylvania Brook; *Wolcott:* Mad River.

Stocked Lakes and Ponds in the Southwestern Corner of the State

Fairfield County *Brookfield:* Candlewood Lake; *Derby:* Picketts Pond; *Fairfield:* Mohegan Lake; *Hebron:* Gay City Park Pond; *Monroe:* Great Hollow Pond; *New Fairfield:* Ball Pond; *Redding:* Starret Pond; *Shelton:* Nells Rock Reservoir; *Trumbull:* Twin Brooks Pond.

New Haven County *Brandford and East Haven:* Lake Saltonstall; *Guilford:* Quonnipaug Lake; *Meriden:* Baldwin Pond; *Middlebury and Waterbury:* Hop Brook Flood Control Impoundment; *Oxford and Southbury:* Southford Falls Pond; *Prospect:* Prospect Town Park Pond; *Southbury:* Southbury Training School; *Wallingford:* Wharton Pon, *Waterbury:* Upper Fulton Park Pond.

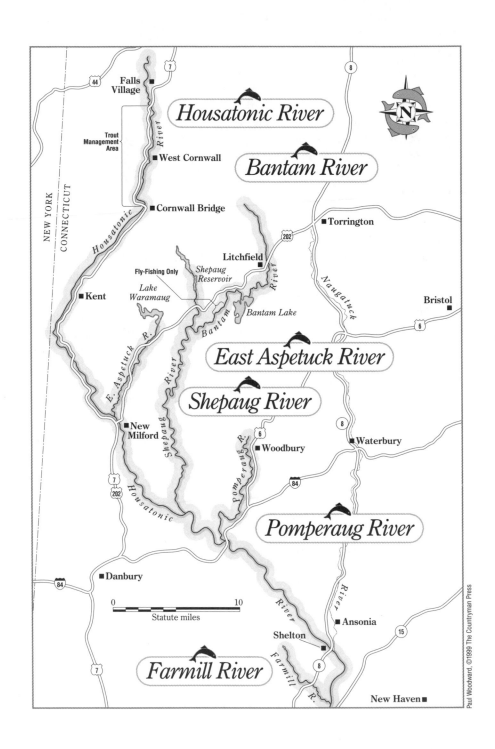

Falls
Village

Housatonic River

Trout
Management
Area

West Cornwall

Bantam River

NEW YORK
CONNECTICUT

Cornwall Bridge

Torrington

Litchfield

Shepaug
Reservoir

Fly-Fishing Only

Lake
Waramaug

Bantam Lake

Kent

Bristol

East Aspetuck River

Shepaug River

New
Milford

Woodbury

Waterbury

Pomperaug River

Danbury

0   10
Statute miles

Ansonia

Shelton

Farmill River

New Haven

Paul Woodward, ©1999 The Countryman Press

8 | Housatonic River Watershed

HOUSATONIC RIVER

Maps *USGS (from Long Island Sound upstream):* Milford (Stratford), Ansonia (Stratford to Shelton), Long Hill (Shelton to Oxford), Southbury (Oxford to Newtown), Newtown (Newtown to Brookfield), Danbury (Brookfield to Boardman Bridge), Kent (Boardman Bridge to Sherman), Dover Plains (Sherman to Bulls Bridge), Kent (Bulls Bridge to Kent), Ellsworth (Kent to Housatonic Meadows State Park), Cornwall (Housatonic Meadows State Park to West Cornwall), South Canaan (West Cornwall to Falls Village), Ashley Falls (Falls Village to Massachusetts line). (*Note:* The Housatonic Trout Management Area [TMA] is covered by the Cornwall and South Canaan maps.)

Description The Housatonic River's place as Connecticut's greatest trout destination may have been eclipsed by the Farmington River, but it remains a fertile water set in the breathtaking hills of the northwestern corner of the state. Strong hatches of mayflies and caddis emerge over often impressively large holdover trout, and both still lure anglers who must decipher which flies are the current focus of the trout, match them closely, and then present their offerings with delicate precision.

The scourge of the Housatonic is pollution—toxic and thermal—with PCBs still a problem and warm summer water and low flows often lethal to trout. A mid-1990s heat wave and drought killed up to 75 percent of the trout in the Housy, but biologists report that since then the trout have held up well, and the angling has improved. And while the PCB problem is beginning to wane, current negotiations with Connecticut Light and Power Company about water flows have turned contentious. Stay tuned.

Because of these problems, the trout angler's focus is entirely on the TMA in Cornwall, the only section of the river that the state stocks. An experiment with rainbow trout in the TMA has ended (the thermal pollution was too great to support rainbows), and only brown trout are now stocked.

Yet the Housatonic remains an alluring river, reminiscent of the West's great flows. Its beauty, its size, its fertility, its large trout, and its angling challenges all beckon.

Access The Housatonic River is very accessible. US 7 parallels the western bank for the entire length of the TMA, with crossroad access at the north end via CT 112, at the West Cornwall covered bridge (CT 128), and at the tail of the TMA at CT 4. In addition, an access road runs upstream along the east shore from West Cornwall, starting on the east side of the covered bridge, just before the railroad tracks. Downstream on the east shore, another road leads from the covered bridge 500 yards to a parking lot, and a hiking trail follows the river for another ¾ mile. Below this area, known locally as The Flats, access is from the Housatonic Meadows campground, a state-owned facility where you can park and/or camp. Trails out of the campground run up- and downstream. For detailed discussions of the named pools on the Housatonic TMA, get the Housatonic Fly Fishermen's Association's fishing guide to the river.

Regulations In the TMA there is no closed season for trout except in those areas within 100 feet of cool feeder streams. These areas—indicated by posters—are closed to all angling from June 15 to August 31 to protect heat-stressed trout. All trout and char must be immediately returned to the water throughout the TMA, and fly-fishing only is allowed in the lower 3 miles and is posted. The rest of the river is under general regulations, but because of PCB pollution, a health advisory on fish consumption is in effect.

Don't miss The autumn fishing in the Housatonic River is unheralded and unparalleled, and the surroundings are nothing short of spectacular. The steep hills are covered with hardwoods that turn brilliant colors early high up on their slopes, and this riot of color progresses downslope for several weeks. In addition, the water temperatures in the river moderate and bring on strong blue-winged olive hatches over rejuvenated trout. And the fancies of most outdoorspeople have turned to bird hunting and autumn chores, leaving the often-crowded banks of the river largely abandoned. It is quite simply the best time to roam the banks and pools of the river.

Best asset At more than 10 miles long, the TMA on the Housatonic River is the longest in the state of Connecticut. Yes, the most well-known and accessible pools can get crowded, especially during May and June, and yes, the state campground at Housatonic Meadows fills up and often requires reservations far in advance. But you can find places to fish at almost any time of year along these 10 miles of river where solitude rules, where strong hatches prevail, and where big, sophisticated trout will challenge you. It helps that the recent bad press about the Housatonic has thinned out the ranks of the fly-fishing wannabes.

Biggest drawback The continued abuse of the Housatonic River in this modern era of enlightened appreciation of our natural resources is unheard of. Years ago, the source of the PCB pollution was identified and stopped, but remedies to removing the existing deposits of this carcinogen have not been found. And while more and more dam owners throughout the country find innovative solutions to appease all river users (who are, after all, their customers), Connecticut Light and Power Company resists compromise to increase the health of the downstream flow. Its attitude toward the river and its users, especially fly-fishermen, is archaic and futile.

Necessary patterns *Underwater:* Pheasant Tail Nymph (#14–20), Hare's Ear Nymph (#12–16), Hendrickson Nymph (#12–16), Caddis Larva (#14–18), Caddis Emerger (#12–18), Stonefly Nymph (#4–10), Woolly Bugger (#4–8), Black–Nosed Dace (#4–10). *Dry flies:* Quill Gordon (#12–16); Hendrickson (#12–16); Red Quill (#12–16); Rusty Spinner (#12–16); March Brown (#12–14); Gray Fox (#12–14); Mahogany Spinner (#10–16); Sulphur Dun (#14–16); Light Cahill (#14–16); Green Drake (#6–10); Brown Drake (#10–12); Cream Variant (#12–14); Dun Variant (#12–14); Tan, Yellow, Brown, or Green Caddis (#12–18); Housatonic Quill (#14–16); Blue-Winged Olive (#12–24); Cream Midge (#18–22); Trico (#18–24); Alder (#16–18); Cricket (#10–14); Hopper (#4–12); Black or Cinnamon Ant (#10-20).

Stocked feeder streams worth a look East Aspetuck River (see below), Shepaug River–Bantam River (see below), Pomperaug River (see below), Farmill River (see below), Blackberry River, Carse Brook, Furnace Brook, Macedonia Brook, Pond Brook, Pootatuck River.

Other tributaries within the TMA Reed Brook, Preston Brook, Adams Brook, Mill Brook, Pine Swamp Brook, Ivy Brook, Hatch Brook.

The Housatonic River is a long and glorious flow that deserves a much better fate than we have given it. The 130-mile-long river originates in Massachusetts' Berkshire Hills and flows through western Connecticut to Long Island Sound. Yet only the TMA in Cornwall in the northwest corner of the state is of interest to fly-fishermen in Connecticut.

This unhappy state of affairs can be laid at the feet of pollution: long-lasting PCB sediment pollution from an electrical manufacturing plant in Pittsfield, Massachusetts, and thermal pollution from a small hydroelectric facility in Falls Village, Connecticut. The PCBs make the entire river de facto catch-and-release water, with the trout especially susceptible to accumulating the toxic substance through their dependence on silt-born insects. And the top-release dam in Falls Village holds back water, often causing it to warm to lethal levels in summer, and then dumps it into the river in reduced amounts. The result is low flows of warm water that can cause extreme stress

The Housatonic River Trout Management Area is big, western-type water that harbors big fish and strong hatches, as here at the Birches Pool.

to the holdover trout upon which the Housatonic relies.

That's the bad news. The good news is that both problems are being addressed. The PCB pollution source was eliminated years ago, and the persistent substance has begun to ebb in the river. Fish species other than trout have begun to show lower levels of the substance in their flesh, but not the trout, yet. And the state has been in sometimes contentious negotiations with Connecticut Light and Power about the water releases at the Falls Village dam as relicensing looms.

Along the 10.4 miles of the TMA, however, in spite of the persistent problems, the angling can often be best described as spectacular. The scenery is dramatic, the hatches of insects varied and strong, and the trout, currently mostly browns, are receptive yet demanding. And when a few years of adequate flows of water are strung together, as they have been since the mid-1990s, the holdover trout grow to impressive sizes, with many exceeding 18 inches and some more than 20.

Access to the Housatonic TMA proper is excellent (see above), even though getting to the river requires a long drive from most of southern New England's major population centers. But the trip is worth it, especially if the water levels and temperatures are right and the fish active.

Help in determining whether the long drive will produce good angling is available from two telephone numbers. The first is a water-release schedule: 1-888-417-4837. It gives flow rates and water temperatures (most regulars prefer flow rates of less than 400 cubic feet per second [cfs] and water temperatures below 70 degrees). The second is maintained by the Housatonic Fly Fisherman's Association: 203-248-8616. This is a regularly updated fly-fishing information hot line that specifies hatches, fish activity, fly patterns, and general suggestions, and it's invaluable. It's worth being a member of the HFFA just to help defray the expense of the phone line. (Information on membership is available at the end of the telephone report.)

The Housatonic River is one of the truly legendary rivers in the Northeast. Could it be improved? Certainly. Does it deserve its legendary status? You bet. Should you ply its waters? Yes. You simply cannot know how good fly-fishing for trout can get in southern New England unless you've been on the Housatonic when it's fishing well.

East Aspetuck River

The East Aspetuck River originates in New Preston, at the outlet of Lake Waramaug, and flows for 10 miles due south until it empties into the Housatonic in New Milford. (Do not confuse the East Aspetuck with the Aspetuck River, which flows into the Saugatuck River near Westport.) The waters of the East Aspetuck are pure and cold, holding trout throughout the year, and the state does stock it well. There are some very impressive holdover rainbow trout here and some of them travel up- and downstream far enough to become available to anglers. Unfortunately, access is limited to several crossroads, with up- and downstream sections of water cut off by private land posting, not an unusual circumstance in Connecticut. But these off-limit sections serve very nicely as havens for the holdover trout, where they grow large on ample supplies of caddis and mayflies.

The major crossroad accesses to the East Aspetuck are near its origins, at the CT 45 and US 202 bridge; the bridge about a mile downstream on US 202; Wheaton Road (turn east); Little Bear Hill Road (turn west); and along Paper Mill Road between Hickory Haven and New Milford on the west side of the river. Generally, the downstream sections have the better holdover water, particularly along Paper Mill Road, but it is easier to get onto the water upstream. General fishing regulations apply.

Shepaug River–Bantam River

The main attraction of the Shepaug River drainage is the fly-fishing-only section of the Bantam River, which feeds into the Shepaug in Washington. The Shepaug does get a few trout from the state in Roxbury, but access to it is limited, and occasional contentious disagreement about what access there is makes it an uncertain destination. The Bantam receives more fish and has the more interesting water and better access.

Find the fly-fishing-only section of the Bantam by turning south onto

West Morris Road from US 202 just west of the center of the little community of Bantam, which itself is just west of the well-preserved colonial town of Litchfield. While there is a bridge and access on Stoddard Road, a left turn (east) off West Morris, the fly-fishing-only section starts a bit farther along, at the bridge on West Morris Road proper. Walk downstream here, or drive a mile farther to Smoky Hollow Road, take a right, and find where the river crosses under the road. This is the downstream limit of the fly-fishing-only zone.

The Bantam River comes under general regulations throughout its run, with the only extra rule being fly-fishing only in the section so marked. It's not a large stream, but it has an almost palpable rural charm that makes it very attractive.

Pomperaug River

The Pomperaug River is an attractive river with a variety of water types, good access, decent holdover trout, and good hatches. It meanders through a wide valley and the towns of Woodbury, Southbury, and South Britain before draining into the Housatonic near the I-84 overpass. It is most accessible and most interesting upstream from the CT 172 bridge in Southbury all the way to the CT 47 bridge in North Woodbury, a distance of some 10 miles. US 6 parallels the east shore of the river for this entire stretch, and many crossroads to the west bring you to the river, with good angling up- and downstream.

General fishing regulations prevail, with the season closed from the last day in February to the third Saturday in April. All legal methods are allowed.

Farmill River

The Farmill River offers a pleasant surprise near the mouth of the Housatonic in Stratford. Yes, there is plenty of development nearby, and the city of Bridgeport is just a stone skip away, but wise seers in Stratford have acquired a strip of land along the west bank of the Farmill and set it and its hiking trail aside. And it provides perfect access to a pretty little river that holds trout well and has good insect hatches to match.

The one major drawback is the lack of parking near where the hiking trail leads upstream from the CT 110 bridge over the Farmill. There are some small shopping centers nearby that might let you use their spaces, but be sure to secure permission first so your vehicle doesn't get towed. And then step onto the surprisingly wild environs along the west shore. The trail meanders along the river upstream for about 2 miles, and there are numerous riffles and pools with a few short waterfalls to explore. The trout can hold in any of a number of places, and the distance upstream to the CT 8 overpass is not so far that you can't hike it up and back in an afternoon.

The Bantam River is small and intimate, and very picturesque.

The river above CT 8 is less interesting and has poorer access, but it also has fewer anglers. If you find too many folks downstream, travel west on Mill Street from CT 8 and fish along Commerce Avenue.

NAUGATUCK RIVER

Maps *USGS:* Ansonia (Shelton to Seymour), Naugatuck (Seymour to Naugatuck), Waterbury (Naugatuck to Thomaston), Thomaston (Thomaston to Campville), Torrington (Campville to Torrington), West Torrington (Torrington to East and West Branches of the Naugatuck).

Description The Naugatuck River is a major tributary of the Housatonic that flows due south from Torrington through Waterbury and Naugatuck to Shelton. It has two distinct personalities—the urban downstream used and abused river and the rural, protected, and nearly pristine upstream section. The dividing line between these two personalities is Waterbury, but if the state and river advocates have their way, the distinction will blur in the near future. In time, the river may well become one of the shining stars of Connecticut trout and Atlantic salmon angling, perhaps even rivaling the Housatonic as a prime fly-fishing destination.

The curse of the river below Waterbury is an antiquated wastewater plant in that city that pumps undertreated and smelly water back into the river. Yet even as this is being written, construction is under way to upgrade the plant, with a target completion date of late 1999. And with its comple-

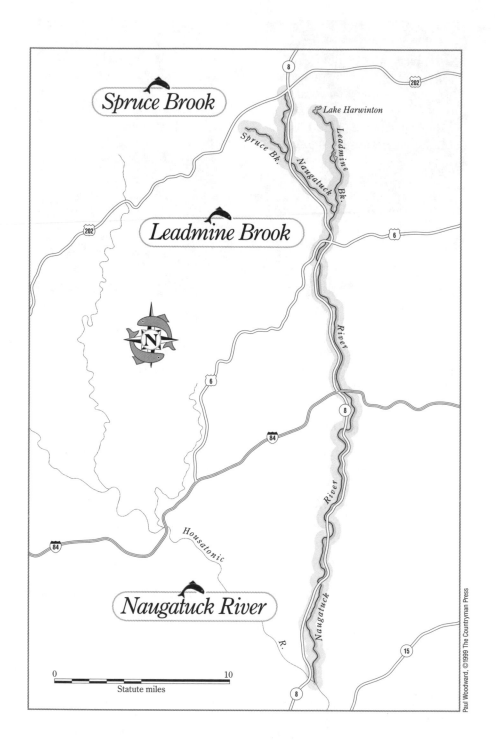

Spruce Brook

Leadmine Brook

Naugatuck River

Lake Harwinton

Spruce Bk.

Naugatuck Bk.

Leadmine Bk.

River

River

Housatonic

Naugatuck R.

N

0   10

Statute miles

tion, all of the communities along the Naugatuck will have modern, efficient plants that return nearly pure water to the river.

In addition, an invigorating plan to remove or breach five antiquated dams in Thomaston, Waterbury, and Naugatuck, and to build fish ladders on two others, will dramatically improve the Naugatuck as a trout stream. This work has already begun, and it has a target completion date of 2000.

The rejuvenation of the lower Naugatuck and the careful stewardship of the upper river are of importance to anglers, both because the river can become a major trout fishery and because it is currently the second river in the state receiving surplus Atlantic salmon. Brood-stock salmon, some reaching 20 pounds and more, are released in late fall upstream in the Corps of Engineers' Thomaston dam flood-control area and downstream between the Union City dam (also known as the Hop Brook Dam, now slated for removal) and Beacon Falls. Trout are currently only released above the Thomaston dam, but when the Waterbury facility goes online, the state intends to stock the entire river.

Access Access to the Naugatuck is an interesting blend of easy drive-up pools and several remote hike-in areas. CT 8, a four-lane, limited-access highway, parallels the river for its entire length, providing a quick means of getting close to the river. In many cases, as with the lower Atlantic salmon area, you can park beside the river and wade right in. At the Union City dam in Naugatuck, for instance, parking is available at Linden Park at the southbound on-ramp of Exit 28 of CT 8, directly adjacent to the dam. Farther downstream, however, the river flows beside CT 8, but you must exit the highway in Beacon Falls, turn west over the bridge, and follow Cold Spring Road into Naugatuck State Forest. Once there, you can hike down a steep hill onto the river, or walk upstream—either along the banks of the river or along the railroad tracks—to get to the more remote and lightly fished sections.

Above the Thomaston dam in Thomaston, access is almost entirely by foot. The Army Corps of Engineers operates the dam as a dry-bed, flood-control facility, meaning that water backs up behind the dam only during spring runoff and when storms might produce flooding downstream. There is vehicle parking at the dam, just upstream near Leadmine Brook, and 4 miles farther upstream at the Campville section of the river adjacent to CT 8 Exit 41. But the good water along this 4-mile run must be accessed via foot (trail bikes can be used).

Regulations The Naugatuck is currently governed by general regulations, closed to all fishing from March 1 to the third Saturday in April. There are no limitations on tackle for trout, and the daily limit is five fish. If targeting Atlantic salmon, only fly-fishing is allowed and a one-fish-a-day limit prevails. If a salmon is caught by other means—lures or bait—it must be immediately released.

Don't miss Fishing for Atlantic salmon in the Naugatuck provides the same contrasts as the river itself. In Union City, a section of the city of Naugatuck, you can cast to them in the shadows of superhighways and urban sprawl. Downstream in the state forest you can wait for a deer to cross a pool before you cast. In the Corps of Engineers project in Thomaston, you'll be fishing for Atlantics in a countryside that rivals even the remote Canadian coast. Regardless of your preferences for company or solitude, however, fish for these Atlantic salmon. They are quite simply the most spectacular fish that you can catch on a fly.

Best asset To give them their due, the U.S. Army Corps of Engineers appears to be truly involved with the maintenance and improvement of the wild area they control here. More than 1,000 acres along the river are theirs to manage, and they've opted for wildlife, for outdoor sports (including hunting and fishing), and for habitat improvement. The Corps has even become actively involved with stream improvement on the Naugatuck by helping to restore riparian habitat with bank stabilization and in-stream structure. Would that the entire Corps understood its place in the natural world as well as they are beginning to in New England.

Biggest drawback Most Connecticut waterways are well within earshot of modern internal combustion contraptions. The Naugatuck is no exception, with CT 8 nearby and plenty of urban reminders available in Torrington, Waterbury, Shelton, and environs. The Corps of Engineers could help provide some relief from the eternal racket of racing engines by keeping their acreage free from any and all vehicles. But alas, they court not only snow-mobiles and moto-cross–type trail bikes, they've also allowed model airplane aficionados to buzz the sky with screaming miniatures. Luckily, the planes fly only near the dam, but the bikes and snowmobiles have access to the entire length of the floodplain.

Necessary patterns *Underwater:* Pheasant Tail Nymph (#14–20), Hare's Ear Nymph (#12–16), Leadwing Coachman (#12–14), Caddis Larva (#14–18), Caddis Emerger (#12–18), Black–Nosed Dace (#4–10), Mickey Finn (#4–12). *Dry flies:* Quill Gordon (#12–16); Hendrickson (#12–16); Red Quill (#12–16); Rusty Spinner (#12–16); March Brown (#12–14); Light Cahill (#14–16); Green Drake (#6–10); White Mayfly (#12–14); Royal Wulff (#10–14); Tan, Yellow, Brown, Green, or Black Caddis (#12–18); Stimulator (# 6–12); Elk Hair Caddis (#12–18); Blue-Winged Olive (#12–20); Cricket (#10–14); Hopper (#4–12); Black or Cinnamon Ant (#10–20). *Atlantic salmon flies:* Mickey Finn (#0/2–6), Cossaboom (#2–6), Green Highlander (#2–12), Bomber (#0/2–4), Black Bear–Green Butt (#4–12), Green Machine (#6–14).

Stocked feeder streams worth a look Leadmine Brook (see below), Spruce Brook (East Litchfield, see below), Little River, Bladens River, Beacon Hill Brook, Long Meadow Pond Brook, Hop Brook, Mad River, Hancock Brook, West Branch of the Naugatuck, East Branch of the Naugatuck.

Other feeder streams (from downstream to upstream) Beaver Brook, Kinneytown Brook, Nickel Mine Brook, Mud Brook (South Seymour), Globe Mill Brook, Mud Brook (North Seymour), Rimmon Brook, Swamp Brook, Hockanum Brook, Egypt Brook, Mulberry Reservoir Brook, Hopeville Pond Brook, Haul Brook, Steele Brook, Turkey Brook, Spruce Brook (Waterville), Nibbling Brook, Jericho Brook, Purgatory Brook, Northfield Brook, Pudding Brook, Pickett Brook, Gulf Stream.

The Naugatuck is a river that's full of potential. It's nearly a great water for angling for Atlantic salmon and trout. It has an extensive mosaic of state or federally protected watershed that offers the chance for solitude. Access is good all along it. And it's "this close" to providing the quality habitat that cold-water species like trout and salmon need and that is necessary for abundant and varied forage.

This potential is that much closer to being realized because every community along the river has demanded, and for the most part received, the attention of the local, state, and national powers to provide the funds and the impetus to clean up the water being returned to the river. Waterbury—just upstream from the city of Naugatuck and the last and most problematic municipality regarding water quality—is in the process of building a modern facility that finally will make the Naugatuck River flow as clean as modern technology allows.

With this in mind, it's important to realize that stream life downstream from Waterbury is currently possible, but not very pleasant. The river smells, and local respect for it is not good. The shores along the urban stretches are littered, and evidence of trash dumping, littering, and general disrespect are abundant. Yet a scant 1½ miles downstream from Naugatuck, where the Naugatuck State Forest protects the river's banks, the aura of wilderness improves, even if the odor doesn't.

The current strongest attraction of the Naugatuck is the stocking of Atlantic salmon by the state in late autumn. In the lower section, from Union City to Beacon Falls, the water has the look of a classic salmon stream. Riffles feed into pools that rival good salmon water anywhere on the continent, and holding water is abundant. It is a popular fishery in early and midwinter, but making the hike down to the water in the state forest and then upstream can leave the crowds behind.

Upstream, in the Thomaston flood-control project, the salmon water is

Downstream from the Thomaston Dam, the Naugatuck is good trout water, and it's soon to be better with the removal of five antiquated dams.

smaller and more intimate. And with the habitat protected from development, you can step into a section of stream that immediately reminds you of remote Canadian headwaters where the salmon search for their redds. The salmon pool where Spruce Brook enters the Naugatuck in the upper reaches of the Corps of Engineers land requires a hike, but it can reward you with a pod of salmon to cast over.

Throughout these two sections, hooking a salmon will transport you into fly-fishing nirvana. These are Atlantic salmon: big and strong and the most spectacular game fish in the world for fly-fishermen. But the trout fishing will continue to improve, too, as the water quality comes back. Already there are impressive hatches of caddis up and down the river, and the strong hatches of mayflies upstream will repopulate the entire river as it becomes cleaner. With the forage species expanding, the ability of the river to hold trout throughout the year will improve, and the trout angling may soon rival that in any of the other waters in the state.

The Naugatuck River is good now, and it may not be long before it becomes great. Keep an eye on it.

Leadmine Brook

Leadmine Brook, in spite of its name, is a gem of a stream that hides next to the Naugatuck River, emptying into it just above the Army Corps of Engineers dam in Thomaston. Much of its lower flow is within the protection of the Corps' domain, making it pristine and remote. And even its upper reaches are rural, shaded, cool flowing, and fertile.

To fish the lower Leadmine, get off CT 8 at Exit 40, the northern Thomaston exit, and drive north on CT 222 past the Corps of Engineers headquarters at the dam. (The Corps has a detailed map of its land and the trails on it, which is available at the headquarters.) Less than a mile along, on the west side of the highway, a well-marked Corps road leads down into its property. You'll cross the Leadmine and can park at the lot that's used by the model plane enthusiasts. Fish the stream up from this lot and bridge all the way back to the highway, or downstream (if there aren't a bunch of miniature screaming fighter planes buzzing your head) to the Naugatuck. You might even latch onto an eye-popping Atlantic salmon here.

The floodplain of the Leadmine extends back upstream past CT 222, and you can fish the upper reaches by turning right (north) at the top of 222's big oxbow corner onto Poverty Hill Road, also know as South Road. It parallels the river into its headwaters, to the town of Harwinton. The state-owned Roraback Wildlife Management Area protects much of this section and provides access. General regulations and seasons apply, with the special Atlantic salmon rules in effect.

Spruce Brook (East Litchfield)

Spruce Brook is included here for a pair of good reasons. First, in its lower reaches, it is lightly fished and the home of a strong population of native, stream-born brook trout. (It is not stocked by the state.) It is remote, hard to get to, and a joy for any angler seeking solitude in wild places. Second, where Spruce Creek joins the Naugatuck River, an important Atlantic salmon pool is formed that epitomizes the qualities anglers everywhere seek. Again, the pool is remote, but it also is deep and attractive, and it gathers salmon.

The directions for finding Spruce Brook are simple. Exit CT 8 in East Litchfield and travel west on CT 118, over the Naugatuck Bridge. Turn south almost immediately onto East Litchfield Road. Park your vehicle and hike down the railroad tracks for 1.5 miles to Spruce Brook. Hike up the brook for brook trout or down to the salmon pool on the Naugatuck.

Other Stocked Streams in the Northwestern Corner of the State

Litchfield County *Barkhamstead:* Beaver Brook and Morgan Brook; *Bethlehem and Woodbury:* Nonnewaug River and Weekeepeemee River; *Canaan and Cornwall:* Wickwire Brook; *Cornwall:* Mohawk Brook and Potter Brook; *Goshen:* Ivy Mountain Brook and Marshepaug River; *Kent and Warren:* Kent Falls Brook; *Litchfield:* Butternut Brook; *New Hartford:* Bakersville Brook and Torringford Brook; *New Milford:* Morrisey Brook; *North Canaan:* Whiting River; *Plymouth:* Todd Hollow Brook; *Salisbury:* Riga Brook; *Thomaston and Watertown:* Branch Brook; *Torrington and Goshen:* Hall Meadow Brook; *Warren:* Lake Waramaug Brook; *Washington and Woodbury:* Sprain Brook; *Winchester:* Taylor Brook.

Stocked Lakes and Ponds in the Northwestern Corner of the State

Litchfield County *Barkhamstead and New Hartford:* Lake McDonough and West Hill Pond; *Colebrook:* Colebrook Flood Control Impoundment; *Cornwall and Goshen:* Mohawk Pond; *Goshen:* Tyler Pond and West Side Pond; *Litchfield:* Mount Tom Pond; *Plymouth:* Hancock Brook Impoundment and Lake Winfield; *Salisbury:* East Twin Lake and Wononscopmuc Lake; *Thomaston:* Northfield Flood Control Impoundment; *Thomaston and Watertown:* Black Rock Flood Control Impoundment; *Torrington:* Stillwater Pond; *Watertown:* Black Rock Pond; *Winchester:* Highland Lake and Mad River Flood Control Impoundment.

9 | Connecticut River Watershed

FARMINGTON RIVER

Maps *USGS:* Tariffville (Connecticut River to Simsbury), Avon (Simsbury to Farmington), New Britain (Farmington to River Glen), Collinsville (Unionville to New Hartford), New Hartford (New Hartford to Pleasant Valley), Winstead (Pleasant Valley to Hogback dam).

Description If there is a true destination-type trout river in Connecticut, it is the Farmington River. Its water comes from the base of two dams, making it cold and pure. Its insect hatches are predictable and strong. It receives more stocked trout, in total and per mile, than any other water in the state, and the trout hold over well and enjoy excellent growth rates. In addition, the Farmington has two long TMAs, and even though they allow bait fishing (which has been proven to kill many more fish than artificial lures), the upstream, older area calls for the release of all fish all of the time, and the lower section is catch and release only from March 1 to the third Saturday in April.

Access There are no secret pools on the Farmington because the access to all of the best fly-fishing is easy and obvious. The most attractive angling, however, is on the West Branch. US 44 parallels the main stem from Nepaug State Forest in Collinsville upstream, north, into New Hartford to where the East and West Branches converge. The highway then follows the West Branch upstream to CT 181 and along it to the town of Pleasant Valley. From Pleasant Valley, take East River Road, which leads north through the People's State Forest to Riverton and on up the West Branch to Hogback Dam, near the Massachusetts border.

Downstream from Collinsville, there are still several runs of the river with good holdover trout. CT 179 follows the river here for a couple of miles until it meets CT 4, which parallels the river downstream to the town of

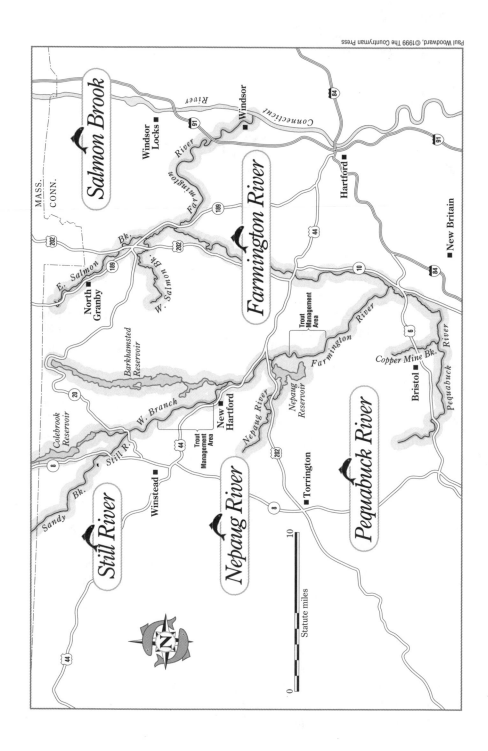

Salmon Brook

Farmington River

Pequabuck River

Nepaug River

Still River

MASS.
CONN.

Windsor
Locks

Windsor

Connecticut

River

Hartford

New Britain

Farmington

E. Salmon

North
Granby

Bk.

W. Salmon

Bk.

Trout
Management
Area

Farmington River

Copper Mine Bk.

Pequabuck River

Bristol

Barkhamsted
Reservoir

Colebrook
Reservoir

W. Branch

New
Hartford

Nepaug River

Nepaug
Reservoir

Torrington

Still R.

Trout
Management
Area

Sandy

Bk.

Winstead

10

Statute miles

0

N

Farmington. Here the river makes a 180-degree swing back to the north, with CT 10 running alongside to Avon, and CT 10 and US 202 together following it to Taconic Mountain State Park near Tariffville. Cut across CT 315 to Tarriffville and on up CT 189 for good access to the East Branch of Salmon Brook (see below), a nice little trout stream in itself.

Regulations On the West Branch from Hogback dam to the TMA, and from the junction of the East and West Branches of the Farmington in New Hartford all the way downstream to the Rainbow Reservoir dam below Tariffville, the minimum length for trout and char is 9 inches, and the daily limit, where allowed, is five fish. (Smolts traveling downstream to the sea because of the Connecticut River Atlantic salmon restoration program are generally less than 9 inches long.)

The West Branch–Farmington River TMA runs from 1 mile upstream from the CT 318 bridge in Pleasant Valley downstream to the CT 219 bridge in New Hartford, a distance of about 4 miles. There is no closed season on trout and char in this area, barbless hooks must be used, and all trout and char caught must be immediately released back into the river. Bait, lures, and flies are allowed.

The lower Farmington River TMA starts at the base of the lower Collinsville dam and runs downstream approximately 3 miles to the CT 4 bridge. There is no closed season on trout here, but from March 1 to the third Saturday in April, the daily creel for trout and char is zero. From the third Saturday in April to the last day of February, the limit is five fish. All methods of angling are legal throughout the year.

The rest of the river is under general regulations with an open season from the third Saturday in April to the last day in February and a daily creel limit of five fish.

Don't miss Anyone who has ever fished the Farmington has heard of and fished the TMA between Pleasant Valley and New Hartford, and it deserves its reputation. Yet the regulars on the river will tell you that the stretch of river from the end of the TMA 10 miles downstream to Collinsville, which has a large variety of water types and excellent access, is at least as productive and often much less crowded than the TMA. It has stronger hatches, good holdover trout, and the chance to fish in rural settings, even if they don't mirror the pastoral wilderness of the People's State Forest.

Satan's Kingdom is especially interesting. Once the stronghold of murderers and thieves, it's now an isolated flow that begins at a gorge near the upstream US 44 bridge in New Hartford and ends 3 miles downstream at the US 202 bridge in Canton. Best access is via a road on the west side of the US 202 bridge. Traveling west on US 202, take the first right and an immediate left and travel upstream to the gorge. The road becomes dirt.

Best asset Because of bottom-release dams on both the West and East Branches of the Farmington, the water stays uniformly cold in the summer and warm in the winter (no anchor ice here). The result is the best growth rates for trout anywhere in southern New England. And the dams are for flood control and drinking water, not peak power generating, so the water levels are not prone to the extremes of high and low water that plague other streams. Yes, the water can stay higher for longer periods of time in the spring when the runoff is captured behind the dams and released over time, but it is held back long enough for the murky sediments to settle out, which helps maintain trout and insect habitat at optimum levels. Perfect temperatures and the best possible water levels mean prime forage growth and fat fish.

Biggest drawback This is a designated Wild and Scenic river, and the label means that there are development restrictions and strict water-quality controls. That's good. But the publicity, to say nothing of the scenic beauty of the river, does attract a large number of other users—canoers, kayakers, tubers, and adventurers—especially during the summer months.

Tradition holds that anglers have no use for the proponents of these flotillas, but more and more, all users are becoming educated to the fact that there is power in numbers. And all users quickly become river stewards. So, yes, you'll see many other river users. And yes, they'll sometimes drift their crafts and their bodies right through a pod of rising trout. But rather than squabble and alienate this bunch, let's educate them and thank them for their care for the river. Maybe our respect for their recreational preferences will breed their respect for our angling. And we can all keep the voice of wise river management and use at the top of any river considerations.

Necessary patterns *Underwater:* Pheasant Tail Nymph (#14–20), Hare's Ear Nymph (#12–16), Hendrickson Nymph (#12–16), Leadwing Coachman (#12–14), Stonefly Nymph (#4–12), Caddis Larva (#14–18), Caddis Emerger (#12–18), Black-Nosed Dace (#4–10), Mickey Finn (#4–12). *Dry flies:* Quill Gordon (#12–16); Hendrickson (#12–16); Red Quill (#12–16); Rusty Spinner (#12–16); March Brown (#12–14); Gray Fox (#12–14); Mahogany Dun (#12–16); Mahogany Spinner (#10–16); Sulphur Dun (#14–16); Light Cahill (#14–16); Green Drake (#6–10); Brown Drake (#10–12); Golden Drake (#8–12); White Mayfly (#12–14); Tan, Yellow, Brown, Green, or Black Caddis (#12–18); Blue-Winged Olive (#12–20); Cream Midge (#18–22); Trico (#18–24); Alder (#16–18); Cricket (#10–14); Hopper (#4–12); Black or Cinnamon Ant (#10-20).

Stocked feeder streams worth a look Pequabuck River (see below), Still River and Sandy Brook (see below), Nepaug River (see below), East and West Branches of Salmon Brook (see below), Mill Brook, Roaring Brook, Unionville Brook, Cherry Brook.

The Farmington River has plenty of room to roam and plenty of named pools, as here at the head of Ovation Pool.

Other feeders (from downstream to upstream) Rainbow Brook, West Brook, Griffon Brook, Munnisunk Brook, Saxton Brook, Owens Brook, Lucy Brook, Hop Brook, Powder Mill Brook, Still Brook, Russell Brook, Minister Brook, Nod Brook, Thompson Brook, Swamp Brook, Great Brook, Rice Brook, Pope Brook, Pequabuck Brook, Hyde Brook, Hawley Brook, Punch Brook, Burlington Brook, Rattlesnake Brook, Thorne Brook.

The Farmington River is a great fishery. Period. It has the trout, the hatches, and the high quality of water that most southern New England anglers only dream about or must travel great distances to find. The river has followed a common historical cycle since European settlement—virgin river to dammed and polluted sewer to restored watershed—and has survived to become a better trout stream than it was in colonial times.

Because it originates on the severe slopes and tortured hills of the Berkshires, the Farmington historically suffered from disastrous flooding, both in spring and from hurricanes. Mountainous ice flows and gushing flood waters scoured the river of forage, drove trout downstream, and ultimately cost companies and citizens millions of dollars. When flood-control and water-reservoir dams were built on the West and East Branches, the horror of the floods ceased. And wisdom prevailed about the release of water back into the river below the dams. Yes, there is a hydroelectric generator at Hogback dam on the West Branch, but its use is secondary to the steady, constant flow of water into the river. You'll find no peaks and valleys in the flow here, and it's a bottom-release facility, so it keeps water temperatures optimal year-round. The result is a constant flow of water that raises an abundance of insects and forage, as well as handsome, well-fed, and receptive trout.

Most anglers fish the Farmington from Collinsville, upstream, concentrating on the two TMAs (see "Regulations"). Easy access to these areas, plus their abundant hatches and fish, make them perfect for anglers new to the river, but there are miles and miles of good water that lie outside the TMAs and should not be ignored. As Dave Goulet of Classic and Custom Trout Flies in New Hartford commented to me, "There are no secret pools on the Farmington. Park your vehicle and follow the well-worn trails. They all lead to good fishing."

A strong river stewardship group, the Farmington River Anglers Association, has produced a 65-page booklet, *A Guide to Fishing the Farmington River*, which describes in detail all of the important stretches of the river from Hogback dam to Tariffville, including road and trail access, particular hatches, nuances of pools and their trout, and cautions and warnings. It would be ludicrous to try to summarize the contents of this guidebook, so if you're serious about exploring all of the fishing in the river, get the book at local fly shops and bookstores. But if you're a casual or occasional visitor to the Farmington, just wade right in. You'll probably be over trout.

Still River and Sandy Brook

Many Farmington regulars insist that the strong hatches and best angling over rising fish begins below the confluence of the Still River with the Farmington in Riverton. Because of the Goodwin and Colebrook Reservoirs above the Hogback dam, most of the nutrients in the West Branch of the Farmington leach out of the water before it is released below the dam, making the water downstream relatively infertile, although pure and cold. The

Still River introduces a slug of nutrients back into the Farmington about 2 miles below Hogback.

About a mile upstream from the Farmington, the Still River makes a hard turn to the south, upstream, back toward its headwaters near Torrington. The river upstream of here is of little interest to anglers, but Sandy Brook is well worth exploring. It joins Still River at the hard turn south and can be found by taking the Robertsville Road out of Riverton. The road becomes the Riverton Road in Colebrook, but keep following it west to CT 8 north, then turn onto Sandy Brook Road, which quickly leads into the Algonquin State Forest and beyond. Sandy Brook parallels all of these roads, has plenty of trout, and—once in the state forest—is tree lined and beautiful.

Nepaug River

The Nepaug offers some interesting water above the Nepaug Reservoir and particularly above Maple Hollow. There is some good angling above and below the bridges along US 202 in the villages of Nepaug and Browns Corner, and there's more upstream. Take Dings Road—a right turn in Nepaug—across the Nepaug River and follow it along to Maple Hollow Road. A right turn here takes you to another good bridge access to the river, and a left turn takes you to Winchester Road. Take a right on Winchester, and shortly look for an unimproved dirt road, Shady Brook Road, on the right, which parallels the river, really just a brook here, through some attractive countryside and decent small-stream angling. Park anywhere along this lane.

The attraction of the Nepaug is its variety. The river immediately above the reservoir has some quick-water stretches intertwined with some slow-water meanderings. Holdover trout can find undercut banks in the backwaters and can grow to good sizes. Farther upstream the river becomes a woodland rill with small pools divided by short runs of riffles.

Pequabuck River

The Pequabuck River flows due east out of the hills to the west of Bristol, directly through the city of Bristol before turning north and feeding into the Farmington River in Farmington. Its main claim to fame is that its best fishing is urban, with good trout found right in downtown Bristol.

While the Department of Environmental Protection does not stock catchable-size trout into the Pequabuck, it does put in fingerling trout, and stream surveys have revealed that these trout do exceptionally well. In fact, a 17½-inch brown trout was electroshocked near the mouth of Copper Mine Brook recently. The factors affecting this good growth of juvenile trout include water that stays cool throughout the season and a forage base that may be boosted by the nutrients in the river supplied by the water treatment plants upstream and by local industry.

The best angling is a mile upstream and a mile downstream from the mouth of Copper Mine Brook, which flows into the Pequabuck near the Hubbell School and the St. Matthews School. A quick fishing journey to the river might even make a great field trip for school kids. But remember, these are stream-grown trout, so limit your catch.

East and West Branches of Salmon Brook

Salmon Brook is a major tributary that joins the Farmington River at the top of the oxbow just above Tariffville. From its confluence all the way upstream to Manitook Lake, just north of Granby, it's a meandering stream with a fertile mix of deep undercut banks, long pools, some quick water, good hatches, and a strong population of both holdover (a few to 20 inches) and stocked trout. The West Branch is smaller, joins the East Branch just south of Granby, and has its own small-stream charms.

The lower end of Salmon Brook is crossed by a number of roads that provide easy access. As with so many of southern New England's streams, short walks up- or downstream from these bridges quickly bring you onto some good water and away from the crowds, especially after the push of the first two or three weekends of the season. From Tariffville, CT 189 follows the flow of the river all the way upstream to Massachusetts.

Upstream from Mechanicsville, at the southern tip of Manitook Lake, the East Branch bends to the west and then back north and is a smaller stream that quickly becomes a cold headwater in the Berkshires. While general regulations do apply along its entire length, a 9-inch-minimum-length rule is enforced because of the Connecticut River Atlantic salmon restoration program.

SALMON RIVER

Maps *USGS:* Deep River (Connecticut River to Pine Brook), Moodus (Pine Brook to confluence of Blackledge and Jeremy Rivers).

Description The Salmon River originates where the Blackledge River and the Jeremy River join in Colchester. Much of its run is through the Salmon River State Forest, making it very accessible for a river so near the Connecticut shore and New York City. A long TMA near its origins keeps the season open for the entire year, even if it doesn't protect the fish year-round as it should.

In addition, the lower river is accessible to those willing to walk a bit, and because it is not part of the TMA, it receives much less attention and fishing pressure than does the upper section in midseason. In fact, I visited the Salmon River on a June weekend and found not one angler on the lower 5 miles of the river. This section of the river holds the best water, being more fertile and larger than above, with better holdover trout.

Strong hatches, plenty of holdover and stocked trout, a beautiful wooded setting, and easy and plentiful access all make the Salmon River exceptionally attractive.

Access The Salmon River runs from just south of CT 2, a four-lane, limited-access highway, downstream to the Connecticut River, a distance of about 10 miles. Reach the upstream area via Exits 15 or 16 on CT 2, River Road being your goal. Find River Road at Exit 15 off Main Street, Marlborough. Take a left turn onto South Road (which becomes Bull Hill Road), and turn left onto River Road. From Exit 16, take CT 149 south and turn right onto River Road. The River Road bridge crosses the Blackledge River, with the entrance to the Salmon River State Forest and the Salmon River TMA just west of the bridge. It is well marked.

Beyond the entrance to the state forest, the country road soon becomes dirt and passes under an elegant arched sandstone railroad bridge, now abandoned, and in another 100 yards comes into view of the river. The dirt road closely follows the river, with plenty of turnouts for parking, all the way through the TMA downstream to Dickinson Road (paved) and then to the Comstock covered bridge, which is open only to foot traffic.

Within view of the Comstock covered bridge is the CT 16 highway bridge. Cross the bridge, and take the second right to reach the downstream entrance to the Salmon River State Forest and the lower river. Drive past the picnic and parking areas (or stop here for lunch) on the right, past the Atlantic salmon acclimatization pools on the left, and up the dirt road. Go slowly, for the road is often rutted, and you need to pick your way up the hills; in dry weather you should be able to get through, even in a passenger vehicle. The river is now on the right (west), 100 yards to ¼ mile from the road. As you hike in, be aware that in some places the river lies down steep banks that you will have to climb back up, but the extra effort will be rewarded with plenty of pools, riffles, and pocket waters virtually to yourself.

Regulations The Salmon River TMA runs from the juncture of the Blackledge and Jeremy Rivers downstream to the Old Browns Mill dam, a distance of just more than 3 miles. Posters indicate fly-fishing only in the lower two-thirds of this area. There is no closed season in the TMA. From the third Saturday in April to the last day in August, the creel limit is five and the minimum length is 9 inches for trout and char. From September 1 to 6 AM on the third Saturday in April, the water is catch-and-release only. The rest of the river is governed by general regulations.

Don't miss Fish in the TMA, but don't ignore the river below CT 16. It is more difficult to get to, but the river matures below the highway, gains water volume and character, and is as attractive as any water in southern New England.

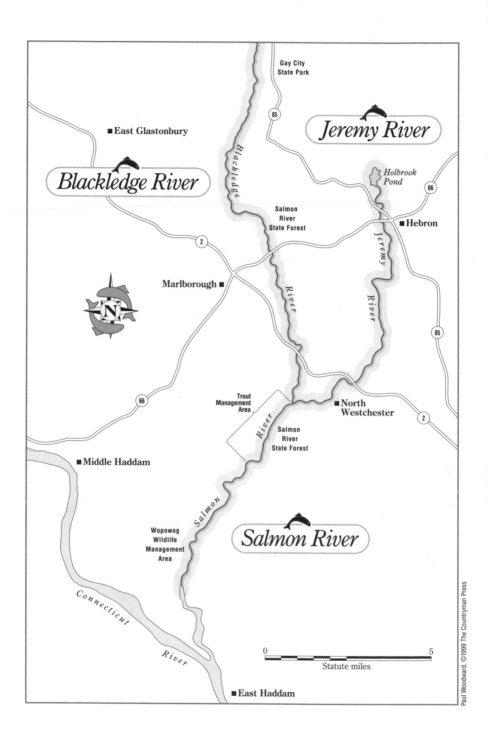

East Glastonbury

Blackledge River

Jeremy River

Gay City
State Park

85

Blackledge

Holbrook
Pond

66

Salmon
River
State Forest

Hebron

N

River

Jeremy River

Marlborough

85

2

66

Trout
Management
Area

North
Westchester

River

2

Salmon
River
State Forest

Middle Haddam

Salmon

Wopowog
Wildlife
Management
Area

Salmon River

Connecticut

River

0   5

Statute miles

East Haddam

Paul Woodward, ©1999 The Countryman Press

Best asset The man-made structures on the upper Salmon River illustrate how it is possible for the good intentions of a society to return a damaged river to its natural state and even to improve it with effort. At the head of the TMA, an abandoned yet elegant arched sandstone bridge gives mute testimony to the architectural skill of 19th-century railroad builders. The access road passes under the bridge, which has graceful lines and close-fitted stones that rise up in the midst of a mature forest. Farther downstream, more modern builders have erected two handicap-access ramps and casting platforms right in the middle of the fly-fishing-only zone; they overlook a long, enticing trout pool without upsetting its character. The downstream end of the TMA is identified by the Old Browns Mill dam, and between the river and the road stands the stark shell of the mill itself: a large building, long abandoned, with the roof caved in and the windows missing, but still with four strong walls standing as straight and plumb as when they were built. Just below the TMA, adjacent to the picnic park at CT 16, the Comstock covered bridge still sheds rain and snow, although it is limited nowadays to foot traffic. And it too, has a very good trout pool under it.

Biggest drawback So if you're in southern Connecticut, where pavement and people prevail, in the midst of one of the most highly populated regions in the country, and you're an ATV or dirt bike fan, where do you find dirt roads to terrorize? Right—the state parks! Even though these vehicles are officially banned from Salmon River State Park, the lure of churning up the roads must be just too great to ignore; or maybe there's a separate competition to see who can run the roads and not get caught; or maybe the parks are so understaffed that there is no enforcement. But there are certainly ATVs and dirt bikes cruising the roads.

Necessary patterns *Underwater:* Pheasant Tail Nymph (#14–20), Hare's Ear Nymph (#12–16), Hendrickson Nymph (#12–16), Caddis Larva (#14–18), Caddis Emerger (#12–18), Black–Nosed Dace (#4–10), Woolly Bugger (#4–12). *Dry flies:* Quill Gordon (#12–16); Hendrickson (#12–16); Red Quill (#12–16); Rusty Spinner (#12–16); March Brown (#12–14); Gray Fox (#12–14); Sulphur Dun (#14–16); Light Cahill (#14–16); Tan, Yellow, Brown, Green, or Black Caddis (#12–18); Blue-Winged Olive (#12–20); Cream Midge (#18–22); Trico (#18–24); Cricket (#10–14); Hopper (#4–12); Black or Cinnamon Ant (#10–20); Green Inchworm (#12–16).

Stocked feeder streams worth a look Blackledge River (see below), Jeremy River (see below), Pine Brook, Safstrom Brook, Flat Brook.

Other feeders (from downstream to upstream) Elbow Brook, Day Pond Brook, Wolf Brook.

The Comstock covered bridge on the Salmon River offers a pleasant park and picnic area, and some decent fishing, about midway along the river's run.

The Salmon River is an unexpected joy. Its location in southern Connecticut, near the asphalt urban sprawl of the northeast corridor, would indicate that it might be channeled, dammed, or owned by some multibillionaire for his own use. Yet there it is, flowing freely but for one dam near its mouth, through publicly owned forest land that's open to all, its waters cooled by the mature forest canopy, fertile, and full of trout.

This jewel of a stream is in Colchester and for nearly all of its length runs through the Salmon River State Forest, which protects its watershed and keeps its waters running cool for most of the year. The combination of an extensive and mature forest along its shores and the decision to leave the road that parallels the river unsurfaced leaves the area in a wild state, oozing the rural flavor favored by anglers and other users.

The state has instituted an unusual array of restrictions on the TMA in the upper run of the river. While much, but not all, of the TMA is restricted to fly-fishing only year-round, from opening day in April until the end of August all anglers may keep five fish per day. From September 1 to the third Saturday in April, the TMA reverts to catch and release only for all anglers.

The wisdom of this mix of restrictions may not be obvious at first, but this area is in southernmost New England, and the river is subject to low water flows and near lethal temperatures in summer, so most of the stocked trout would not survive. In essence, the state is saying the stocked trout should be taken from the waters. Those few holdovers and natives survive by getting up into the feeder streams, and the cool spring seeps are given a break through autumn and winter with catch-and-release regulations. But the jury is still out as to whether this is a wise use of an excellent resource or an attempt to satisfy the entire array of angler/consumers.

The sleeper area of the Salmon River is its downstream section, below CT 16. It's a climb to get down onto the water from the access road in most places, but it is really the better trout water. The best way to enjoy this 4-mile-long stretch is to spend the entire day fishing downstream from the CT 16 bridge and the state forest parking lot. Either use a drop vehicle at the end of the dirt road, or figure on walking back to the parking lot.

Blackledge River

The Blackledge River rises up near Shenipsit Lake in Rockville and flows due south toward its junction with the Jeremy River to form the Salmon River. Along its course it offers anglers a full complement of opportunities to fish. Its smaller headwaters, in Gay City State Park and Meshomasic State Forest, are attractive for brookies and are easily accessible because of the state-owned property.

Farther downstream, the middle section of the Blackledge flows through the northernmost plot of the Salmon River State Forest just north of CT 66, where there is some parking near the bridge. A well-used trail follows the river's east shore. This midsized water has plenty of pocket water and pools, with attractive riffles and occasional meadow undercuts to hide good holdover brown trout.

The downstream section of the Blackledge is found via the same River Road in Marlborough that leads to the Salmon River TMA. The bridge just south of the state forest access road spans the Blackledge, and the state forest envelops the river all the way back upstream past CT 2, the limited access highway, and then downstream to the Jeremy River and the Salmon River.

This lower section closely resembles the Salmon River; indeed, but for the quirks of our ancestors' naming of rivers, it might be more rightly called the Upper Salmon River. As such it shares many of the same qualities as the Salmon, including the strong hatches and good holdover trout. And the state

The Blackledge River provides respite from the sometimes crowded conditions found on the Salmon River.

stocks it well. The entire river is governed by general regulations, but with a 9-inch minimum length to protect Atlantic salmon smolt below Parker Road in Marlborough.

Because of the public ownership of much of the shoreline of the Blackledge and its high-quality trout habitat, it is well worth any time spent on it. The Blackledge might, in fact, provide better angling than the Salmon because it is so relatively unknown. In short, if you've made the trip to the Salmon River TMA, you should also try the Blackledge.

Jeremy River

You'll find good angling on the Jeremy for about a mile upstream of its conjunction with the Blackledge where it runs through the Salmon River State Forest. You'll need to hike upstream from the Salmon River TMA access road a couple of hundred yards to find the Jeremy, then fish it upstream. You can continue upstream to where the river crosses under CT 149, or park at that bridge and fish downstream.

Upstream of CT 149 there is good access to the middle section of the river at the Hartford Road bridge just off Exit 16 of CT 2. Even farther up the river, the headwaters are protected by yet another section of the Salmon River State Forest in Hebron. Find these headwaters via the Old Colchester Road by turning west onto Gayville Road. Access is from the bridge.

General regulations apply to the Jeremy River, but there is a 9-inch minimum length on trout and char downstream from the Gayville Road Bridge.

OTHER CONNECTICUT RIVER TRIBUTARIES (NORTH TO SOUTH)

Tankerhoosen and Hockanum Rivers

The Tankerhoosen River near Vernon is unique because of its Wild Trout Management Area (WTMA). Several years ago, biologists identified wild, self-sustaining populations of both brown trout and brookies in the Tankerhoosen River in the Belding Wildlife Management Area (WMA). To the state's credit, they reacted immediately to preserve this unique fishery, and they instituted strict catch-and-release regulations, making only barbless, single-hook flies legal. In addition, the season in this area is closed from midnight on September 30 through December 31 so that spawning trout are not disturbed.

The Tankerhoosen River is a tributary of the Hockanum River, which is an up-and-coming trout stream in its own right. It flows through East Hartford and into the Connecticut River. Find it from Exit 66 of I-84 and take Bolton Road south to the Belding WMA and WTMA.

Coginchaug River

The Coginchaug River runs due north on the west side of the Connecticut River and joins the Mattabesset River just before it feeds into the Connecticut. The state stocks the Coginchaug along CT 17 in Durham and in Wadsworth Falls State Park in Middlefield. Fish in the state park or off Parmalee Road in Durham in the Durham Meadows hunting area. There's also access to the water along CT 77 and via Meeting House Road.

Eight Mile River

Eight Mile River flows from the Devil's Hopyard State Park in East Haddam due south to the Connecticut River in Hamburg. In the state park itself, the river is a delightful small stream stocked with brookies. The access to the attractive middle section of the river is at the bridge on CT 82, with good holding water ¾ mile downstream to the bridge on CT 156. But the best water is another ¾ mile below the CT 156 bridge where the river comes close to the road. Step into the river here and fish it down to the MacIntosh Road bridge, another ½ mile downstream, to just opposite the North Lyme town hall.

Eight Mile River is subject to low water in the summer, but there are some good holding pools, a few cool feeder streams, and some holdover trout. In addition, the state is very liberal in stocking the river, so early to midseason angling is very productive.

Other Stocked Streams in the Connecticut River Valley

Hartford County *Berlin:* Belcher Brook; Hatchery Brook; *Bloomfield:* Iron Ore Brook; *Bristol:* Coppermine Brook; Wash Brook; *Burlington:* Bunnell Brook; *East Windsor:* Johnsons Brook; Scantic River; *Enfield:* Buckhorn Brook; Jawbuck Brook; *Glastonbury:* Dark Hollow Brook; Salmon Brook; *Hartland:* Howell Pond Brook; *Marlborough:* Fawn Brook; *Simsbury:* Stratton Brook; *South Windsor:* Podunk River; *Suffield:* Muddy Brook; Stony Brook; *Suffield and Granby:* Cannons Brook.

Middlesex County *Chester:* Pattaconk River; *Chester and Haddam:* Great Brook; *Clinton and Killingworth:* Indian River; Menunketesuck Brook; *Durham:* Allyn's Brook; Asmans Brook; Parmelee Brook; Wadsworth Brook; *Deep River:* Deep River; *East Hampton:* Cattle Lot Brook; Soestrom Brook; *Essex:* Falls River; *Haddam:* Candlewood Hill Brook; Ponset Brook; Roaring Brook; *Haddam and Middletown:* Bible Rock Brook; Sumner Brook; *Killingworth:* Chatfield Hollow Brook; *Middletown:* Ling Hill Brook; *Middletown and Middlefield:* Laurel Brook; *Portland:* Buck Brook; Cox Brook; Reservoir Brook.

Stocked Lakes and Ponds in the Connecticut River Valley

Hartford County *East Windsor:* Broad Brook Mill Pond; *Enfield:* St. Martha's Pond; *Glastonbury:* Angus Park Pond; Salmon Brook Pond; *Hartland:* Howells Pond; *Simsbury:* Stratton Brook Park Ponds; *Suffield, Massachusetts:* Congamond Lakes.

Middlesex County *Chester:* Cedar Lake; Pattaconk Lake; *Coventry:* Waumgumbaug Lake; *Durham:* Millers Pond; *East Haddam:* Bashan Lake; Shaw (Hayward) Lake; *Killingworth:* Schreeder Pond; *Middlefield:* Black Pond.

10 The Thames River Watershed

WILLIMANTIC RIVER

Maps *USGS:* Willimantic (Shetucket River to US 6), Columbia (US 6 to CT 31 bridge in Mansfield), Coventry (Mansfield to South Wellington), Stafford Springs (West Wellington to Stafford Springs).

Description The Willimantic River forms in Stafford Springs and runs due south. CT 32 parallels it for its entire run to the city of Willimantic, where it meets the Natchaug River to form the Shetucket River. Although it is dammed several times near its mouth in Willimantic, only the Eagleville dam and lake in Eagleville interrupt its attractive flow upstream. The entire river is a series of pools, riffles, and runs that all hold trout well throughout the year. Even when the water flows low in the summer, there are enough deep pools, spring holes, and cool feeder brooks to tide the fish over. It's a keeper.

Access Access to the Willimantic River is excellent all the way from its origins in Stafford Springs to US 6, the Willimantic bypass, in the city of Willimantic. CT 32 meets the river at its origin and parallels its east shore for its entire length. There are numerous crossroads that provide access. In the Trout Management Area (TMA), one of the most popular access sites is the rest area on I-84 on the westbound side between Exits 69 and 70; and there is good access to the TMA on the west bank via North River Road, which is found by traveling west on CT 74 off Exit 69 of I-84. Take your first right (north) onto North River Road, which runs up almost the entire length of the TMA. At its end, a trail leads to the top of the TMA where Roaring Brook enters from the opposite shore.

Regulations The Cole W. Wilde TMA runs from the mouth of Roaring Brook, just north of Exit 70, 3 miles downstream to the CT 74 bridge in West Willington. It is a fly-fishing-only area with no closed season, and all trout

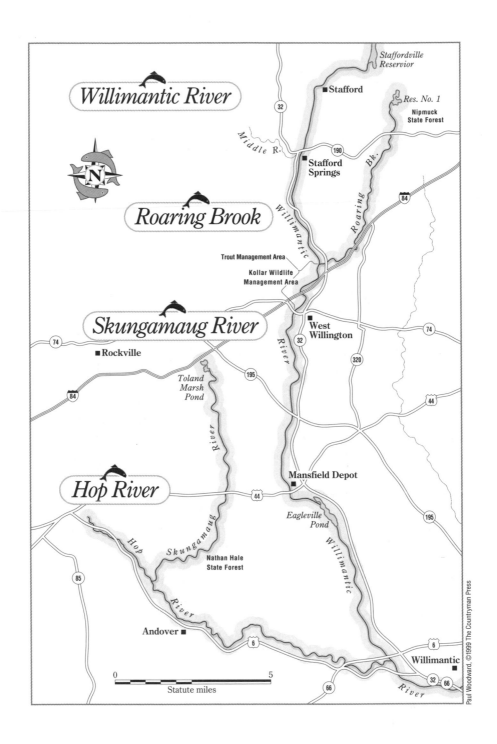

Willimantic River

Roaring Brook

Skungamaug River

Hop River

Staffordville
Reservoir

Stafford

Res. No. 1

Nipmuck
State Forest

32

190

Middle R.

Stafford
Springs

Willimantic

Roaring Bk.

84

Trout Management Area

Kollar Wildlife
Management Area

74

West
Willington

32

74

Rockville

320

Toland
Marsh
Pond

195

84

River

44

Mansfield Depot

44

195

Eagleville
Pond

Hop

Skungamaug

Willimantic

Nathan Hale
State Forest

85

River

Andover

6

6

Willimantic

32

66

River

66

0   5

Statute miles

Paul Woodward, ©1999 The Countryman Press

must be released immediately, with no trout in possession in the water or on its banks. The rest of the river is governed by general regulations, closed to fishing from March 1 to the third Saturday in April.

Don't miss The TMA in West Willington is the only one in Connecticut that is governed by fly-fishing-only, catch-and-release-only rules, with no closed season. The only other TMA to come close is on the Housatonic River (see chapter 8), but even there, portions of the TMA are closed to angling during the summer. This makes the Willimantic's 3-mile long TMA a sure shot any time of the year, and it's worth the trip.

Best asset Much of the river along the west side of the TMA is protected by the Nye-Holman State Forest and the Kollar Wildlife Management Area (WMA), with the management area extending upstream from Roaring Brook for 2 miles. There is no development here, which has allowed the forest to regenerate and grow large. The water is shaded and cooled by huge maple, ash, and hemlock trees, and the feeling is pleasurably remote.

Biggest drawback I-84 has a Jekyll-and-Hyde effect on the TMA. While its presence helps keep the east bank free from development and the rest area on the highway provides easy access to the middle of the TMA, the deep rumble and constant din from the heavily used highway is never out of earshot. It looks like you're in the wilderness, but it sounds like you're in the heart of the city. In addition, the easy flow and lack of rapids makes the Willimantic a popular canoeing destination, especially for less experienced boaters. Too often they can't maneuver their canoe around or behind you and end up cruising right through the pool you're fishing. You need to keep an eye out for them because you could get run over.

Necessary patterns *Underwater:* Pheasant Tail Nymph (#14–20), Hare's Ear Nymph (#12–16), Hendrickson Nymph (#12–16), Caddis Larva (#14–18), Caddis Emerger (#12–18), Black–Nosed Dace (#4–10). *Dry flies:* Quill Gordon (#12–16); Hendrickson (#12–16); Red Quill (#12–16); Rusty Spinner (#12–16); Mahogany Spinner (#12–16); Green Drake (#6–10); Tan, Yellow, Brown, Green, or Black Caddis (#12–18); Blue-Winged Olive (#12–20); Light Cahill (#14–18); Sulphur (#14–20); Cream Midge (#18–22); Alder (#16-18).

Stocked feeder streams worth a look Hop River (see below), Skungamaug River (see below), Roaring Brook (see below), Cedar Swamp Brook (Mansfield), Conant Brook, Middle River, Furnace Brook.

Other feeder streams (from downstream to upstream) Cider Mill Brook, Dunham Pond Brook, Eagleville Brook, Brigham Tavern Brook, Winding Brook, Clark Brook, Newcomb Brook, South Willington Brook, Green Brook, Grapeville Brook, School Brook, LaBonte Brook, Bonemill Brook.

The Willimantic River hides in plain view. Although it is not far from the Hartford metropolitan area, and in fact is closer to the city than any of the other good fishing covered in this chapter, most of the serious fly anglers from Hartford head west toward the Farmington or Housatonic Rivers or south to the Salmon River in Colchester. And anglers west of the Willimantic have a veritable smorgasbord of rivers and streams from which to choose. That leaves the Willimantic's long stretches much more lightly fished than many of the other good waters in Connecticut.

That's not to say that the Willimantic doesn't get fished. It does, especially early in the season and especially in the TMA in West Willington. But there are plenty of miles of this long river that see little pressure compared with the rest of the state, and they are easy to get to. Particularly upstream from the TMA, long, attractive runs of water are largely ignored, even where they run close to the highway. And where some hiking is needed few anglers ever go.

The river is formed by the confluence of the Middle River, itself a pretty, wooded stream for some of its run, and Furnace Brook. They come together in the heart of Stafford Springs. The good angling begins just south of the center of town on CT 32, the route that follows the river for its entire length. Pull over anywhere along the highway between Stafford Springs and Roaring Brook in West Willington, and you are likely to find strong hatches and good angling.

The Cole W. Wilde TMA runs from the mouth of Roaring Brook downstream to the CT 74 bridge in West Willington, where a section of the Nye-Holman State Forest abuts the west bank. A sign announces the TMA, and there are picnic facilities, parking, and river access. This lower section of the TMA is a boggy backwater but wadeable in low water, and the ideal place for presenting Green Drakes over trout that have seen few anglers.

The most popular segment of the TMA, and the more classic riffle-run-pool water, is upstream. Find North River Road (see "Access"), and walk into the Trestle Pool at the abandoned stone bridge abutments. Downstream, you'll need to pick and choose where you wade because some of the pools are deep. Upstream, you'll find the Tarzan Pool and above it, at the mouth of Roaring Brook, the T-pool.

Downstream from the TMA, there are many crossroads that provide access. They do see a number of anglers, especially early in the season, but well-worn trails lead away from the crowds and to some very fine angling.

The Willimantic has miles and miles of good water; it holds trout well and it gets ample stockings; it has strong hatches and an excellent forage base; it is accessible, yet not overcrowded; and it is very nearby. With all this going for it, don't tell your friends. You might spoil a very good thing.

Roaring Brook

Many anglers use the trail along Roaring Brook to get to the top of the Willimantic's TMA. Few think to stop and fish Roaring Brook unless a good

The productive Cole W. Wilde Trout Management Area on the Willimantic River is productive and popular with other river users as well as anglers .

trout splashes in a pool as they pass by. But Roaring Brook has very high-quality water and holds good trout, many of which move into its waters in the summer when the Willimantic warms. In fact, its lower ¾ mile makes an easy and pleasant meander. Park at the commuter lot at the I-84 on-ramp and walk up Village Hill Road to where it crosses Roaring Brook. Fish back down to and across CT 32 to the Willimantic, or vice versa, fishing upstream. And don't miss the pool at the railroad bridge below the highway.

Hop River

The Hop River flows from east to west, from Manchester all the way to the Willimantic River in Willimantic. Its best areas are paralleled by US 6 and are accessed via many crossroads. To get to some of the best angling away from the crossroads, walk along the abandoned railroad bed from Pucker Street on the lower river to the Gauging Station on Hop River Road and upstream to Parker Brook Road.

Skungamaug River

The Skungamaug River is the major tributary to Hop River; indeed, it provides the majority of the water to the Hop in its headwaters and some very attractive pool–riffle–slick-water angling. It meets the Hop River 1.3 miles northwest of the small town of Andover on US 6. Access is via Times Farm Road or upstream from South Street, Case Road, and North River Road.

NATCHAUG RIVER

Maps *USGS:* Hampton (Phoenixville to Chaplin), Spring Hill (Chaplin to North Windham), Willimantic (Chaplin to the City of Willimantic).

Description The Natchaug is a gem of a river, ideal for the fly-fisherman. It has strong hatches, receives an abundance of stocked trout, and has the deep pools to hold trout over during the low-water runs of summer. Its fertility is proven by the fact that the state record rainbow trout was taken here in 1998, a 14-pound, 10-ounce behemoth that broke the record by more than a pound. Access is good, there are several private campgrounds on its shores, and the Natchaug State Forest makes you think you're somewhere in the remote north, not Connecticut.

Access Access up and down the Natchaug River is exceptionally good because CT 198 parallels its best sections—running up its west shore from South Chaplin to its origins—and because much of the abutting land is state owned in WMAs, state parks, and the large Natchaug State Forest. Crossroads and formal access sites are numerous. Below South Chaplin, access to the lower river is gained via Basset Bridge Road in North Windham and a 1½-mile-long trail along the west bank. There is an abundance of good water here, and walking even a short distance up- or downstream leaves the bridge anglers in the dust.

Regulations The Natchaug is governed by general regulations, closed to fishing from March 1 to the third Saturday in April. There are no limitations on tackle, and the daily limit is five trout.

Don't miss The Natchaug State Forest is the state's second largest, with its entrance well marked off CT 198 in Eastford. There are plenty of picnic areas and hiking trails, and you can walk up and down the river to heart's content.

Best asset Diana's Pool is a state-owned fishing access located on the east side of the river at the cement bridge where CT 198 crosses the Natchaug. It's a series of plunge pools overlooked by granite boulders and cliffs, and it is spectacular. After appreciating the beauty of Diana's Pool, where a young lady is rumored to have died in a lover's quarrel in the 19th century, pool-hop upstream, for these are some of the best year-round trout holding waters in the river.

Biggest drawback Alas, Diana's Pool is a well-known and popular spot, particularly with the students from nearby UConn, who regularly invade the area on warm spring weekends and throughout the summer. While swimming is not allowed in the Natchaug, and particularly here, the temptation to jump from the cliffs into the deep, swirling waters of Diana's Pool sometimes overwhelms spring-invigorated kids, often resulting in injuries and frantic rescues.

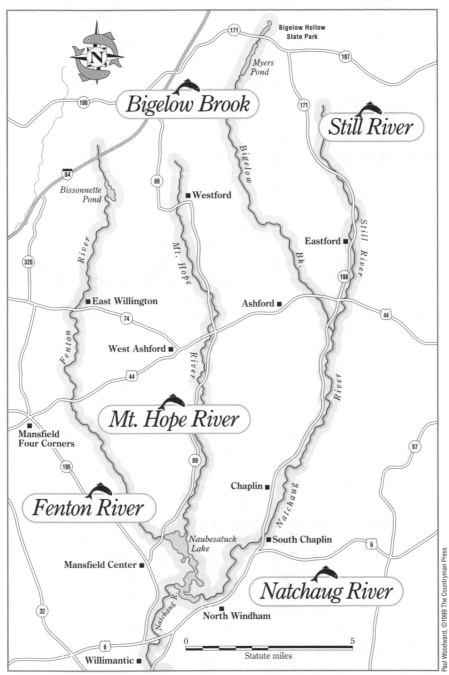

Bigelow Brook

Still River

Bigelow Hollow
State Park

Myers
Pond

171

197

171

190

84

89

Bissonnette
Pond

■ Westford

Bigelow

Still River

Eastford ■

320

Mt. Hope

Bk.

198

■ East Willington

Ashford ■

44

Fenton

River

74

West Ashford ■

River

44

Mt. Hope River

■ Mansfield
Four Corners

89

River

97

195

Chaplin ■

Natchaug

Fenton River

Naubesatuck
Lake

■ South Chaplin

6

Mansfield Center ■

Natchaug River

Natchaug R.

32

■ North Windham

0   5

6

Willimantic ■

Statute miles

Necessary patterns *Underwater:* Pheasant Tail Nymph (#14–20), Dark Hare's Ear Nymph (#12–16), Hendrickson Nymph (#12–16), Cased Caddis (#6–10), Caddis Larva (#14–18), Caddis Emerger (#12–18), Black–Nosed Dace (#4–10). *Dry flies:* Quill Gordon (#12–16); Hendrickson (#12–16); Red Quills (#12–16); Rusty Spinner (#12–16); Mahogany Spinner (#12–16); Green Drake (#6–10); Tan, Yellow, Brown, Green, or Black Caddis (#12–18); Blue-Winged Olive (#12–20); Light Cahill (#14–18); Sulphur (#14–20); Cream Midge (#18–22); Alder (#16–18).

Stocked feeder streams worth a look Bigelow Brook (see below), Still River (see below), Buttonball Brook.

Other feeders (from downstream to upstream) Stonehouse Brook (one of the best native brook trout streams in the state), Turner Brook, Goodwin Brook, Beaverdam Brook, Slovik Brook.

The Natchaug River may well be the best-kept secret in the state of Connecticut. The two streams that form it in Phoenixville, the Still River (see below) and particularly Bigelow Brook (see below), are cold-water sources filled with nutrients and water life. In fact, the source of Bigelow Brook is in the northern end of the Natchaug State Forest, which consists of towering, virginal timber stands that help keep the waters cool and stain them tea colored.

This rich soup of trout water continues to gain volume from other smaller feeder streams, which tumble out of the slopes on both banks of the river all the way downstream to where the Natchaug feeds into Naubesatuck Lake (also known as Mansfield Hollow Lake). In addition, the Natchaug is fed by numerous underground springs, which add to the quality and coolness of the water. The result of these qualities is a free-flowing, fertile trout stream reminiscent of deep-woods Maine.

If you're approaching the Natchaug from the south, find your way to the city of Willimantic and head north on US 6. On the lower river, below the Willimantic Reservoir dam, there is some decent angling, particularly from the accesses at the CT 14 bridge and the US 6 bridge. On the west bank, access is gained via Lauter Park, which is just off CT 195, and you can fish upstream to the good pool just below the I-395 bridge. You can also fish the good stretch of fast water below the Mansfield Hollow dam from the parking lot at the dam, which is found off CT 195 and Mansfield Hollow Road. The Mansfield Hollow dam backs up the water for Naubesatuck Lake, which is entirely surrounded by the Mansfield Hollow State Park and is home to some impressive angling itself. Fly-fishing from a boat or canoe can be very productive in the lake, and there is a boat launch at Basset Bridge along the neck of land that separates the northern basin of the lake

The Natchaug River offers a full array of fishing waters, including riffles, runs, pocket water, and deep plunge pools, like here at Diana's Pool.

from the southern. Note also that both the Fenton and Mount Hope Rivers (see below) feed into the top of the north basin.

The portion of the Natchaug that flows directly above Naubesatuck Lake is also within the confines of the state park, and while its best pools do require a short hike, access can be gained from the bridge at Bates Road in North Windham. Bates Road becomes Bassett Bridge Road in Mansfield. You can hike along the shorelines here, up- or downstream, and there is parking on both the upstream and downstream side of the bridge on the east shore.

By continuing north on US 6, CT 198 meets the highway and continues north along the rest of the length of the Natchaug River. Just after US 6 turns east, Buttonball Brook cuts under CT 198 and you can fish along it until it feeds into the Natchaug a short distance downstream. It's a pretty little mountain brook that often attracts some of the Natchaug's bigger trout. In addition, there is a pair of very attractive pools on the Natchaug just below Buttonball.

Just upstream from the Buttonball bridge, CT 198 crosses over from the east bank to the west bank of the river, and it is at this bridge that Diana's Pool Road cuts off to the east. The state has purchased a fishing access here, and there is parking for a half-dozen cars. A short hike into the woods leads to the famous Diana's Pool, and if you find yourself in the midst of a group of young revelers, either continue hiking upstream or join in the party.

Continuing north on CT 198, you'll find access at the bridges over the river at England Road and North Bear Hill Road. The state owns the land downstream from North Bear Hill Road as part of the Natchaug State Forest, and you can also hike into the river via the Town of Chaplin's town garage just south of North Bear Hill Road. More crossroads, at Marcy Road and Morey Road, provide access farther north on CT 198, and you can fish the water along the privately owned Nickerson's Park Campground property by parking at the campground (and paying a parking fee) and hiking up- or downstream. Nickerson's Park, along with Peppertree Campground and Charlie Brown Campground (which sits at the site of the confluence of Bigelow Brook and the Still River), provide nearly 300 sites and full access to the upper river.

The main access to the state forest and its excellent and extensive river frontage is between Nickerson's Park and Peppertree Campground. A sign shows the way and a road leads down to the river. Plenty of picnic sites, ample parking, and numerous hiking trails are available. You need to remember that the state park is open only from sunrise to sunset, and there is no camping in it. However, the forest here has been preserved and the park is largely undeveloped, so the river and its shores give the aura of being remote and untouched. The fishing benefits from the cooling effects of the huge shade trees, from the tendency of anglers to stay close to the easiest accesses, and from the strong hatches provided by the fertile water.

Bigelow Brook

Bigelow Brook and its more accessible partner, the Still River, meet in Phoenixville to form the Natchaug, but each of them is a worthy fishery in its own right. Bigelow is the more difficult to get to and involves longer hikes. This makes it more attractive to some anglers because it receives less pressure than the Still, but a few crossroads do provide good jumping-off points. US 44 crosses Bigelow Brook just east of Phoenixville. You can hike along the Natchaug Trail both upstream to Ashford Road and downstream, to the Natchaug State Forest, where the Bigelow meets the Still. Above the Ashford Road, the brook meets and follows Westford Road. Following the brook, it shortly crosses under the road and continues north, upstream, to its origins in Bigelow Hollow State Park in Unionville.

The state stocks Bigelow each year, and because of its forested meanderings, there are good holdover trout as well. Use the Natchaug patterns here and pool-hop to your heart's content. General season regulations apply.

Still River

The Still River originates in North Ashford, flows through a number of small man-made ponds, and then follows CT 171 to Kenyonville, where the good fishing starts. Here, CT 171 meets CT 198, which follows the downstream run of the river all the way through Eastford to Phoenixville and its meeting with Bigelow Brook to form the Natchaug. Because the Still is easily accessible from the roads, and because it has a more exposed run through fields and towns, the water is not as high quality, nor does it stay as cool as in the Bigelow. There are, however, annual stockings of trout, mainly rainbows, with some browns put in the lower stretches and fewer brookies in the headwaters. Attractor flies work well in the Still, including Royal Wulffs, Adams, Woolly Worms and Buggers, and even a Stimulator or two. General season regulations apply.

Mount Hope River

The Mount Hope River is one of those hidden jewels of Connecticut's eastern half that has strong hatches of mayflies, caddis, and stoneflies; has an abundance of holdover and stocked trout; and has one of the highest water-quality ratings in the state. It owes this high water quality to two isolated plots of the Natchaug State Forest and the surrounding forests above Warrenville and US 44, where its headwaters emerge from the steep hills of the deep woods. The best angling for fly-fishermen, however, is below Warrenville and particularly above and below the town of Mount Hope.

Access to the Mount Hope is good. CT 89 parallels it for its entire run from its headwaters in Ashford to its mouth in the northeastern corner of the north basin of (Naubesatuck Lake) Mansfield Hollow Lake. Several crossroads provide direct access, but try particularly River Road on the east bank north of the town of Mount Hope and the crossroad between CT 89 and Elizabeth Road just north of Atwoodville.

Use many of the same fly patterns that are listed for the Natchaug River, but adventurous early-season anglers can have good action with the early Little Black Stonefly before the March 1 closing of the season. And note that the state does stock brood-stock rainbow trout in the river each year, so trophy fish are always a possibility. General season regulations apply.

Fenton River

The Fenton River is the mirror image of the Mount Hope River, feeding into the northwestern corner of the north basin of Naubesatuck Lake (Mansfield Hollow Lake). Access is very good, even if there isn't a main highway along its shores, mainly because of the rural Chaffeeville Road, which runs along its east shore from Chaffeeville to Gurleyville, and because the Nipmuck hiking trail follows the river's banks from the mouth all the way upstream to US 44 near Mansfield Four Corners.

The Fenton, like the Mount Hope, has very high-quality water, which translates into good holdover trout populations and excellent insect numbers. And the state recognizes the value of the fishery by stocking ample brookies, brown trout, and rainbows—along with a slug of surplus brood stock—every year.

Access the upper river at US 44 and along Daleville Road, which runs south just west of the US 44 bridge that crosses the Fenton in East Willington. Upstream of US 44, the river becomes a smaller, brook trout–type of stream, but the Moose Meadow Road parallels it from East Willington north to Jared Sparks Road near Gaines Pond.

Mayflies and caddis abound in the Fenton, with stonefly nymphs productive in the faster water sections. And it does have good populations of feed fish, primarily black-nosed dace, so use streamers accordingly, and don't be surprised by the big trout you may find. General season regulations apply.

SHETUCKET RIVER

Maps *USGS:* Willimantic (City of Willimantic to Scotland dam), Scotland (Scotland dam to Baltic bridge), Norwich (Baltic bridge to Thames River).

Description The Shetucket is a large river formed by the meeting of the Willimantic and Natchaug Rivers. It has high water quality, is largely wadeable, produces strong hatches, holds trout well, and receives an annual stocking of Atlantic salmon. The best area is the 4-mile stretch of river below the Scotland dam to the Baltic bridge.

Access The river immediately below Willimantic follows the highway, with pulloffs nearby. Below the CT 203 bridge, short hikes to the river are necessary. The prime 4 miles between the Scotland dam and the Baltic bridge are near roads and parking. As with any popular water, hiking up- or downstream will help you get away from the crowds. There is a large gravel parking lot on the east side of the Baltic bridge.

Regulations The Shetucket is currently governed by general regulations, closed to all fishing from March 1 to the third Saturday in April. There are

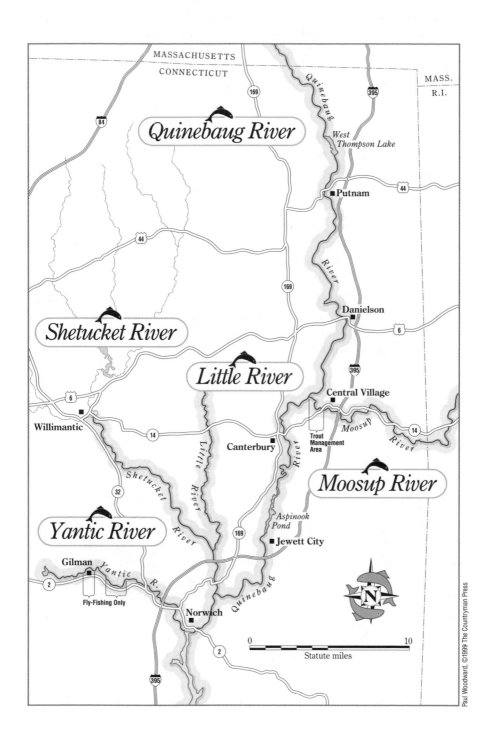

MASSACHUSETTS
CONNECTICUT

MASS.
R.I.

Quinebaug River

West Thompson Lake

■ Putnam

Shetucket River

Danielson

Little River

Central Village

Willimantic

Canterbury

Trout
Management
Area

Moosup River

Moosup River

Yantic River

Gilman

Aspinook
Pond

■ Jewett City

Fly-Fishing Only

Norwich

0   10
Statute miles

N

Paul Woodward, ©1999 The Countryman Press

no limitations on tackle for trout, and the daily limit is five fish. If targeting Atlantic salmon, only fly-fishing is allowed and a one-fish-a-day limit prevails. If a salmon is caught by other means—lures or bait—it must be immediately released.

Don't miss The Atlantic-salmon angling in fall and winter can be an electrifying experience. The fish weigh between 2 and 8 pounds, with some pushing 20 pounds. They are well fed in the hatcheries and in prime condition when they are released, and they respond to the fly and fight with their famed abandon as well as, if not better than, their wild counterparts in Canada. The Shetucket provides an apt setting, and you get all of this for the price of your regular fishing license. No better deal exists anywhere in the United States.

Best asset The Atlantic salmon are unprecedented. Even in the spring, when you're expecting to cast delicate mayfly imitations over feeding trout, a fish pushing 15 pounds can leisurely rise to your fly, suck it in, quickly break you off, and leave you wide-eyed for the rest of your life.

Biggest drawback The Scotland dam is a hydroelectric facility that does not have a terribly large reservoir behind it. It is used primarily as a peak demand supplement to the power grid. This makes for unscheduled water releases, often when families get home in the afternoon and turn on the TVs, the air conditioners, and the ovens all at the same time, or just as the late afternoon hatches are due. And because of the relatively small impoundment behind the dam, water flows below it can be sparse when the managers try to refill the reservoir. The river below the dam often suffers from the "too much or too little" water syndrome throughout the season.

Necessary patterns *Underwater:* Cased Caddis (#6–10), Caddis Larva (#14–18), Caddis Emerger (#12–18), Pheasant Tail Nymph (#14–20), Hare's Ear Nymph (#12–16), Hendrickson Nymph (#12–16), Hornberg (#6–12), Woolly Worm (#6–12), Woolly Bugger (#4–10), Hide and Seek (#4–8), Mickey Finn (#6–12), Black–Nosed Dace (#4–10). *Dry flies:* Quill Gordon (#12–16); Hendrickson (#12–16); Red Quill (#12–16); Tan, Brown, Green, or Black Caddis (#12–18); Blue-Winged Olive (#12–20); Light Cahill (#14–18); Sulphur (#14–20); Cream Midge (#18–22); Alder (#16–18). *Atlantic salmon flies:* Mickey Finn (#0/2–6), Cossaboom (#2–6), Green Highlander (#2–12), Bomber (#0/2–4), Black Bear–Green Butt (#4–12), Green Machine (#6–14).

Stocked feeder streams worth a look Little River (see below), Beaver Brook, Merrick Brook.

Other feeders (from downstream to upstream) Cold Brook (Norwich), Waldo Brook, Indian Hollow Brook, Cold Brook (Franklin), Pigeon Swamp Brook, Larrabe Brook, Obwebetuck Brook, Potash Brook.

The Shetucket River is of major importance in southeastern Connecticut for a pair of reasons. The first is that it receives the flows of two premium watersheds: the Willimantic and the Natchaug. Their confluence, in the city of Willimantic, creates the Shetucket and guarantees a very high quality of water that supports a strong cold-water fishery for the river's 18-mile length. It is also fed by the Quinebaug River (see below) and joins the smaller Yantic River (see below) in Norwich to form the Thames River, which then makes its 15-mile run to the sea.

The second reason that the Shetucket draws attention is its designation as one of only two locations in the state where excess brood-stock Atlantic salmon are released (the other is the Naugatuck). The program was started in 1992 when the federal government decided that they were wasting a valuable resource by killing and discarding unneeded brood-stock fish. Now they distribute the fish throughout the New England region, and only in Connecticut and New Hampshire are the fish released into moving water, their natural habitat. The other New England states generally release them into still-water lakes and ponds.

The salmon are currently stocked in fall and early winter, as many as 600 of them, depending on availability, in each of the two rivers. We can only hope that the Atlantic Salmon Restoration Program, which generates the fish, will remain strong—at least until there are enough naturally returning runs of wild fish to supply much more widespread angling.

Like most major rivers in southern New England, the Shetucket power has been amply tapped, with dams in Scotland, Occum, and Greenville. And the urban areas of Willimantic and Norwich might at first put one off from exploring the river. But south of Willimantic, along CT 32, the river quickly finds its natural streambed, is wide and wadeable, and is largely overlooked. Crossing to the east side of the river on Windham Center Road, CT 203, and traveling the back roads through South Windham, Scotland, and Sprague, the rolling, rural countryside is a true surprise. The fishing for both trout and salmon, particularly below the Scotland dam for 4 miles to the Baltic bridge, is truly outstanding.

Access is excellent by car from Willimantic downstream to just below the CT 203 bridge on the west side of the river because CT 32 parallels it. From the CT 203 bridge down the east bank, there is some limited access along the country lane—Jerusalem Road—which becomes Station Road in Scotland, and then Waldo Road, which meets CT 97 near the Baltic bridge. Near the Scotland dam tailwater, you can hike down a steep bank from the east shore.

For the most part, however, access to the prime lower section between Scotland dam and the Baltic bridge is from the bridge, where CT 97 crosses the river to meet CT 207. You can hike upstream on the east bank for about a half mile before the boulders and steep bank make it treacherous. Or cross the bridge and hike up the path along the river, fishing its many attractive pools, riffles, and runs, for 2 miles. Access to the upper 2 miles is via Holton Road, 2 miles along CT 207 west. A short hike takes you to the tailwater by bearing left at the fork; bear right for the area named, Sandy Beach.

Little River

The Little River feeds into the Shetucket in Versailles/Occum, but it is the 7-mile section from the Hanover Reservoir in Hanover upstream to the Pudding Hill WMA that draws the most interest from anglers. Access is via the WMA and downstream at CT 14 (Westminster Road), the Ulasik Road bridge, Goodwin Road (which is an unpaved road on the east side), and the Hanover Road bridge.

These accesses are heavily fished early in the season, but a short hike away from them puts you into the woods, away from the crowds. There are good holding pools and riffles all along this section, with many of the same hatches as the Shetucket. The river here averages 30 feet wide, and the Thames Valley chapter of TU floats stocking platforms down the stream to insure that the fish are widespread. You'll be surprised at how easy it is to get away from it all and back into some very attractive country. General season regulations apply.

Quinebaug River

The Quinebaug River could easily become one of the major trout streams of eastern Connecticut, but alas, it suffers from poor water management, limited access (especially in its lower reaches), and, if not disrespect for its potential, at least second-class status as a trout stream. The major problems on the river stem from several hydroelectric generating projects—particularly one in Jewett City on the lower river and another in Danielson. Their unpredictable water releases can make wading a dangerous pastime, and their holding back of water behind the dams warms the river to dangerous—even lethal—temperatures for trout and forage in summer. And it's too bad, because the Quinebaug is a big, long river with a very high potential.

Still, there is some trout fishing from the limited stocking that the state does in spring. Much of the lower river can be waded when the river is down, but access is a problem, with only two places actually available to anglers. The first is reached via CT 138 east in Jewett City and by turning right onto Wedgewood Lane, which leads to a gravel parking lot that nestles between a railroad bed and the local water-treatment facility. The second is behind the state highway garage just north of the Shetucket on CT 12. Two other former accesses, one at the Knights of Columbus building in Jewett City and the other off the Bayberry Road cul-de-sac in Lisbon, are no longer available. Brown trout sometimes do show up here and in decent size, but just as often the rise you're fishing to will be a small or largemouth bass, a crappie, or a panfish; and on the bottom, eels or brown bullheads.

If you fish the upper section of the Quinebaug, choose the 9.5 miles from the Danielson dam downstream to the CT 14 bridge in Canterbury near CT 6. Concentrate particularly on the 5 miles from the CT 205 bridge in Wauregan downstream past the mouth of the Moosup River (see below) and through the Quinebaug State WMA. Because the majority of this area is protected from development, most of it provides a pleasant, tree-lined background for casting over stocked and holdover trout. It helps that the cooling waters of the Moosup join the Quinebaug near the Quinebaug Valley State Fish Hatchery in Central Village, and it also helps that the state stocks nearly half the total number of trout for the entire 50 miles of the river in this short run. Excellent access to the lower Moosup and up- and downstream on the Quinebaug is gained via the hatchery, which is found off CT 14.

Along with the Moosup River, three other important tributaries deserve exploring. The first is Pachaug River, which flows from Pachaug State Forest to Jewett City and receives intermittent stockings of trout in the few flowing-water stretches between the six man-made lakes and ponds that interrupt its flow to the Quinebaug. The Pachaug really has better still-water fishing, but do try both Mount Misery Brook and Myron Kinney Brook, which feed into it.

Mount Misery flows out of Phillip's Pond north of the Pachaug River in Pachaug State Forest, and it flows due south entirely in the state forest to Beachdale Pond. Myron Kinney Brook flows due north through the section of the Pachaug State Forest just south of the Pachaug River. The brook runs between CT 201 and CT 49 in Voluntown, and you can get onto it via Hodge Road and fish it downstream all the way to Glasgo Pond.

The second major tributary to the Quinebaug River is Five Mile River, a stream with limited access, some holdover trout, and decent hatches. It runs from Quaddick Reservoir in Thompson through Putnam and into Danielson, where it joins the Quinebaug. The area of most interest to fly-fishermen is in Putnam from US 44 to Five Mile River Road.

The third tributary that might tempt anglers is the French River, which originates in Massachusetts but flows due south through Thompson, paralleling CT 12. It receives ample stockings but runs through the center of the town of North Grosvenor Dale, so there is little solitude. It's fishable, however, from North Grosvenordale Pond downstream to Blain Road.

Moosup River

The Moosup River is a high-quality trout stream that runs from the east, out of Rhode Island, to the west, where it enters the Quinebaug in Central

Village. It originates in the rolling highlands of western Rhode Island (see the Moosup River in Rhode Island) as a pure, fertile headwater, and it gains water from many small tributaries and underground springs. This high water quality is maintained along its entire run and fosters excellent holdover and stream-born trout, as well as strong insect hatches and an excellent feed-fish forage base.

Connecticut has recognized the potential of this stream and has flagged its last 1½ miles—the run below the CT 14 bridge in Central Village—as a TMA, where all trout caught must be immediately released unharmed. In addition, the lower ¾ mile of the management area is for fly-fishing only, whereas the upper ¾ mile allows the use of flies, bait, and lures.

Access to the entire run of the Moosup in Connecticut is excellent. From the CT 14 bridge upstream, there are many pulloffs and parking lots along CT 14 eastbound through the village of Moosup proper and into Almyville and Sterling. Church Street in Sterling gives some access to the river and drops down to CT 14A in the village of Oneco, where the river flows out of Oneco Pond under the road.

The fly-fisherman's main interest, however, remains in the TMA. Access the upper half via the CT 14 bridge and the Old Bridge Turnaround (it's labeled) right at CT 14. The lower access is via a dirt road and a quarter-mile hike adjacent to the hatchery. This road is within the state property, and vehicular traffic is prohibited. The short hike leads not only to the river, but away from any semblance of civilization. Bear left at the fork, and go down to the river, which resembles remote waters from northern Maine, complete with overhanging hemlocks, quick sharp turns in the river, deep pools, and fertile riffles. Bearing right at the fork leads toward the mouth of the river at the Quinebaug.

The Moosup has all of the good hatches—mayflies, caddis, and stoneflies in the faster runs—but it's also a fertile feed-fish factory, making streamers like the Black-Nosed Dace, the Ghosts, Woolly Buggers, and the like particularly effective. Don't miss it.

Yantic River

The Yantic River is not properly a tributary of the Shetucket, but rather joins the Shetucket in Norwich to form the Thames River. It is a smaller, much more intimate stream than the Shetucket, however, and is properly placed here. It also suffers from the problem of being a superb trout stream with sometimes intense angling pressure, and this dilemma has given rise to an unusual set of fly-fishing-only regulations on a pair of sections. The regulations state simply that in these two sections only artificial flies and standard fly-fishing methods may be used, but creel limits and season-open dates remain the same as in general regulation streams. So the special reg-

The Moosup River has high-quality water and holds trout well, especially in the Trout Management Area near the state trout hatchery, shown here.

ulation areas, along with the entire stream, are open to fishing from the third Saturday in April to the end of February. You can kill a standard limit of five fish a day, but you can only use flies in the special regulation areas.

The upstream fly-fishing-only section starts about 200 yards above the "Turnaround" pool, itself about ¾ mile upstream from the intersection of Old Colchester Road and Waterman Road, adjacent to Exit 22 of CT 2, on the north side of the river. The fly-fishing-only area runs downstream for about 700 yards, and it is amply posted on the stream banks. The lower section starts where Stanton Road crosses the river about a mile below the above-named intersection and ends where the Old Colchester Road crosses back across the river from the south shore to the north, at a bridge referred to as Johnson's Bridge. This lower section is about 1½ miles long and is referred to as "Sullivan's Meadows."

Old Colchester Road is the main rural access road to all of the good angling on the Yantic and can be reached from Exits 22, 23, 24, and 25 of CT 2 (a major four-lane highway running east and west from Norwich to Colchester and beyond to Hartford). There is an excellent variety of angling in the fly-fishing-only sections, which simply reflects the qualities of the entire river.

The main aquatic insects in the Yantic include the full array of mayflies, along with some decent stoneflies. A small (size 18–20) black caddis often comes off the water and confounds even experienced fly anglers. Along the meadow pools, terrestrials work well, and small streamers—like the Black-Nosed Dace and the Mickey Finn—work well, especially early in the season.

Other Thames River Tributaries

Hunt's Brook flows through some very pretty countryside from Montville to Waterford. Access is via Unger Road and Fire Street above Lake Cuheca and Miller Pond Road below the lake. Indiantown Brook, also known as Shewville Brook, meanders east from Avery Pond through the Rose Hill WMA through Poquetanuck to Poquetanuck Cove on the Thames River. There's a variety of water with decent access, especially in the WMA.

Other Stocked Streams in Eastern Connecticut

Tolland County *Ellington and East Windsor:* Broad Brook; *Ellington and Somers:* Charter Brook; *Hebron:* Fawn Brook; Raymond Brook; *Marlborough:* Fawn Hill Brook; *Somers:* Abbey Brook; Gillette Brook; Gulf Stream; Hope Valley Brook; Scantic River; Thrasher Brook; Watchaug Brook; Woods Stream; *Stafford:* Cedar Swamp Brook; Crystal Lake Brook; Delphi Brook; *Tolland:* New City Brook; *Windsor:* Broad Brook.

Windham County *Ashford:* Knowlton Brook; *Brooklyn:* Blackwells Brook; *Brooklyn and Pomfret:* White Brook; *Canterbury:* Corry Brook; Kitt Brook; Tatnic Brook; *Eastford and Woodstock:* Bungee Brook; *Killingly:* Whetstone Brook; *Killingly and Plainfield:* Snake Meadow Brook; *Plainfield:* Ekonk Brook; Horse Brook; Lathrop Brook; Mill Brook; *Pomfret:* Mashamoquet Brook; Quaker Meeting House Brook; *Putnam:* Little River; Mary Brown Brook; *Sterling:* Cedar Swamp Brook; Quanduck Brook; *Thompson:* Five Mile Brook; Long Branch Brook; *Woodstock:* Mill Brook; Muddy Brook; Taylor Brook.

New London County *Bozrah:* Gardner Brook; Trading Cove Brook; *Bozrah and Lebanon:* Pease Brook; *Colchester and Marlborough:* Dickinson Creek; *Columbia and Lebanon:* Ten Mile River; *Franklin:* McCarthys Brook; Mountain Brook; *Franklin and Lebanon:* Susquetonscut Brook; *Griswold and North Stonington:* Billings Brook; *Groton:* McGuire Brook; *Groton and Ledyard:* Haley Brook; Joe Clark Brook; *Lebanon:* Bartlet Brook; Exeter Brook; *Ledyard:* Billings Avery Brook; Seth Williams Brook; *Ledyard and Stonington:* Whitfords Brook; *Lisbon:* Blissville Brook; *Lyme:* Roaring Brook; *Montville:* Oxoboxo Brook; Stony Brook; *North Stonington:* Lantern Hill Brook; Pendleton Hill Brook; Wyassup Brook; *Preston:* Broad Brook; Choate Brook; *Stonington:* Anguila Brook; Copps Brook; *Voluntown:* Denison Brook; Great Meadow Brook; Lowden Brook; Wood River; *Waterford:* Jordan Brook.

Stocked Lakes and Ponds in Eastern Connecticut:

Tolland County *Ellington:* Shenipsit Lake; *Ellington and Stafford:* Crystal Lake; *Mansfield:* Bicentennial Pond; *Somers:* Bald Mountain Pond; *Union:* Bigelow Pond; Mashapaug Lake; *Vernon:* Walkers Reservoir.

Windham County *Killingly:* Alexander Lake; Wauregan Reservoir; *Mansfield:* Mansfield Training Ponds; *Plainfield:* Childrens Pond (Quinebaug Valley Hatchery); Moosup Pond; Public Fishing Ponds (Quinebaug Valley Hatchery); *Thompson:* Keach Pond; Little Pond; *Windham:* Beaver Brook Pond; *Woodstock:* Black Pond; Roseland Lake.

New London County *Bozrah:* Gardner Lake; *Colchester:* Day Pond; *East Lyme:* Dodge Pond; *Ledyard and North Stonington:* Lantern Hill Pond; Long Pond; *Lyme:* Norwich Pond; Uncas Lake; *Lyme and Old Lyme:* Rogers Lake; *Montville:* Fort Shantock Pond; *North Stonington:* Billings Lake; Godfrey Pond; Hewitt Pond; Wyassup Lake; *Norwich:* Mohegan Park Pond; *Preston:* Amos Lake; *Salem:* Horse Pond; *Voluntown:* Beach Pond; Green Falls Reservoir.

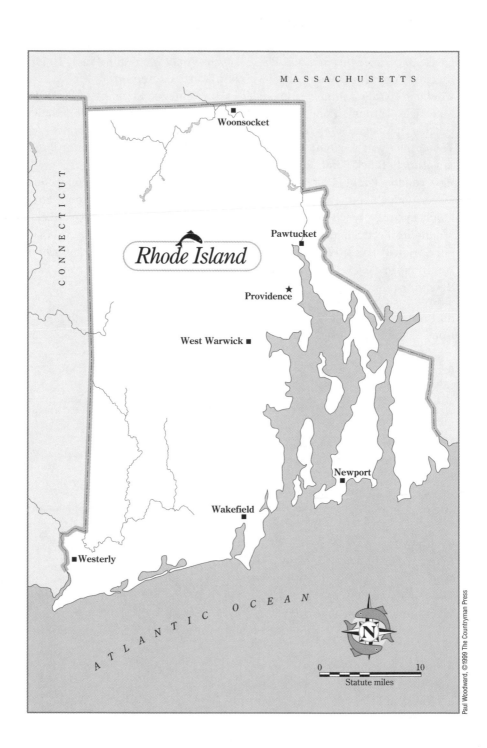

III | RHODE ISLAND

Rhode Island is a deceptively small, seemingly overpopulated state. It ranks dead last in size and is the second-most densely populated state (to New Jersey) in the Union. No angler in his right mind could hope to find trout, much less decent fly-fishing for trout here, right? Wrong.

Rhode Island does have its share of problems in dealing with too many people in too few acres, but it does a commendable job of providing some superb trout fishing. The state even has a few reaches of streams that allow a person to get back into the country, to get away from it all. And there are not only good trout in these streams, but decent hatches of mayflies and caddis. True, cold-water-loving stoneflies that require highly oxygenated water are not abundant, but in some of the streams, they are not only present, but provide a substantial portion of the trout's diet.

While Rhode Island's two most famous rivers, the Moosup and the Wood, are first-class, blue-ribbon waters, other much less well-known waters can offer hours and days of pleasure. The Pawtuxet River has high-quality water and huge potential. The two streams that form the Wood River—the Falls River and the Flat River—have all of the qualities of the Wood, if on a smaller scale, and flow through wooded, protected watersheds. The Ponaganset River has a deep-woods, remote feel to it. And even the Blackstone is making a remarkable comeback and now holds trout.

In addition, the Division of Fish and Wildlife is itself stocked with biologists and workers who tirelessly devote themselves to the improvement of Rhode Island's inland waters. They are not and never have been content with the status quo, and they endlessly sample waters, work at improving habitat, and ensure that there are plenty of trout to go around. As with fish and wildlife department rank-and-file members throughout southern New England and the country, they are to be commended for their selfless efforts and genuine concern for the resources. I applaud them.

The twelve rivers that are discussed below represent the best flowing-water trout streams that Rhode Island has to offer. They are certainly the cream of the crop of the state's rivers. But don't ignore any of the trout streams or lakes and ponds within the confines of the Ocean State. They can all provide good angling and plenty of self-fulfillment for anyone willing to get out there and ply their waters.

Rhode Island Trout Waters: North to South

BLACKSTONE RIVER

Maps *USGS:* Providence (Pawtucket), Attleboro (Pawtucket to Woonsocket), Franklin (Woonsocket), Uxbridge (Woonsocket to Massachusetts border).

Description The Blackstone River in Rhode Island is urban. It runs through what can only be called a naturalist's worst nightmare. Factories back up to it, along with the tenement housing that inevitably grew along with the factories. And highways, shopping malls, department stores, gas stations, and all of the support that a large population demands line both shores of the river. The corridor that is the Blackstone Valley is widely known as being the birthplace of the Industrial Revolution, and that designation made the Blackstone also the first river to be truly abused, polluted, and ignored.

With the growth of the environmental movement, however, the Blackstone became a prime target for cleanup, and years of effort have made the river clean flowing again and pleasurable to fish. Although the identification and elimination of sources of pollution was (and is) a huge undertaking, it has been successful to the point to which the Rhode Island Department of Fish and Wildlife began stocking trout into it in 1995.

As with many urban flows, the Blackstone now offers something of an island of nature amidst the follies of man. Shoreline vegetation has returned and matured, attracting with it a surprising abundance of wildlife. And with the river clean and fertile again, wildfowl and wading birds have returned, too.

While this turnabout seems to offer nothing but good news, the river is still highly manipulated, with numerous dams backing up and warming the water. Trout do not hold well over the hot summer, and cold-water-loving mayflies are scarce. There is an abundance of caddis life for hatch matchers, however, and enough forage in the form of minnows, suckers, chubs, and the like, that the stocked trout quickly adapt and respond well to imitations.

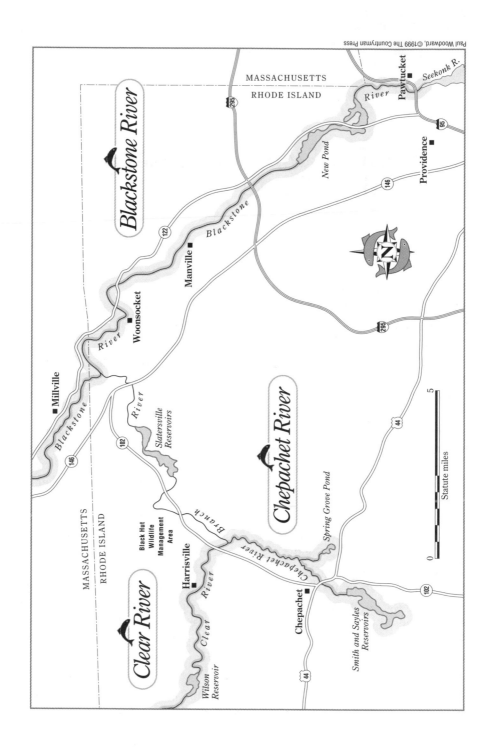

Access Access to the Blackstone River is good and improving. As a National Heritage River Valley Corridor, much has been done to ensure access to the river. State parks have been established, and a bike path along the river has begun to be built. Currently it runs from the Whipple bridge on Mendon Street (RI 122) in Cumberland, upstream to the Ashton dam just above the high-arching RI 116 bridge some 4 miles away. Plans in the near future call for unlimited access to the entire river, not only in Rhode Island, but all the way to the river's origins in Worcester, Massachusetts.

Regulations The Blackstone River falls under general Rhode Island regulations, with a trout season opening date of the second Saturday in April, closing on the last day in February. From December 1 to the close of the season the daily limit is two fish; the limit is six fish during the rest of the season.

Don't miss The best fishing is at the base of and directly downstream from the dams. The trout congregate here and in the good water flows below the dams, and the forage does, too. The best angling is below four of the seven dams in the state: near River Island Park in Woonsocket at the South Main Street bridge; the run at Albion bridge on Albion Road in the Albion section of Lincoln; at the base of the Ashton dam just above the RI 116 bridge (George Washington Highway) in the Blackstone River State Park; and just below the sluice gates at the Old Pratt dam in Lonsdale.

Best asset The Blackstone River has been saved because the large number of corridor users came together to demand, and get, water quality and recreational improvements. Hikers, bikers, canoers, fishermen, and everyday people formed a coalition whose voice could not be ignored, and together they have seen vast improvements along and in the river. They aren't done yet, and in the future full access to the river will become a reality. Anglers can even hope that the thermal pollution of the river—from warm-water returns and obsolete dams—will be addressed, too. Keep an eye on the Blackstone. It has the potential to be the best trout river in the state.

Biggest drawback Being an urban flow is a mixed blessing. Water power attracted industrialists and caused the pollution of the river. The combined voices of the large populace have helped restore it. But when you put this many people this close to a natural asset, you are going to get heavy use. And when you get heavy use, you're bound to have conflicts. Canoers and tubers might float through the best trout pools. Bikers and joggers will vie for rights of way. And always there'll be litter, in spite of everyone's best efforts to prevent it. The Blackstone is not pristine and probably never can be.

Necessary patterns *Underwater:* Pheasant Tail Nymph (#14–20), Hare's Ear Nymph (#12–16), Caddis Larva (#14–18), Caddis Emerger (#12–18), Black-Nosed Dace (#4–10), Mickey Finn (#4–12). *Dry flies:* Adams (#12–20); Royal Wulff (#10–14); March Brown (#12–14); Mahogany Dun (#12–16);

Mahogany Spinner (#10–16); Tan, Yellow, Brown, Green, or Black Caddis (#12–18); Blue-Winged Olive (#12–20); Trico (#18–24); Alder (#16–18); Cricket (#10–14); Hopper (#4–12); Black and Cinnamon Ant (#10-20).

Stocked feeder streams worth a look Sylvester Pond (Woonsocket, directly adjacent to the Blackstone); Harris River (Woonsocket, the outflow of Harris Pond in Blackstone, Massachusetts), Clear River (see below), and Chepachet River (see below) join in Oakland to form the Branch River, which feeds into the Blackstone in Woonsocket; Aldrich Brook (Butterfly Pond).

Other feeders (from downstream to upstream) Happy Hollow Pond outlet; Monastery Brook; Sneech Brook; Rochambeau Ponds Brook; Crookfall Brook; Peters River; Fox Brook.

The Blackstone River originates in Massachusetts and runs for 17 miles through Rhode Island along the urban landscape from Woonsocket to Pawtucket before draining into the Seekonk River and Providence Harbor at the top of Narragansett Bay. The river here is rarely far from the back of a factory, the arches of some busy road bridge, or the hubbub of urban life. Yet down by the river's edge, a swath of green nature has reclaimed the shores of this once highly polluted—even deadly—flow.

Even with the reemergence of the appreciation for clean-flowing rivers in the 1960s and '70s, the Blackstone River was considered all but impossible to reclaim. Municipal sewage ran untreated into it, industrial outflows were unnoticed or ignored, and the river was universally shunned. Its inherent beauty and intrinsic value were finally recognized with the creation of the Blackstone National Heritage River Valley Corridor and innumerable grassroots organizations and individuals. Slowly the river has regained its health.

Now, not only does the river flow cleanly, but increasingly longer sections of its banks are being protected by the Blackstone River State Park and by the creation of a bike path along its shores from the Massachusetts line to its mouth. The work isn't done yet, but there is an impressive start, especially along 4 miles of river from Lonsdale upstream to Ashton, where the bike path has been completed.

For trout anglers, plying the waters of the Blackstone is a relatively new experience. Only since 1995 has the water quality been good enough to support the trout that the Division of Fish and Wildlife stock into it. The river is stocked before the season opens and again during spring and fall, but lethal water temperatures are a glaring problem during the height of summer.

These high water temperatures are a function of the heavy use of the river both now and in the past. Seven dams block the flow in Rhode Island, and behind each the water sits there and heats up. There is still industrial use of the water, too, and the water is not always returned to the streambed

You're never very far from cities or suburbia on the Blackstone River, but there are man-made features to appreciate, too, like the high arching bridge of CT 116 shown here.

at or below its original temperature. And of course there is the simple fact that urban areas are hot themselves. Rain falling on asphalt streets and roofs gets a quick temperature boost, then runs into the river.

When the water temperatures are optimal in spring and fall, however, the stocked trout are active and they acclimate very quickly. And make no mistake, the Blackstone River is now very attractive to fish. It's big enough to offer plenty of refuges for the trout, making searching them out challenging, and its water volume is ample to support insect life—particularly caddis—and a variety of forage fish. Indeed, if you put the Blackstone into a rural setting, it would rival any of the famous trout waters of southern

New England—waters like the Housatonic, Farmington, or Deerfield Rivers. It has the potential to be that good.

As it is now, the river is a very pleasant surprise. You can easily spend several days investigating it, and you'll find plenty of trout, especially in the runs and rapids below the dams (see "Don't miss," above). If there is a problem, it's the increased awareness of all who live nearby (see "Biggest drawback," above), but better to have an abundance of river stewards, as there is now, than to have none, as there was before.

Will the Blackstone ever gain the status of a destination-type trout stream? It's difficult to tell. But it is a certainty that all of the work that has gone into revitalizing and rejuvenating the river has resulted in huge rewards. If this zealous interest and work continues, it just might become the teeming river it once was.

Clear River

The Clear River is the major tributary of Wilson Reservoir in the Bridgeton section of Burrillville. It flows from the reservoir due east through Graniteville and Harrisville to its meeting with the Chepachet River (see below) in Oakland to form the Branch River, a major tributary of the Blackstone River.

Both the Clear and Chepachet Rivers are worth exploring for trout, but the Clear is the better of the two, being more extensive with better access and a higher quality of habitat, fish, and forage.

As is typical of most flowing water in Rhode Island, the Clear River has been amply tapped for its waterpower. There are no less than five dams on it in its 6-mile run from Wilson Reservoir to Oakland. They provide only a minor inconvenience, however, and the waters behind them can produce some decent still-water angling from a belly boat or canoe. The flows below the dams generally are attractive and productive.

The stretch from Harrisville to Oakland is the lower end of the river, is larger, and provides some good fly-fishing in a generally rural setting. Get onto the river via RI 107 (Sweets Hill Road) in Harrisville or downstream via Whipple Avenue, which turns south off RI 107. Clear River Drive also parallels the river's south bank and is reached off RI 102 (Bronco Highway) in Oakland.

The Fish and Game Department flags the Clear River as an excellent trout water, and it receives fish before the season and all through it. Attractor flies, like a Royal Wulff, a March Brown, or an Adams, will work well, and there are a few mayfly hatches to match and a good supply of caddis.

Chepachet River

The Chepachet River originates out of Spring Grove Pond, itself an excellent trout fishery, in the Chepachet section of Glocester and flows due north to its meeting with the Clear River in Oakland. From its source to its mouth it's less than 4 miles long, but much of its run is tree lined and rural.

Access the best section of the river from Douglas Hook Road, which is an extension of Jack's Way, an east turn from the center of Chepachet. Fish downstream, north, from tiny Malbourn Pond and the bridge. This remote stretch runs for about 2 miles to the Gazza Road bridge in Gazzaville, or if you want to, you can hike up to the Gazza Road, to the east, by using Gazza Hill as a landmark. The hill sits about halfway between the two bridges. At the Gazza Road bridge, the water flow slows as it enters Gillcran Pond. The short stretch of river between Spring Grove Pond and Malbourn Pond also holds fish.

Ponaganset River

The Ponaganset River is lovely little sweet-water stream in Foster that rises up on the slopes of Mount Hygeia and runs through some pretty country southeastward before draining into the Barden Reservoir and then the Scituate Reservoir. Its best fishing is in the headwater run upstream from the Barden Reservoir, which is best accessed from the top of Hopkins Mill Pond, itself adjacent to the Old Danielson Pike in South Foster. You can also hike down to the stream along Winsor Brook, which is adjacent to Winsor Cemetery on Windsor Road. Find Windsor Road by turning north off the Old Danielson Pike in South Foster. The cemetery and brook are about 1½ miles along.

The Fish and Wildlife Department also owns a public fishing area in the headwaters of the Ponaganset in North Foster. Find this half-mile-long run of water by turning east onto Pine Tree Road from Mount Hygeia Road (RI 94), which is called Foster Center Road south of US 6. You can also find the access from the opposite shore off Windsor Road.

The run from the public fishing access to Hopkins Mill Pond is about 2 miles long through a forest that makes you think that you're miles from civilization. And the stream has plenty of riffles and runs, and in a few places some nice plunge pools where trout are likely to hold. There is a decent March Brown hatch and a few smaller mayflies at the height of spring, but caddis make up the bulk of the hatching activity. In late spring and early summer, try some small black and cinnamon ant patterns; medium-sized attractor patterns work well the whole season. The state stocks the Ponaganset before the season, throughout spring, and again in fall.

Pawtuxet River

The North Branch of the Pawtuxet River has the potential to be an outstanding tailwater trout fishery. Unfortunately, except for the short run of river below the Kent dam of the Scituate Reservoir in the Hope section of Scituate, the river has little access and few, if any, trout. Indeed, the only section of any part of the Pawtuxet River system, North or South Branches included, that the state stocks is the North Branch of the Pawtuxet River above the dam of Hope Pond in Hope. And the flow of water into Hope Pond is highly variable because of irregular releases of water from the reservoir, making the stream above the pond a hit-or-miss proposition.

This short section, from the reservoir to the Hope Pond dam, is only about 2 miles long, and better than half of it is the still water of the pond itself. The 1 mile of flowing water is accessible only by paddling a canoe up to the inflow and then hiking upstream, or by asking permission from one of the local landowners to cross their property to the river. Fish and Wildlife officials advise caution when you are near the Kent dam, because the reservoir police are extremely strict about enforcing the no-fishing restriction that applies to their jurisdiction.

Yet even with these problems, this little section of pond and river can be very enjoyable to fish. The water is pure and cold, bringing with it nutrients and supporting forage very well. And because of the Hope Pond dam and the high-water quality, the still-water angling can be exceptional.

Find the state-owned boat launch ramp in Hope on Old Furnace Road near the fire station. Turn west onto the road, and the paved ramp is about 400 feet along on the right. Old Furnace Road turns off East Road (RI 116) near the Coventry–Scituate line. Note that no outboard motors of any kind, except electric trolling motors, are allowed.

In Hope Pond and in the river above it, there are some decent hatches of mayflies and a few caddis, but mostly midges prevail. In the still water, brightly colored streamers—like Cardinelles, Mickey Finns, or Marabou Muddlers—work well. The state does recognize the high quality of this short fishery and stocks it before the season and during spring and fall.

Moosup River

The Moosup River is one of Rhode Island's most attractive trout streams for a number of reasons. First, it is free flowing with no dams to impede its progress, an almost unheard of accomplishment in this state. Second, the Moosup is as remote as a river can be in the nation's second-most densely populated state. Sitting out on the western border with Connecticut, in Foster and Coventry, rural is the rule, and the river flows through some very pretty, unspoiled country. Third, the water is very high quality and fertile, with plenty of spring seeps and canopy cover to help keep it cold, giving the trout and the ample forage a chance to survive summer's heat. Last, the very best angling on the Moosup in Rhode Island is protected from development because the lower flow is contained within the boundaries of the Nichol's Farm Wildlife Management Area (WMA), a fact that also makes access assured.

The Moosup originates out of Clark Pond near the North Sterling section of the town of Foster as a tiny rill. It quickly picks up volume from a half-dozen small feeders and becomes fishable at the Harrington Road bridge. Harrington Road connects Cucumber Hill Road on the west to Green Bush Road on the east. The river is not large here, and just downstream it flows into a marsh, but there are some stocked trout in this run and an occasional holdover if you can get to them downstream.

In the Moosup Valley section, which is really nothing much more than a bend in the road at the end of Cucumber Hill Road, the Moosup Valley Road crosses the river, giving access. And on the east side, Potter Road turns south and parallels the river downstream to Vaughn Hollow, where Barb's Hill Road turns west and over the river. Continue south past Vaughn Hollow and the road intersects with RI 14, the Plainfield Pike. Turn west to the bridge, and fish downstream.

While the river to this point is attractive and fertile, it is this lower section, starting at the RI 14 bridge, that is the most attractive and provides the best fly-fishing. The Moosup is still not a large river here, but it is large enough to harbor decent trout, plenty of mayflies and caddis, an occasional stonefly, and good feed fish. Use flies that approximate what's on or in the water and small streamers like Black-Nosed Dace and Muddlers for best results when the water is running high or is roiled.

The run from RI 14 to the Connecticut border is about 3½ river miles long, but about halfway along, the river makes a sharp west turn, changing from its due-south flow for the first time. Except for the very elbow of this run, the Moosup is entirely contained within the Nichol's Farm WMA. You can hike and fish downstream from the RI 14 bridge, or you can take the first south turn on the west side of the river and hike down an old dirt road to the river. If you want, you can keep hiking downstream to an old railroad grade bed, which in turn leads east out to Lewis Farm Road, which connects to RI 17 north and back to RI 14 at Fairbanks Corner just east of the bridge over the river. Or you can park at the end of the railroad bed and fish up- or downstream.

The railroad-grade bed parallels the north bank of the river right to the Connecticut line and is easy to follow. Or, you can turn west onto Nicholas Road from Lewis Farm Road, park at the dirt road a half mile along, and hike north to the river. It's pretty much your choice, because the river is full of fish, being stocked throughout the season, and it has good holding water all up and down this stretch. Get away from the easiest accesses, and you'll have the stream to yourself. You may just think that you've discovered one of those pristine north country trout streams. The Moosup is just plain that good.

And by the way, Carbuncle Pond, just west of the RI 14 bridge, is one of the few pure cold-water ponds in the state. It holds trout exceptionally well throughout the season.

Hunt River

The Hunt River is the extreme opposite of the Moosup River. It's on the opposite side of the state, flowing mostly as the border between East Greenwich and North Kingstown. It flows mostly from south to north. You'll never feel like you're in the wilds of Rhode Island—the Hunt is urban and coastal, skirting the urban areas of East Greenwich and feeding into the Potowomut River and Narragansett Bay.

The Hunt is interesting, however, because it has a long natural flow, interrupted only by Potowomut Pond, and its slow flow creates some nice, deep holding water. In addition, access to the Hunt is good, with several bridges providing jumping-off points—notably at both the RI 403 (Davisville Road) and 402 (Frenchtown Road) bridges and at the US 1 bridge.

The water quality is fairly decent in the Hunt for being so urban, and the state stocks it with trout throughout the season. Look for some big mayflies, brown and green drakes, late in spring, but deep-running nymphs and streamers will work best most of the time.

Falls River

The Falls River is hidden in the west-central side of Rhode Island and contains the state's only catch-and-release, artificial-lure-only section of a trout stream. It is a pretty, unspoiled stream that is not large but has plenty to offer fly-fishermen, who can often find refuge along its shores in early spring when many of the state's other streams are overrun with anglers. That's one of the primary benefits of a no-kill stream.

The Falls River can be difficult to find because most maps mislabel this little jewel of a stream as the Wood River (see below), which is perhaps the state's finest trout river. But the Wood River starts at the junction of Falls River and Flat River just upstream from RI 165, Ten Rod Road, in the heart of the Arcadia WMA in West Exeter. The Falls River runs upstream from this juncture toward the northwest and its origins out of Hazard Pond.

Fish this upper mountain stream section by either hiking upstream from Plain Road or downstream from Falls River Road, which can be reached by turning north onto Escoheag Road from RI 165 1½ miles west of the Wood River bridge.

This pure, cold-flowing stream has plenty of decent hatches—mostly caddis, but a few mayflies. Fishing some of the plunge pools with the tandem rig of an indicator fly—an Adams or a March Brown—above a Hare's Ear Nymph is exceptionally productive, but the fish respond well to small streamers, too, like a Black-Nosed Dace or a small Muddler.

The catch-and-release section of Falls River runs for 2 miles from the bridge at Plain Road, a western extension of Austin Farm Road in the Lewis

City section of Exeter, downstream to the bridge off Brook Trail on a road locally known as Twin Bridges Road. Find this downstream access by using the main entrance to the WMA on the north side of RI 165, just west of the West Exeter Church. Brook Trail offers vehicular access upstream, with only short hikes to the stream.

Fishing in the catch-and-release section is allowed only with single, barbless-hooked artificial flies and lures, and all fish caught must be immediately released.

Flat River

The Flat River is the eastern counterpart to the Falls River, except that general fishing regulations apply to it—namely, the daily creel limit is six fish between the second Saturday in April and the last day November, when the two-fish limit prevails to the end of the season, the last day of February. The Flat originates at the juncture of Phillips Brook and Acid Factory Brook just south of Eisenhower Lake. It flows for a little more than 2 miles to where it meets the Falls River to form the Wood River.

The primary attraction of the Flat River is that it flows entirely within the confines of the Arcadia WMA and thus suffers no development along its shores. In fact, the 1¼-mile run of the river between the Plain Road bridge and the Twin Bridges Road bridge is like stepping out of the northeast and into the forest primeval. The forest is mature and helps keep the water in the river (it's really a brook) cold. There are decent hatches of mayflies and caddis, and an occasional stonefly nymph turns up. Because both the Wood and the Falls rivers are so nearby, the Flat is often ignored.

WOOD RIVER

Maps *USGS:* Carolina (Alton to I-95), Hope Valley (I-95 to junction of Falls and Flat Rivers).

Description The Wood River is Rhode Island's most famous and productive trout stream. It has earned this reputation by providing anglers with a nearly 17-mile-long, fertile run of river that is rural, accessible, and productive. The river also provides the rare opportunity to get away from it all, with long lengths of it flowing through swamps and backwaters that can only be easily reached via a canoe. In fact, while the 3½- mile-long stretch at its origins flows through the Arcadia WMA and is beautiful, another 3½-mile-long reach of river downstream, from the I-95 overpass to Woodville, is remote and very attractive, both to canoers and fly-fishermen. And from Woodville to Alton, another 2½ miles of river echoes the other two upstream stretches.

As if to balance these remote areas for noncanoers, much of the rest of the river is easy to get onto for walk-in anglers. There are bridges and access

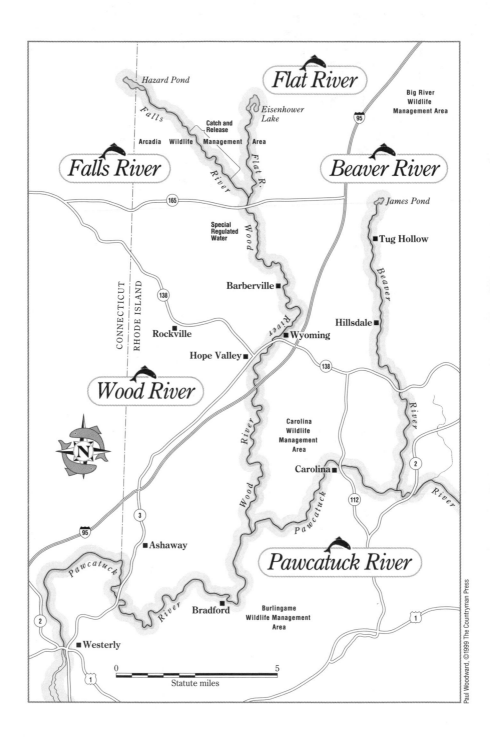

Flat River

Hazard Pond

Eisenhower Lake

Big River Wildlife Management Area

95

Falls

Catch and Release Management Area

Arcadia Wildlife Management Area

Falls River

Flat Ri.

Beaver River

James Pond

165

River

Wood

Special Regulated Water

Tug Hollow

CONNECTICUT

RHODE ISLAND

138

Barberville

River

Beaver

Hillsdale

Rockville

Wyoming

Wood River

Hope Valley

138

N

River

Carolina Wildlife Management Area

River

Carolina

2

Wood River

112

3

95

Ashaway

Pawcatuck River

Pawcatuck

River

2

Pawcatuck

River

Bradford

Burlingame Wildlife Management Area

1

Westerly

0   5

Statute miles

2

1

Paul Woodward, ©1999 The Countryman Press

points near the headwaters in Barberville, in Hope Valley, in Woodville, and in Alton.

Access Access onto the Wood River is relatively easy. In the Arcadia WMA, you can park on either the east or west bank on state-owned land just downstream from the RI 165 bridge, and fish up- or downstream. You can hike all the way downstream to Barberville and its dam through public land, or you can canoe it, a distance of about 3½ miles. While there is a good ½ mile of flowing water below the Barberville dam that can be waded, the river at the Skunk Hill Road bridge downstream has slowed and deepened, a result of the backwater behind the Wyoming dam. There is a state-owned public boat launch right at the Wyoming dam, which is convenient for canoing back up into this still-water section of the river. Find it adjacent to the inter-section of RI 3 and RI 138. Fish the immediate downstream section, too, which is wadeable and productive.

Below Hope Valley, the river is difficult to wade, but canoe access is superb and some very big holdover trout hide out in the deep flows and undercut bankings. Put in your canoe at the gravel ramp just downstream from the I-95 overpass and float downstream to the dam in Woodville. Do the same again from Woodville to Alton.

Regulations From about May 15 each year (check the abstracts as this date can vary) to the last day in February, the section on the Wood from the RI 165 bridge downstream to Arcadia Road (Barberville dam) has a reduced—two fish—creel limit on trout, char, and domestic (landlocked) Atlantic salmon. The rest of the river, and the stretch above before May 15, are governed by general regu-lations: six fish daily from opening day to the end of November, then two fish daily to the close of the season, the last day of February.

Don't miss The run of river in the Arcadia WMA is pristine and a nearly per-fect place to fly-fish. With the two excellent cold-water rills that form the river—the Falls and the Flat—providing high-quality trout water themselves, the Wood here begins and continues as the best wading trout water in the state. And while a more severely restricted daily bag limit on trout would be a huge benefit on this reach (it fairly screams to be a catch-and-release, artificial-lure-only stretch), the state has at least restricted the kill to two a day after the middle of May and the opening day gush of meat anglers. So target this run of water, especially after the middle of May.

Best asset The protection of the Wood River from development—both by the hand of man where the state owns the land in the Arcadia WMA, and by Mother Nature via some lovely swamps and bogs—has so far kept the river wild looking and fertile. Yes, there are some old dams on the river, but they are something of a plus, because they help add variety to the angling and help limit development along the shores. And being able to point to a wild, fertile trout stream anywhere in Rhode Island is a huge asset.

Biggest drawback Because this is southern New England, and because the Wood River is almost as far south as you can go in the region, the water does warm up in the summer. Local wisdom dictates fishing farther and farther downstream as water temperatures rise, and during unusually low-water years, the flows in the upper river can become meager. But the trout, especially the browns, can usually survive in the deep-water pools and behind the dams, and when water levels return to normal, they will migrate back up into the flowing-water sections.

Necessary patterns *Underwater:* Pheasant Tail Nymph (#14–20), Hare's Ear Nymph (#12–16), Hendrickson Nymph (#12–16), Leadwing Coachman (#12–14), Caddis Larva (#14–18), Caddis Emerger (#12–18), Black–Nosed Dace (#4–10), Mickey Finn (#4–12). *Dry flies:* Quill Gordon (#12–16); Hendrickson (#12–16); Red Quill (#12–16); Rusty Spinner (#12–16); March Brown (#12–14); Gray Fox (#12–14); Mahogany Dun (#12–16); Mahogany Spinner (#10–16); Sulphur Dun (#14–16); Light Cahill (#14–16); Green Drake (#6–10); Brown Drake (#10–12); Golden Drake (#8–12); White Mayfly (#12–14); Tan, Yellow, Brown, Green, or Black Caddis (#12–18); Blue-Winged Olive (#12–20); Cream Midge (#18–22); Trico (#18–24); Alder (#16–18); Cricket (#10–14); Hopper (#4–12); Black or Cinnamon Ant (#10–20).

Stocked feeder streams worth a look (from downstream to upstream) Brushy Brook, Roaring Brook and Ponds, Falls River (see above), Flat River (see above).

Other feeders (from downstream to upstream) Canonchet Brook, Diamond Brook, Canob Pond Brook, Baker Brook, Parris Brook.

The Wood River makes the heartstrings of southeastern New England fly-fishers sing. In the midst of the northeast corridor of urban sprawl, here flows a rural, pure river that offers up a panoply of fly-fishing opportunities. Whether your forté is deep-woods bushwhacking, civilized stream-bank meandering, canoe fishing along moving or still water, or stocked-trout chasing at obvious sites, the Wood offers it all. And all this is contained within 17 river miles of water.

The Wood River proper is formed just north of RI 165, Ten Rod Road, in Exeter where the Falls River and the Flat River join. This juncture is currently mislabeled on the USGS Hope Valley map, an important mistake to notice. The actual juncture is ⅓ mile upstream from the highway. The USGS map calls the lower section of the Falls River the Wood River, and with strict catch-and-release regulations on the Falls, you must know where that river runs.

To fish this lovely stretch and the 3½ miles downstream as it flows through the Arcadia WMA to Barberville, park on the south side of the highway on either side of the river. You'll know you are in the right spot because of the Quonset hut that Fish and Game uses as a deer-check station. Many anglers fish downstream, and this is indeed fertile holding water. But the fly-fishing can be better upstream for the ⅓ mile of the Wood and on into both the Flat and Falls Rivers (see above).

If there is a drawback to this area, it is its popularity. The Arcadia WMA is the largest in the state at more than 13,000 acres, and as such, it has received ample publicity. Division of Fish and Game managers have voiced some concern about the overuse of the area. It's a favorite destination for anglers, tubers, canoers, hikers, ATV users, and almost anyone looking for a swatch of the great outdoors. At times it may seem to be loved to death. An easy solution to this popularity is not simple to formulate or implement, so sometimes the river and its environs can seem crowded.

At the Barberville dam, which is just above the bridge on Arcadia Road, be sure to visit the offices of the Wood-Pawcatuck Rivers Watershed Association. (Another mistake by the USGS, Arcadia Road is mislabeled as Old Nooseneck Road.) They're located right at the dam. Also, spend a silent moment here. Two people drowned in a canoeing accident at the base of the dam in the spring of 1994 when the river was at full spate and the back currents below the dam dangerous. Let their fate serve as a reminder that we should always respect the waters we so love.

Below the bridge, the Wood shows its true value as a trout stream. The rock-strewn riverbed offers countless trout-holding spots, and the big pool on the downstream sweep just reeks of trout and mayflies and hatch matching. This attractive water continues downstream for about a half mile until the river begins to back up behind the Wyoming dam.

Still-water fishermen will be glad of this pause in the flow, however. While the pond behind the dam is not large, it does slow the water enough to give the trout a deep-water refuge for the entire year, but especially during the summer, when water temperatures can border on unbearable for the trout. This backwater and the others downstream are where the biggest trout in the state come from.

There is a state-owned boat launch area at the dam of Wyoming Pond, so fishing upstream from the dam is easy. Downstream from the dam is a wading section that's often overlooked, probably because it's the one section of the river that has a more urban feel to it with a factory, a few shops, and the intersection of RI 3 and RI 138 nearby. In addition, there's another dam a mile downstream near another factory.

But below this factory dam, the river regains its wild feel. In spite of its presence, I-95 signals the start of this pretty section of river. Although you can wade a few sections below the I-95 overpass, this is really an ideal canoeing run. The water flows along at a leisurely pace, but the banks are boggy. Trout hiding spots are innumerable, and you can either anchor the canoe and fish from it, or get out and wade prime sections as you come upon them. Float along to the still water behind the dam at Woodville, take out there, or portage around the dam and continue along to Alton Pond in Alton, just above where the Wood joins the Pawcatuck River (see below). You'll be sure to enjoy this last run on Alton Pond because no motors of any kind are allowed on it, not even electrics on canoes. A state-owned boat ramp and parking lot, the Lewis Memorial Boat Launch, is on the west shore at the dam.

The Wood River is truly a river for all fly-fishing tastes, and it's beautiful to boot. People who live near it revel in its closeness, and increasingly, anglers are traveling to it because of the many options they can find along its miles.

Beaver River

The Beaver River heads up in Exeter out of James Pond and follows an almost due-south course to its meeting with the Pawcatuck River in the Kenyon section of Richmond, just west of the Great Swamp Wildlife Reservation. It is notable because of its length, because of the surprisingly remote run that it makes, and because it holds trout well and supports a very surprising variety of aquatic insects and forage.

Access, especially to the lower river, is very good with a number of crossroads and bridges, notably at Shannock Hill Road, and then upstream along Beaver River Road to RI 138, the Kingston Road. You can also get onto the river about halfway along at Beaver River Schoolhouse Road. Upstream from RI 138, Hillsdale Road parallels the river almost to its source. Find Hillsdale Road about a mile west of the bridge over the Beaver River on RI 138 and turn north. The river is a short hike back to the east. When Hillsdale Road crosses over the river in Hillsdale, there is good access—now to the west—down the hill to the river. It flows no more than a few hundred yards away.

Although the lower section of the Beaver is slower water and deeper, it holds trout fairly well into the season. The upper section, above RI 138, is more a freestone-type brook with plenty of pools and riffles. The state stocks the Beaver River before the season opens, during spring and again in autumn.

Pawcatuck River

The Pawcatuck River cuts across the bottom of Rhode Island, gathering the waters of many of the state's south-flowing streams—including the Wood

The Wood River below the Barberville Dam has an abundance of varied trout water.

River (see above) and the Beaver River (see above)—before becoming the border between Connecticut and Rhode Island below Potter Hill and dumping into the sea at Little Narragansett Bay. In its lower reaches, say from Bradford downstream to the sea, it's a slow-flowing, warm-water river, meandering in and out of swamps and the backwaters behind dams. But in its upper reaches, it's a sleeper of a trout stream.

Technically, the Pawcatuck begins where the outlet of Worden Pond in the Great Swamp Wildlife Reservation (known by some as the Charles River) joins the waters of the Usquepaug River just upstream from Biscuit City Road in Richmond. But local wisdom dictates that the Pawcatuck begins as the outlet to Worden Pond. Regardless of exactly where the river starts, it is this section—from Great Swamp to Bradford—that contains the best trout water. And specifically, the reaches of river from Shannock to the backwaters behind the dam in Carolina, from Carolina to the RI 91 bridge, and from Alton through Burdickville to Bradford have the best moving water, trout holds, and forage.

Access to each of these sections is relatively easy. In Shannock, get onto the river at Shannock Road or at the railroad bridge just downstream. There's also a bridge just downstream on the west side of Shannock, where the west end of Shannock Road crosses. In Carolina, RI 112 (Carolina Main Street) crosses the river just below the dam, and this is a good place to find schooling trout and feed fish. Downstream, you can get onto the river at RI 91, the Alton-Carolina Road, but the river is slow moving from here downstream to where the Wood River joins it. It does hold trout and makes an excellent canoe-fishing run. And the run from the Wood River to Bradford is very productive, especially where the river necks down and speeds up in Burdickville. Unfortunately, there is no formal access in Burdickville, and plenty of no parking signs, so a canoe run must begin in Alton, at the ramp at the dam on the Wood River, and end below Burdickville in Bradford at the state boat-launch ramp there on RI 91 and RI 126. It's about 5 miles between the two landings, so a day's meander down the river offers plenty of time for fishing. And this run may contain the most attractive water on the entire river.

Many areas in this entire upper river can be very fruitfully waded, but a canoe trip along this section is particularly attractive. There is camping allowed in the Carolina WMA, which abuts the river for about a half mile just downstream from the dam in Carolina. There is plenty of good trout fly-fishing.

The Pawcatuck River is very fertile, with an abundance of caddis and some substantial mayfly hatches, but early in the season use big attractor dry flies—like Wulffs, March Browns, or Adamses—and flashy but not overly large streamers—like Mickey Finns or Marabou Muddlers in the size 8–12 range. Enjoy this river. It's productive and pretty and largely overlooked.

Other Stocked Streams in Rhode Island

All listed waters are stocked with trout before the season begins, some are stocked again during spring (S). Streams that are also stocked in fall are discussed above. The Falls River (see above) is the only stream in the state that has a catch-and-release section.

Providence County Abbots Run Brook, Brandy Brook, Dolly Cole Brook (S), Harris River (S), Meshanticut Brook (S), Peeptoad Brook, Round Top Brook (S), Silvy's Brook, Winsor Brook (S), Woonasquatucket River.

Kent County Big River (S), Buck's Horn Brook (S).

Washington County Ashaway River (S), Breakheart Brook (S), Brushy Brook (S), Chickasheen Brook (S), Log House Brook (S), Meadow Brook (S), Parris Brook, Roaring Brook and Ponds (S), Saugatucket River.

Newport County Adamsville Pond and Brook, Dunderry Brook.

Stocked Lakes and Ponds

All listed waters are stocked with trout before the season begins, some are stocked again during spring (S), and some also receive fall plantings (F). A few ponds are listed as fly-fishing only (FFO), and some are restricted to anglers 14 years of age and younger (Y).

Providence County Cass Pond (Y), Dexter Pond, Foster Green Acres Pond, Geneva Brook and Pond (Y), Hopkins Mill Pond (S), Lapham Pond (Y), Memorial Park Pond (Y), A. L. Mowry Pond (S, FFO), Mowry Meadow Pond (S, FFO), Olney Pond (S, F), Peck Pond (S), Round Top Ponds (S, F), Seidel's Pond (Y), Shippee Saw Mill Pond (S), Silvy's Pond (Y), Slater Park Pond (Y), Spring Grove Pond (S, F), Sylvester Pond, Tarkiln Pond (S), Upper Rochambeau Pond (S, FFO), Wallum Lake (S, F).

Kent County Breakheart Pond (S, F), Carbuncle Pond (S, F), Carolina Trout Pond (S, F).

Bristol County Brickyard Pond (S).

Washington County Alton Pond (S), Ashville Pond (S), Barber Pond (S, F), Beach Pond (S, F), Biscuit City Pond (Y), Deep Pond (S, FFO), Frosty Hollow Pond (S, Y), Lloyd Kenney Pond (Y), Meadow Brook Pond (S, F), Silver Spring Lake (S, F), Tucker Pond, Watchaug Pond, Wyoming Pond (S).

Newport County Melville Ponds (S, F), Saint Mary's Pond (S), Simmon's Mill Pond, Stafford Pond (S, F), Tiverton Trout Pond.

APPENDIX I: SOUTHERN NEW ENGLAND HATCH CHART

Species	March	April	May	June	July	August	September	October
Little black stonefly (A. minima)	●———●							
Quill Gordon (E. pleuralis)	●———●							
Blue-winged olive (B. vagans)		●————————●			●		●—————●	
Black caddis (C. aterrima)		●————————●						
Hendrickson (E. subvaria)		●———————●						
Am. Grannom (B. numerosus)			●———●					
Black quill (L. cupida)			●———●					
March brown (S. vicarium)			●————●					
Tan caddis (G. nigrior)			●————————●					
Gray drake (S. quebecensis)			●——————————●					
Green sedge (R. fuscala)			●————————————●					

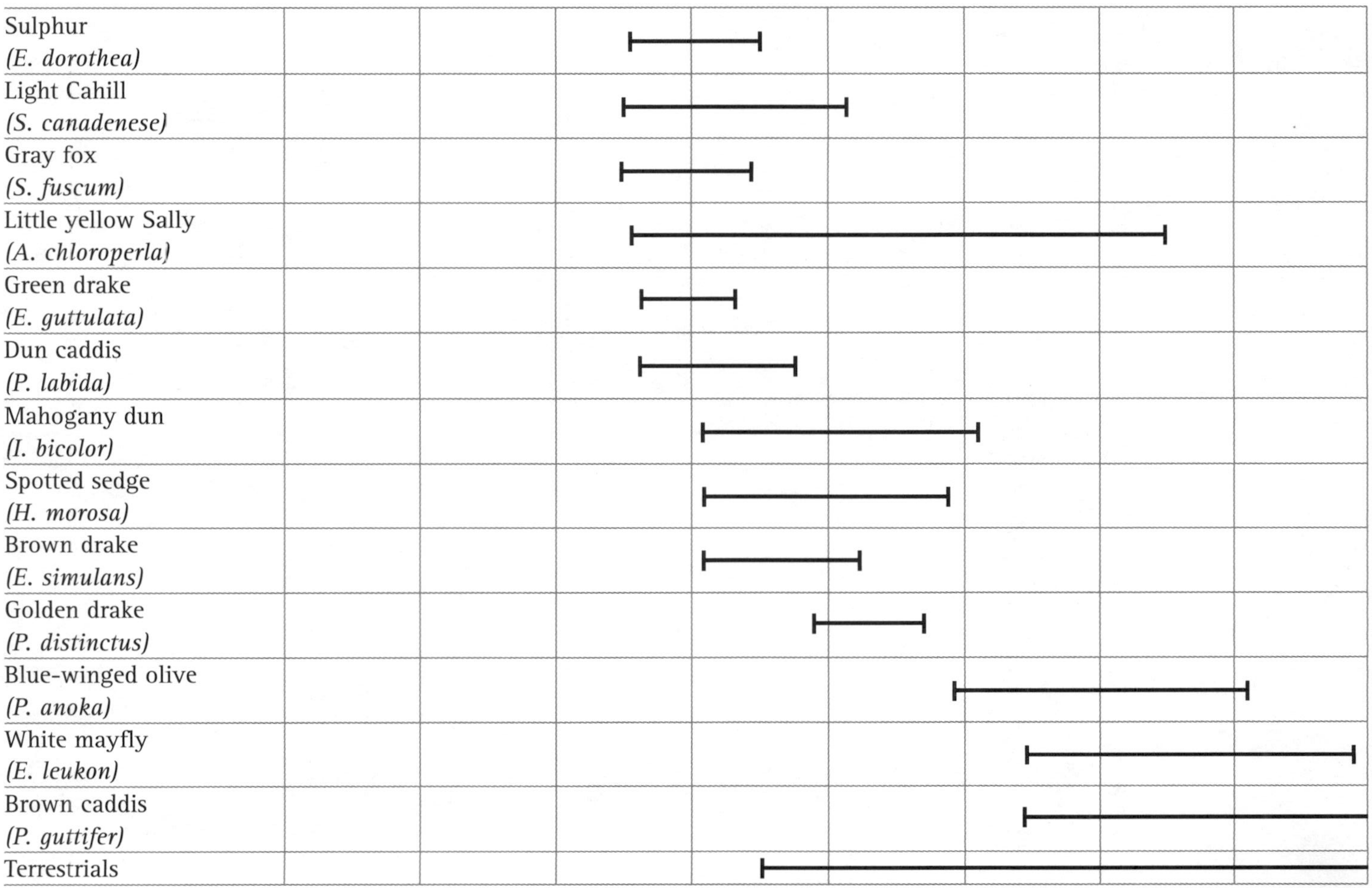

Sulphur
(E. dorothea)

Light Cahill
(S. canadenese)

Gray fox
(S. fuscum)

Little yellow Sally
(A. chloroperla)

Green drake
(E. guttulata)

Dun caddis
(P. labida)

Mahogany dun
(I. bicolor)

Spotted sedge
(H. morosa)

Brown drake
(E. simulans)

Golden drake
(P. distinctus)

Blue-winged olive
(P. anoka)

White mayfly
(E. leukon)

Brown caddis
(P. guttifer)

Terrestrials

APPENDIX 2:
FLY PATTERNS OF SOUTHERN NEW ENGLAND

See tying instructions beginning on page 225.

Underwater Mayflies
Baetis Nymph (#18–20)
Hare's Ear Nymph (#12–16)
Hare's Ear Wet Fly (#12–16)
Hendrickson Nymph (#12–16)
March Brown Nymph (#8–16)
Pheasant Tail Nymph (#14–20)
Teeko Bug (#8–12)
Zug Bug (#8–18)

Underwater Caddis
Caddis Emerger (#12–18)
Caddis Larva (#14–18)
Cased Caddis (#8–14)
Deep Sparkle Pupa (#14–16)
Leadwing Coachman (#12–14)
Tellico (#10–14)

Underwater Stoneflies
Early Black Stonefly Nymph (#10–14)
Giant Black Stonefly Nymph (#2–8)
Golden Stonefly Nymph (#4–8)
Montana (#4–10)
Ted's Stonefly (#6–12)
White Stonefly Nymph (#4–10)

Streamers
Nine-Three (#2–6)
Ballou Special (#2–8)
Black Ghost (#2–6)
Black-Nosed Dace (#4–10)
Clouser Deep Minnow (#2/0–6)
Erskine (#2–10)
Gray Ghost (#2–6)

Hornberg (#6–10)
Jerry's Smelt (#2–6)
Joe's Smelt (#2–6)
Llama (#4–10)
Marabou Muddler (#4–10)
Matuka (#2–6)
Mickey Finn (#4–12)
Muddler Minnow (#4–10)
Pink Ghost (#2–6)
Sculpin (#2–6)
Threadfin Shad (#2–4)
Woolly Bugger (#4–10)
Woolly Worm (#4–10)

Atlantic Salmon Flies
Black Bear–Green Butt (#4–10)
Bomber (#2–6)
Cossaboom (#2/0–10)
Green Highlander (#4–10)
Green Machine (#4–10)
Mickey Finn (#2/0–6)

Dry Flies—Mayflies
Adams (#8–22)
Ausable Wulff (#10–18)
Black Quill (#12–14)
Blue Dun (#10–18)
Blue Quill (#12–20)
Blue-Winged Olive (#12–20)
Brown Drake (#10–12)
Cream Midge (#18–22)
Cream Variant (#12)
Dark Hendrickson (#12–16)
Dun Variant (#12)

Female Hendrickson (12–16)
Ginger Quill (#12–18)
Golden Drake (#8–12)
Gray Fox (#12–14)
Green Drake (#6–10)
Griffiths Gnat (#14–22)
Housatonic Quill (#12–16)
Humpy (#8–18)
Light Cahill (#14–16)
Light Hendrickson (#12–16)
Mahogany Dun (#12–16)
Mahogany Spinner (#10–16)
March Brown (#12–14)
Pale Evening Dun (#14–20)
Quill Gordon (#12–16)
Red Quill (#12–16)
Royal Wulff (#8–16)
Rusty Spinner (#12–16)
Sulphur Dun (#14–16)
Trico (#18–24)
Usual (Natural or Olive) (#10–20)
White Mayfly (#12–14)

Dry Flies—Caddis

Alder (#16–18)
Elk Hair Caddis (#12–18)
Mottled Caddis (#12–18)
Slate Caddis (#12–18)
Tan, Yellow, Brown, Green, or Black
    Caddis (#12–18)

Dry Flies—Stoneflies

Picket Pin (#8–14)
Stimulator (#6–14)
Yellow Stonefly (#14–18)

Dry Flies—Terrestrials

Black or Cinnamon Ant (#10–20)
Cricket (#8–14)
Green Inchworm (#14–16)
Hoppers: Madam X (#4–12), Letort
    Hopper (#8–16)

Tying formulas

Underwater Mayflies

BAETIS NYMPH

Hook: 3X long
Thread: black
Tail: pheasant tail barb tips
Abdomen: olive thread with pheasant
    barb shanks over top
Thorax: peacock herl
Wingcase: dark mottled turkey tail
Legs: wood duck
Head: pheasant tail barb

GOLD-RIBBED HARE'S EAR NYMPH

Hook: 1X–3X long
Thread: tan
Tail: partridge hackle barbs
Abdomen: hare's ear dubbing
Rib: oval gold tinsel
Thorax: hare's ear dubbing
Wingcase: dark turkey wing quill
Legs: picked-out fur
Head: tying thread

HARE'S EAR WET FLY

Hook: standard wet
Thread: tan
Tail: partridge hackle barbs
Abdomen: hare's ear dubbing
Rib: oval gold tinsel
Thorax: hare's ear dubbing
Wing: mottled turkey wing, quill section
Throat: wood duck flank

HENDRICKSON NYMPH

Hook: 1X or 2X long
Thread: brown
Tail: wood duck flank barbs
Abdomen: reddish brown fur
Rib: copper wire
Thorax: reddish brown fur
Wingcase: black turkey tail section
Legs: brown partridge

MARCH BROWN NYMPH

Hook: 1X or 2X long
Thread: brown
Tail: three pheasant tail barbs
Abdomen: dark amber fur
Rib: brown thread
Thorax: same as abdomen
Wingcase: dark turkey tail
Legs: brown partridge hackle

PHEASANT TAIL NYMPH

Hook: 1X long
Thread: brown
Tail: pheasant tail barbs
Abdomen: pheasant tail barbs
Rib: copper wire
Thorax: peacock herl
Wingcase: pheasant tail barbs
Legs: pheasant tail barbs from thorax

TEEKO BUG

Hook: 2X–4X long
Thread: tan
Tail: brown hackle barbs
Abdomen: green or gray dubbing
Rib: none
Thorax: same as abdomen, built up
Wingcase: wood duck flank feather tied in at head and swept back over thorax and abdomen, ending midway along tail
Legs: rabbit fur with guard hairs spun on tying thread and palmered over thorax

ZUG BUG

Hook: 1X–2X long
Thread: black
Tail: three peacock sword feathers
Body: peacock herl tied full
Rib: oval silver tinsel
Wingcase: mallard flank tied in at head
Legs: brown hackle

Underwater Caddis

DEEP SPARKLE PUPA

Hook: dry fly
Thread: primrose yellow

Weight: tin wire
Underbody: gold Antron yarn mixed with brown fur
Overbody: gold Antron yarn tied in at bend, pulled forward top and bottom
Legs: wood duck barbs
Head: brown fur

EMERGENT SPARKLE CADDIS PUPA

Hook: dry fly
Thread: to match adult (orange, tan, yellow, brown, green, black)
Tail: Antron yarn
Underbody: Antron and fur to match adult (orange, tan, yellow, brown, green, black)
Overbody: Antron yarn as above tied in at tail and pulled forward, top and bottom
Wing: natural light deer body hair
Head: yellow thread

LARGE DARK CADDIS EMERGER

Hook: 1X long (#6 or 8)
Thread: black
Tail: none
Abdomen: orange to brown dubbing
Rib: orange thread
Wing and legs: dark furnace hackle on each side
Head: black ostrich herl

SMALL CADDIS EMERGER

Hook: nymph (#14–20)
Thread: to match color of body of natural
Tail: Z-lon
Abdomen: dubbing to match color of body of natural
Rib: copper wire
Wing: dark dun *cul de canard*, over which are wood duck barbs
Legs: wood duck flank barbs
Head: dark brown ostrich herl

Caddis Larva

BASIC LARVA

Hook: curved nymph hook
Thread: brown

Underbody: tin wire
Abdomen: dubbing to match natural (orange, tan, yellow, brown, green, black)
Head: dark brown dubbing
Legs: wood duck barbs

BRASSIE

Hook: nymph
Thread: black
Abdomen: copper or brass wire, same diameter as hook
Head: Black to gray fur, picked out

CASED CADDIS

Hook: 6X long (#8–12)
Thread: black
Underbody: tin wire
Case: peacock herl
Hackle: brown, palmered over peacock herl
Rib: copper wire, counter-wound
Body: band of cream fur just behind head
Head: black ostrich herl

LEADWING COACHMAN

Hook: wet fly
Thread: black
Tag: flat gold tinsel
Body: peacock herl
Hackle: dark ginger
Wing: mallard wing quill segments

TELLICO

Hook: nymph, 1X–2X long
Thread: black
Tail: brown hackle barbs
Rib: peacock herl
Shellback: peacock herl pulled over top from bend
Legs: brown hen hackle

Underwater Stoneflies

EARLY BLACK STONEFLY NYMPH

Hook: 1X–3X long
Thread: black
Tail: brown goose biots

Abdomen: dark brown sparkle fur
Rib: black thread
Thorax: same as abdomen
Wingcase: black goose wing quill segment
Legs: dark blue dun

GIANT BLACK STONEFLY NYMPH

Hook: 6X long, bent
Thread: black
Underbody: tin wire
Tail: black goose biots
Abdomen: black sparkle fur
Rib: copper wire
Thorax: brown sparkle fur
Wingcase: dark mottled turkey tail sections
Legs: dark grizzly hen hackle
Head: same as thorax
Antennae: black goose biots

GOLDEN STONEFLY NYMPH

Hook: 4X–6X long, bent
Thread: brown
Tail: ginger goose biot
Abdomen: gold sparkle fur
Rib: brass wire
Thorax: same as abdomen
Wingcase: light mottled turkey quill
Legs: ginger goose biots
Head: same as abdomen

MONTANA

Hook: 4X–6X long
Thread: black
Tail: black hackle fibers
Abdomen: black chenille
Thorax: yellow chenille
Wingcase: black chenille
Legs: black hen hackle

TED'S STONEFLY NYMPH

Hook: 3X long
Thread: black
Tail: brown goose biots
Abdomen: brown chenille
Thorax: orange chenille
Wingcase: brown chenille
Legs: black hen hackle

WHITE STONEFLY NYMPH

Hook: 3X–4X long, bent
Thread: white
Tail: wood duck flank barbs, divided
Abdomen: light cream fur
Rib: clear monofilament
Thorax: same as abdomen
Wingcase: light mottled turkey wing quill
Legs: bleached grizzly hackle
Head antennae: wood duck flank barbs, divided

Streamers

BALLOU SPECIAL

Hook: 4X–8X long
Thread: black
Tail: golden pheasant crest curving down
Body: flat silver tinsel
Wing: peacock herl over white marabou plumes over sparse red bucktail
Cheeks: jungle cock

BLACK GHOST

Hook: 4X–8X long
Thread: black
Tail: yellow hackle barbs
Body: black wool
Rib: flat silver tinsel
Throat: yellow hackle barbs
Wing: four white hackles
Cheeks: jungle cock

BLACK-NOSED DACE

Hook: 3X–4X long
Thread: black
Tail: red wool
Body: flat silver tinsel
Rib: oval silver tinsel
Wing: brown bucktail over black bear hair over white bucktail

CLOUSER DEEP MINNOW

Hook: 2X–3X long
Thread: gray
Eyes: tin dumbbell eyes painted red with black pupils

Throat: orange-dyed squirrel tail
Wing: natural gray squirrel tail over silver krystal flash

ERSKINE

Hook: 2X–6X long
Thread: white
Body: white floss
Rib: oval silver tinsel
Throat: white calf tail
Wing: light badger
Eyes: glass taxidermy eyes

GRAY GHOST

Hook: 6X–8X long
Thread: black
Body: golden yellow floss
Rib: flat silver tinsel
Wing: four gray hackles over golden pheasant crest over peacock herl
Throat: sparse white bucktail and a short golden pheasant crest
Shoulder: silver pheasant body feather
Cheeks: jungle cock

HORNBERG

Hook: 2X–3X long
Thread: black
Body: flat silver tinsel
Underwing: yellow hackle tips
Wing: mallard flank feathers on sides of fly
Cheeks: jungle cock
Collar: hen grizzly hackle

JERRY'S SMELT

Hook: 6X long
Thread: black
Tail: red calf tail
Body: pearlescent Mylar tubing tied in back with red thread
Throat: red paint
Wing: pintail flank feather tied flat
Head: black tying thread
Eyes: yellow paint with black pupil

JOE'S SMELT

Hook: 6X long
Thread: black

Tail: red calf tail
Body: silver Mylar tubing tied in back
with red thread
Throat: red paint
Wing: pintail flank feather tied flat
Head: black tying thread
Eyes: yellow paint with black pupil

LLAMA

Hook: 2X–6X long
Thread: black
Tail: grizzly hen hackle barbs
Body: red floss
Rib: oval gold tinsel
Wing: woodchuck guard hair, including
the underfur
Collar: grizzly hen hackle
Eyes: white with black pupils

MARABOU MUDDLER

Hook: 3X–4X long
Thread: white
Tail: red hackle barbs
Body: oval silver tinsel
Wing: peacock herl over white marabou
Head and collar: spun natural deer hair,
trimmed

MATUKA

Hook: 2X–4X long
Thread: black
Body: chenille
Rib: oval silver tinsel
Throat: red wool
Wing: four hackle feathers secured with
the rib along the top of the fly

MICKEY FINN

Hook: 3X–6X long
Thread: black
Body: flat silver tinsel
Rib: oval silver tinsel
Wing: yellow bucktail over red bucktail
over yellow bucktail
Cheeks: jungle cock

MUDDLER MINNOW

Hook: 3X–4X long
Thread: brown

Tail: mottled turkey wing quill sections
Body: flat gold tinsel
Wing: mottled turkey wing quill sections over gray squirrel tail
Head and collar: natural deer hair, head
clipped, collar splayed back along
body

NINE-THREE

Hook: 4X–8X long
Thread: black
Body: flat silver tinsel
Wing: two black hackles over two green
hackles tied flat over sparse white
bucktail

PINK GHOST

Hook: 6X–8X long
Thread: black
Body: red floss
Rib: flat silver tinsel
Wing: pink saddle hackles
Throat: white bucktail
Shoulders: silver pheasant body feathers
Cheeks: jungle cock

SCULPIN

Hook: 3X–6X long
Thread: yellow
Body: cream dubbing
Rib: brass wire
Wing: four olive saddle hackles
Pectoral fins: ringneck pheasant body
feathers
Collar and head: natural over bleached
deer body hair, head clipped, collar
splayed back along body

THREADFIN SHAD

Hook: 2X–4X long
Thread: white
Underbody: folded and shaped metal
tape or shaped toothpick
Body: pearlescent Mylar tubing, high-
lighted with red paint for gills
Wing: two olive and two silver badger
hackles
Eyes: small plastic doll eyes

WOOLLY BUGGER

Hook: 4X–6X long
Thread: olive
Tail: olive marabou
Body: chenille
Rib: brass wire counter-wound
Hackle: olive saddle hackle, palmered
Collar: two turns of palmered saddle hackle

WOOLLY WORM

Hook: 2X–4X long
Thread: black
Tail: red wool yarn
Body: black chenille
Rib: copper wire counter-wound
Hackle: grizzly saddle hackle, palmered

Atlantic Salmon Flies

BLACK BEAR–GREEN BUTT

Hook: wet salmon
Thread: black
Tag: fine oval silver tinsel
Butt: fluorescent green wool
Tail: black bear hair
Body: black wool
Rib: oval silver tinsel
Throat: black bear hair
Wing: black bear hair

BOMBER

Hook: dry or low-water salmon, 4X–6X long
Thread: black
Tail: brown deer hair
Body: spun deer hair, clipped to a cigar shape
Rib: brown saddle hackle, palmered
Head: brown deer hair, pointing forward over eye

COSSABOOM

Hook: wet salmon
Thread: red
Tag: embossed silver tinsel, tied well down on bend
Tail: pale olive floss
Body: pale olive floss

Rib: embossed silver tinsel
Wing: gray squirrel tail
Collar: lemon yellow hackle
Head: red

GREEN HIGHLANDER

Hook: wet salmon
Thread: black
Tag: silver tinsel
Tail: mallard flank feather barbs over golden pheasant crest, turned up
Butt: black ostrich herl
Body: *first quarter:* golden-yellow floss; *remainder:* fluorescent green floss
Rib: oval silver tinsel
Hackle: green, palmered over green floss
Throat: lemon hackle barbs
Wing (from hook shank to top): golden pheasant tippet fibers, yellow then orange then green bucktail, red squirrel tail, golden pheasant crest turned down
Cheeks: jungle cock

GREEN MACHINE

Hook: wet salmon
Thread: black
Tag: fluorescent green wool
Body: green deer body hair, spun and clipped
Hackle: brown, palmered

MICKEY FINN

Hook: wet salmon or streamer, 4X–6X long
Thread: black
Butt: fluorescent red wool
Body: flat silver tinsel
Rib: oval silver tinsel
Wing: yellow over red over yellow bucktail
Cheeks: jungle cock

Dry Flies—Mayflies

ADAMS

Hook: dry fly
Thread: gray
Tail: mixed grizzly and brown hackle barbs

Body: gray dubbing
Wing: grizzly hackle tips
Hackle: mixed grizzly and brown

AUSABLE WULFF

Hook: dry fly, 2X long
Thread: fluorescent orange
Tail: woodchuck tail
Body: rusty orange dubbing
Wing: white calf tail
Hackle: mixed brown and grizzly

BLACK QUILL

Hook: dry fly
Thread: black
Tail: black hackle barbs
Body: stripped peacock herl
Wing: dark gray mallard wing quill
  segments
Hackle: black

BLUE DUN

Hook: dry fly
Thread: gray
Tail: blue dun hackle barbs
Body: gray dubbing
Wing: gray mallard wing quill segments
Hackle: medium blue dun

BLUE QUILL

Hook: dry fly
Thread: gray
Tail: blue dun hackle barbs
Body: stripped peacock herl
Wing: dark gray mallard wing quill
  segments
Hackle: medium blue dun

BLUE-WINGED OLIVE

Hook: dry fly
Thread: olive
Tail: blue dun hackle barbs
Body: olive dubbing
Wing: dun hackle tips
Hackle: blue dun

BROWN DRAKE

Hook: dry fly
Thread: tan

Tail: dark moose hair
Body: yellow-tan dubbing
Rib: yellow floss
Wing: light brown elk hair
Hackle: brown and grizzly

CREAM MIDGE

Hook: dry fly
Thread: cream
Tail: cream hackle fibers
Body: cream dubbing (fine)
Hackle: cream

DARK HENDRICKSON

Hook: dry fly
Thread: gray
Tail: dark blue dun hackle barbs
Body: dark gray dubbing
Wing: wood duck flank feather
Hackle: dark blue dun

DUN VARIANT

Hook: dry fly, 1X–2X short
Thread: gray
Tail: dark blue dun hackle barbs
Body: brown hackle stem
Hackle: oversized dark blue dun

FEMALE HENDRICKSON

Hook: dry fly
Thread: gray
Tail: dark blue dun hackle barbs
Butt: ball of lemon dubbing
Body: dark gray dubbing
Wing: wood duck flank feather
Hackle: dark blue dun

GINGER QUILL

Hook: dry fly
Thread: gray
Tail: light ginger hackle barbs
Body: stripped peacock herl
Wing: light gray mallard wing quill
  segments
Hackle: light ginger

GOLDEN DRAKE

Hook: dry fly, 2X long
Thread: gold

Tail: light ginger hackle barbs
Body: light amber dubbing
Rib: yellow monocord
Wing: natural deer hair
Hackle: mixed brown, grizzly, and ginger

GRAY FOX

Hook: dry fly
Thread: primrose yellow
Tail: light ginger hackle barbs
Body: light fawn-colored fox fur
Wing: mallard flank
Hackle: mixed light grizzly and light
  ginger

GREEN DRAKE

Hook: dry fly
Thread: olive
Tail: moose hair
Body: olive elk hair, tied reversed to
  form a bullet head and extended past
  hook bend
Rib: tying thread
Wing: natural deer hair, as a post
Hackle: yellow grizzly hackle, tied para-
  chute style

GRIFFITHS GNAT

Hook: dry fly
Thread: olive
Body: peacock herl
Rib: fine gold wire
Hackle: grizzly, palmered

HOUSATONIC QUILL

Hook: dry fly
Thread: cream
Tail: light badger hackle barbs
Body: stripped peacock herl
Wing: wood duck flank feather
Hackle: light badger

HUMPY

Hook: dry fly
Thread: red
Tail: moose hair
Body: red floss or thread
Overbody: natural elk hair
Wing: natural elk hair

Hackle: mixed grizzly and brown

LIGHT CAHILL

Hook: dry fly
Thread: cream
Tail: cream hackle barbs
Body: cream dubbing
Wing: wood duck flank feather
Hackle: cream

LIGHT HENDRICKSON

Hook: dry fly
Thread: tan
Tail: blue dun hackle barbs
Body: light fox belly fur
Wing: wood duck flank feather
Hackle: medium blue dun

MAHOGANY DUN

Hook: dry fly
Thread: brown
Tail: olive hackle barbs
Body: dark brown dubbing
Wing: mallard flank feather, dyed brown
Hackle: grizzly hackle, dyed brown

MAHOGANY SPINNER

Hook: dry fly
Thread: gray
Tail: blue dun hackle barbs, divided
Body: red brown dubbing
Wing: dun hen hackle tips, tied spent

MARCH BROWN

Hook: dry fly
Thread: orange
Tail: ginger hackle barbs
Body: light fawn-colored fox-fur dub-
  bing
Wing: mallard flank feather, dyed brown
Hackle: grizzly and dark ginger

PALE EVENING DUN

Hook: dry fly
Thread: cream
Tail: light blue dun hackle barbs
Body: pale yellow dubbing
Wing: gray duck wing quill segments
Hackle: medium blue dun

QUILL GORDON

Hook: dry fly
Thread: gray
Tail: blue dun hackle barbs
Body: stripped peacock quill
Wing: wood duck flank feather
Hackle: blue dun

RED QUILL

Hook: dry fly
Thread: gray
Tail: blue dun hackle quills
Body: coachman brown hackle quill,
  stripped
Wing: wood duck flank feather
Hackle: blue dun

ROYAL WULFF

Hook: dry fly
Thread: black
Tail: elk hair
Body: peacock herl, then red floss, then
  peacock herl
Wing: white calf tail
Hackle: coachman brown

RUSTY SPINNER

Hook: dry fly
Thread: brown
Tail: blue dun hackle barbs, divided
Body: reddish brown dubbing
Wing: blue dun hackle tips, tied spent

SULPHUR DUN

Hook: dry fly
Thread: primrose yellow
Tail: light blue dun hackle barbs
Body: cream dubbing
Wing: cream hackle tips
Hackle: light blue dun

TRICO

Hook: dry fly
Thread: black
Tail: blue dun hackle barbs, divided
Body: black dubbing
Wing: light blue dun hackle tips
Hackle: black

USUAL

Hook: dry fly
Thread: olive
Tail: snowshoe rabbit foot hair, dyed olive
Body: snowshoe rabbit underfur, dyed
  olive
Wing: same as tail, tied full and upright

WHITE MAYFLY

Hook: dry fly
Thread: white
Tail: wood duck flank feather barbs
Body: white dubbing
Wing: white hackle tips
Hackle: light blue dun

Dry Flies—Caddis

ALDER

Hook: dry fly
Thread: black
Body: peacock herl
Rib: gold wire, counter-wound
Wing: wood duck flank feather, tied tent
  style
Hackle: coachman brown

ELK HAIR CADDIS

Hook: dry fly
Thread: tan
Body: hare's ear dubbing
Rib: fine gold wire, counter-wound over
  hackle
Wing: light elk hair
Head: tips of elk hair from wing
Hackle: dark brown, palmered
Note: elk hair caddis are tied in a vari-
  ety of body colors—tan, yellow,
  orange, brown, green, and olive

MOTTLED CADDIS

Hook: dry fly
Thread: olive
Body: hare's ear dubbing
Wing: light mottled turkey wing quill
  tied tent style over body
Hackle: brown

SLATE CADDIS

Hook: dry fly
Thread: black
Body: dark gray dubbing
Wing: dark mallard wing quill segment, tied tent style
Hackle: dark blue dun

Dry Flies—Stoneflies

PICKET PIN

Hook: dry fly, 2X–3X long
Thread: black
Tail: brown hackle barbs
Body: peacock herl
Rib: brown hackle, counter-wound over the body
Wing: natural deer hair, angled back over body
Head: peacock herl, in front of wing

STIMULATOR

Hook: dry fly, 2X–4X long
Thread: fluorescent orange
Tail: elk hair
Abdomen: fluorescent orange dubbing
Thorax: amber dubbing
Rib: fine gold wire, counter-wound over abdomen hackle
Hackle: furnace palmered over abdomen, grizzly palmered over thorax
Wing: elk hair, tied in front of and angled over abdomen

YELLOW STONEFLY

Hook: dry fly, 2X–4X long
Thread: yellow
Tail: dyed yellow deer hair
Abdomen and thorax: sulphur dubbing
Rib: light blue dun hackle feather palmered over abdomen, trimmed on top
Wing: light gray duck wing quill segment, tied in front of and flat over abdomen
Hackle: light blue dun, palmered over thorax

Dry Flies—Terrestrials

ANT (CINNAMON OR BLACK)

Hook: dry fly
Thread: red or black
Body: cinnamon or black dubbing tied as an abdomen and thorax
Hackle: black or coachman brown, tied between abdomen and thorax, as legs

CRICKET

Hook: dry fly, 2X long
Thread: black
Body: black dubbing
Wing: black-dyed deer hair, swept back over body
Head: black-dyed deer hair, spun and clipped

GREEN INCHWORM

Hook: dry fly
Thread: light green
Body: light green–dyed deer hair, tied as a bullet head and swept back along hook shank, beyond bend
Rib: green tying thread

Hoppers

LETORT HOPPER

Hook: dry fly, 1X–3X long
Thread: yellow
Body: yellow dubbing
Wing: mottled brown turkey wing quill segment, tied flat over body
Overwing: natural deer body hair
Head: natural deer body hair, spun and clipped

MADAM X

Hook: 2X–4X long
Thread: yellow
Tail: bleached elk hair
Body: fluorescent yellow floss
Legs: brown rubber legs, tied to form an X with band of yellow tying thread behind head
Head and wing: bleached elk hair tied reversed style to form head in front of legs and wing behind legs

Index